MILLIRON
Abbott "Pete" Smith, D.V.M.
The Biography

Gina McKnight

Illustrations by Terry Fortkamp

Monday Creek Publishing
Ohio USA

With love to
Jody, Jessica, Pat,
Karen, Rich,
AJ, Grant and Noah

Foreword

Abbott Pliny Smith III, D.V.M., better known as Pete to anyone he ever met, was a man who took pride in all aspects of his life. Highly skilled in his craft, Pete was one of the most respected veterinarians in his field, and never quit learning about his life's work.

As Pete's life unfolded, Milliron Clinic was his prized possession and where most people's stories with him took place. However, in the following pages, you will see the story of a man who lived every day to its fullest potential, and always had time to help someone in need: the story of a man who spoke just as easily with university professors about foreign films as he did logging equipment with a client of the clinic. Whether it be a fit of rage, an inappropriate limerick or his speaking of his deeply rooted religion, you always knew he was being himself. Pete was authentic and that is what people respected.

Thanks to many friends, clients, and most importantly, his family and author Gina McKnight, this book is filled with countless stories that accurately describe the personality of Pete Smith. He lived simply and dreamed big, and there is no doubt that his legacy and impact on the lives he touched will live on for generations to come. This is his story.

Grant W. Smith
Grandson of Abbott "Pete" Smith, D.V.M.

Introduction

You are holding in your hands a book about a life lived passionately. My father, Pete Smith D.V.M., knew from an early age that he wanted to be a veterinarian, a great veterinarian! My brother, Pat Smith, was inspired when he commissioned the author, Gina McKnight, to write this book about our father. Gina has lovingly created this book for you to read, to enjoy, to learn something about yourself and the world we all share as this story about our father unfolds. Gina and my mother, Jody Smith, and many others, have collaborated, wholeheartedly, to bring you this glimpse into Dad's life.

The journey of creating this book has been a healing experience, as we move forward with our lives since Dad passed away February 22, 2010. In this book, and in many of our lives, Pete Smith continues to live on, inspiring each of us to have an active calling. An active calling in our lives helps us to summon the energy required to live fully the width as well as the length of our lives, as Dad lived his life. It is our prayer that you enjoy the journey you are about to embark on, as you read this story of a life well lived.

Jessica Smith Fox
Daughter of Abbott "Pete" Smith III

Contents

Sit tall in the saddle; Hold your head up high
Keep your eyes fixed where the trail meets the sky
And live like you ain't afraid to die
Don't be scared, just enjoy the ride.
'The Ride' Chris LeDoux

———————

Prologue

THE MONTE FOREMAN saddle eased onto Bud's back, just as it had a hundred times before. The leather squirmed as Pete shoved the toes of his logging boots into the stirrups. They almost fit. Almost.

Bud was a stout horse, standing at about 15.2 hands high; he was one of Pete's favorites. His bay coat was traditional for a half Arabian, half Quarter Horse lineage. He was named after Bud Strouss D.V.M., a longtime colleague and friend of Pete's. Bud was a polo player and avid equestrian. Equine Bud didn't know that this particular day was going to be a challenge - both for him and Pete.

It was the summer of 1991. The riding trails around Pete's busy southeastern Ohio enclave, which included his Milliron Veterinary Clinic, his farmyard, and his sawmill, were in dire need of thinning. Fallen limbs, protruding trees, unruly underbrush, and overgrown brambles were overtaking Pete's trails. Every so often he would solicit the help of one or more of his farmhands to help clear the trails so that he, his family, and whoever else might happen to be horseback riding with them, would have a pleasurable ride. Today was another trail clearing day. Nothing special. Pete had cleared the trails many times before.

1

The farmhand for this adventure was Ibrahim Schubert, a neighborhood teenager who worked for Pete during the summer months and sometimes after school. Pete really liked Ibrahim, his work ethic, love of horses, and youthful energy. They were standing in the clinic parking lot early that morning.

"Hey, I want to show you something," Pete said as he gently lowered his bearded face toward his right pants pocket. Ibrahim and another farmhand were intrigued with the object Pete lifted in his right hand. "I bought this at the vet meeting in Chicago last week," Pete grinned. "It's a wallet gun; two shot 22." Pete pointed his wallet to a faraway hay bale and fired two shots. The farmhands were startled at Pete's quick draw exhibition. Pete grinned and enjoyed their reaction, then remembered he had trails to clear. "Come on, Ibrahim, let's get to work."

The walk up the hill to the barnyard was quiet. Ibrahim was in charge of Junco, nicknamed Junie, Jody's beautiful white New Forest Pony. Ibrahim strapped Junie with breeching and crupper, and then added three chainsaws to Junie's pack saddle. Ibrahim and Junie followed Pete and Bud through the barnyard.

Pete gathered Bud to a trot at the trailhead, just above the house. Ibrahim was close behind with Junie. They worked their way to the cliff pasture below the Negro Den, a locally famous cave where slaves hid during the Underground Railroad. Riding above the edge of the cliff, to the top meadow, Pete decided to stop and secure his raincoat. The raincoat was neatly folded and securely tied to the back of his saddle cantle. *Crunch. Crumble...*

The crumbling noise of the raincoat on his haunches was more than Bud could take. This time the Arabian side of Bud's brain took over and he spooked! Whirling in a panic, throwing Pete off balance. *"Whoa!"* Pete tried to make a quick dismount and was able to free his boot from the right stirrup, but the left boot wouldn't budge! The move alarmed Bud even more and he was off on a dead run back to the barn, unmercifully dragging Pete.

Pete's left special-order logging boot was wedged in the Monte Foreman stirrup. The quarter-inch logging spikes gripped the stirrup without signs of release. This would be the point where it is suggested that you do not wear logging boots while riding

2

horseback.

Custom made by White Boots, USA, Pete's boots had metal toe cleats, spikes screwed into the soles for added traction and durability. Not just ordinary boots, the shafts came up to Pete's calves. Secured by nylon laces, these boots did not easily come off.

Pete was in a precarious situation. His six-foot frame was in peril. *"Whoa*!!" Pete yelled again emphatically, along with some other explicit interjections. Bud didn't recognize the desperate timbre of Pete's voice. Pete's arms and head bounced wildly as the horse plunged through the dense forest. Pete tried to slide back into the saddle, but his hand couldn't reach the saddle horn. It was so far away! Reins flying, branches cracking, brambles groping, hooves pounding; it was no use. Bud mistook Pete's flailing arms as a signal to run harder and faster.

Ibrahim and Junie looked on in disbelief as Pete and Bud raced by; jumping fallen trees, weaving through prickly thickets, and dodging pendulous grapevines. Pete was being perilously dragged. Both arms flew over his head, his right leg pounding onto the saddle with Bud's every stride. He looked like a ragdoll tossed to the wind.

Wham! Pete's body slammed into a large fallen tree as Bud raced by. Mouth agape and in shock, Ibrahim followed in chase to stop the runaway horse, but to no avail. Running through the dense woodland, Ibrahim spotted Pete's new wallet gun lying on the forest floor. It must have fallen out of Pete's pocket. Ibrahim was thinking how lucky Pete was that he hadn't been shot in the foot! He grabbed the gun and kept running.

Thoughts popped into Pete's head. When a man is down and out, and on a runaway horse, his life flashes before his eyes. After everything he had been through, would he meet his demise on a gentle saddle horse? Jody would miss him; Jessica and Pat would be respectful and understanding. Everyone at the clinic and hundreds of clients would be upset with him. How could he be so careless? *Lord, please help! Bud! Stop*! The sunshine was gleaming through the canopy of trees, spinning and swirling above Pete's head.

After Bud's 300-yard agonizing gallop and Pete's skyward prayer, Pete's left boot finally broke free from the stirrup. Pete dropped to the ground with an unceremonious *thud*. Bud didn't stop; he continued his wild trek back to the barn. Pete was still in the un-cushioned soil. He was finally free. Ibrahim ran up to Pete, almost out of breath.

"*God...,*" Pete wearily tried to say. He was a little raspy; the air had been knocked out of him, but finally got the words out. "*Goddamn it!*" this time with perfect diction.

Tremendous pain racked Pete's body. Pete looked through the dense forest to see if he could figure out their location. How far was the barn? *Lord, help me*, he thought.

"Don't move!" Ibrahim insisted as Pete began rolling and swearing.

"*Damn horse,*" Pete said.

Pete used a nearby stump to dizzily stand. Ibrahim didn't know what to say. The shock of the event and the dramatic ride through the forest left both men speechless. Ibrahim solemnly handed Pete his wallet gun. The leather had been torn by the brawn of brambles, but Pete didn't notice.

While Pete was trying to gain his balance and composure, Ibrahim ran back to get Junie, who never moved an inch and had looked on complacently during the entire incident. Meeting up with Pete, Ibrahim and Junie helped Pete hobble back to the barn. Bud was waiting with an "*uh oh*" look back, a little uncertain of what had occurred. But Pete with his vast horseman's wisdom, gave Bud a pat, a few choice words, and sent him out to pasture. Beat up and worn out, Pete called it a day.

Over the next few days, Pete's backside turned black, then green, then blue, collecting to a luminous yellow with a fulgent purplish tint. At the clinic, Pete was proud of his war wounds and was not shy to show anyone his colors.

"Hey! Do you want to see something?" Pete offered while pulling down pants and undershorts, mooning anything within viewing distance. He was purple from his mid-back down to his ankles, just like the "sunset over the Tetons" as he referred to the bruising.

The romp through the woods has become legendary among the locals. To Pete it was no big deal, just another day in the saddle.

Abbott Pliny Smith, III
Date of Birth: June 16, 1938
Birthplace: Augusta, Maine
Father: Abbott Pliny Smith, II
Mother: Elizabeth Cooper Saunders Smith
Physician: Dr. L. D. Herring, MD
State of Maine
Certified Abstract of Record of Live Birth

Like arrows in the hand of a warrior,
so are children of one's youth.
Psalms 127:4

---

1 STRONG BOW

ABBOTT PLINY SMITH III was the second of five children of Abbott Pliny Smith II and Elizabeth Cooper Saunders Smith. To differentiate between father and son, and at the advice of a neighbor woman, Abbott III quickly became known as "Pete"; a handsome, round faced, charismatic little lad who grew to be the delight of his parents and siblings. His mother, Elizabeth, also known as Betty, was born May 22, 1912, in Creston, Montana. She was the daughter of homesteaders Sarah and Arthur L. Saunders. Her father was a WWI Colonel and an accomplished Civil Engineer, recognized for his role in the construction of Going to the Sun Highway, a road through Glacier National Park. Her father kept a daily journal of the road construction which the family later donated to the Montana Historical Society.

Surrounded by the scenic views of Echo Lake, Betty embraced her Montana heritage. She learned the joys of horsemanship and rode her horse to school every day. In the summer months she wrangled the boarded horses at Echo Lake Ranch. After the highway was completed, her father accepted a position with Standard Oil Company in the east. The family eventually migrated to Lewiston, Maine. There, Betty enrolled as an English major at Bates College in Lewiston. She was a dynamic woman, a talented writer, an energetic equestrian, and an eager scholar.

Pete's father was born Abbott Rand O'Brion, July 28, 1912, in New Bedford, Massachusetts. Pete knew his father as a rather eccentric man; a stranger to no one, he was generous, debonair, traditional, with a passion for horses. His father was an avid thinker, an Episcopalian, and a gardener, who created profound impressions on all of his children. Abbott's New England heritage was rooted in the American dream – work hard, play hard, and enjoy the benefits. Abbott was a precocious child, growing up in luxury.

Pete told the story of how, in 1929, his father Abbott arrived home from then Choate School, a private college-preparatory boarding school in Wallingford, Connecticut, for Thanksgiving holiday. As was customary, the butler announced Abbott to a roomful of guests. But the butler called him "Master Smith" rather than "Master O'Brion". Abbott dismissed the butler's announcement as senility. The following morning when he came down to breakfast, the same butler announced him as "Master Abbott Smith."

Abbott asked his maternal grandfather (Pete's great-grandfather), who was eating his oatmeal, "What's this Smith bit?" His grandfather replied without looking up, "Your name has been changed." Grandfather Smith had enough substance to do what he pleased; not only did he own the local bank, A&P, local warehouse, and whaling business, he also had influence with local judges. So, Abbott was no longer an O'Brion. His mother (Pete's grandmother) Ruth Smith O'Brion, had divorced her estranged northern Irish Protestant husband, Rand O'Brion, and changed the family name to her maiden name of Smith. Mr. O'Brion was off selling tractors in the Soviet Union rather than raising his children, which was a disappointment to Grandfather Smith. This all happened one month after the great stock market crash of October 1929. Grandfather Smith had visited Choate for Father's Day weekend the Saturday after the crash. Walking on campus with his son Abbott, Grandfather

Smith closed his black book and said, "I lost $15 million this week, which leaves only $1 million."

Pete's father was a handsome college playboy. Prominent chin, thick black hair, and his charismatic personality could melt a heart at first glance. Abbott was provided every extravagance by his aristocrat grandfather and his doting mother. He was a passionate equestrian and polo player, having learned the skill of horsemanship at a very early age. "Dad's grandfather tied him and his brother to their saddle to teach them how to ride horseback," Pete's elder sister Carol remembers, "Dad's brother would cry all the while. That was the mentality in the 1930's; that generation of our family was well-educated and financially privileged. That was the era when the attitude was that those who could afford children should have children. They also came from the family background of raising kids with an iron fist. But our dad enjoyed the thrill of the horse, a trait that would follow him throughout his lifetime and that he would instill in his own children."

Abbott arrived at Harvard College in the family Rolls Royce. A chauffer drove him to his dormitory, providing a forbidden case of alcohol that was finessed into his room. Evidence shows that this would contribute to the end of Abbott's college career at Harvard, as he was later dismissed for lack of studying and too much partying. Pete's sister Susie doesn't mince words, "Dad flunked out of Harvard. He went to too many debutante parties." Maybe he'd been spoiled by his grandfather's mega wealth and importance in New Bedford.

"Dad was a Greek major," Susie continues. "He asked the counselor when he was kicked out 'Where can I go to study Greek?' The only school in New England is Bates. So, he went to Bates, transferring as a sophomore."

His future wife, Betty, was attending Bates, too. One day during required chapel attendance, she was sitting in a pew in front of him. "Dad leaned up and over in his pew and asked her if she wanted to go riding," Susie says. "Mom said, 'Yes.' They were absolutely in love right away, although mom probably acted a little bit coy."

Abbott had made the perfect pitch: as a Maine local, Betty lived at home, had horses, and rode constantly. The couple graduated together in the Class of 1934, Abbott having redeemed himself with Cum Laude honors. He then enrolled in Harvard Business School, at least partly to correct his record there, and they moved to Cambridge, Massachusetts. "I believe they might have been living together," Susie says, "which would have been unusual in 1934. They married, and in 1935 after he was finished at Harvard, they moved to Maine."

In Portland, Maine, Pete's father developed two real estate companies - Maine Lakes and Coast Realty. He also sold life insurance to farmers, fisherman, and loggers, a market overlooked by other insurance companies. Later, he purchased a lobster boat and WMTW radio station.

The five Smith children - Carol, Pete, Susie, Janet, and Jim - were born while living in New Gloucester, Yarmouth, and Freeport, Maine. The Freeport farmhouse holds posterity for the Smith children. The 160 seaside acreage, known as Little River Farm, is located on Burnett Road, in Casco Bay.

In addition to being an outstanding horsewoman, Pete's mother, Betty, was an accomplished artist and well known for her artistic endeavors. In 1948, while Abbott was away on business, Betty decided to paint a mural on the dining room horsehair-plaster wall of their two-story farmhouse. The landscape she chose was of Casco Bay as seen from nearby Pritham Bridge, also known as the Little River Bridge where Pete and his siblings used to dive and swim. Pete had the fondest memories of the place. He loved it there.

The mural was rediscovered when the farmhouse was renovated in 2002. It had been covered by plywood for almost 35 years. Two local Freeport artists have restored the mural to its original grandeur. It can still be seen there to this day and is a testament to Pete's amazing cultural heritage. Today, the farmhouse is a Maine State Park, renamed Wolf's Neck Farm.

Mostly an agricultural state, Maine is known for producing some of the most independent, determined, and strong people. Mainers embody ruggedness, fearlessness and passion, traits that Pete would assimilate during his childhood. From tiny hands at his mother's breast, feeling for his life's journey, he grew into a childhood of love, sibling rivalry, animals, seashells, curiosity, and moonlight. All these things would guide his life's path. Bursting with energy, an arrow in flight, Pete grew to be a stalwart young man. He was put to work at an early age, mingling with the animals, garden and countryside. He was a handsome fellow, like all the Smith children. Pete inherited more of his Mother's facial features; steady brow, kind eyes, and olive complexion.

The countryside hemmed by the Atlantic Western Seaboard provided ample opportunity for building physical as well as mental acuity. Maine's summer weather patterns collide pleasantly in the coastal regions and along the water. Rolling fog is prominent, especially in the western part of Casco Bay, where Pete played. Casco Bay is known for its mesmerizing landscape and nautical breezes. It is a pivotal point on Maine's coastline where vast beaches of Maine's southern coast end and rocky bluffs jut out into the sea. It is where the Atlantic coast divides into dramatic islands and curves downward to Florida. Light breezes, bitter winds, and ferocious gales create a component for thrilling playscapes and childhood memories. Blending with the countryside, Pete embraced his natural surroundings. He learned of God, love, nature, and the sea.

Carol, Pete's oldest sister, was two years old when Pete arrived. As he grew, Pete became the delight of his family. He was ornery, bright, and witty. Living then on West Elm Street in Yarmouth, Maine, was every child's dream. It was a Norman Rockwell picture of baseball, horseback riding, a family dog, walks on the beach, and beginning school. It was where Pete learned to love animals. He befriended dogs, horses…and geese. He took a goose to the county fair and won a blue ribbon.

"Little River Bridge is a saltwater bay off the Atlantic Ocean that came up to our property, but then beside the property a stream that fed into that body of water was called Little River," Carol explains. "Our farm was named Little River Farm." Carol remembers their mother as a terrible housekeeper who would rather be writing her newspaper columns. "None of us were very interested in her writing because she wasn't very interested in us," Carol admits. "I don't know; that's a pretty harsh thing for me to say. We were kind of a nuisance half the time. Pete and I were raised by two intelligent, creative people. They created five kids that they didn't have a clue what to do with."

Carol and Pete were twenty-one months apart. Then Susie came along, but trailed Pete by five years. Then came the rest of the brood, Janet and Jim. "We called them 'the little kids'," Carol reminisces. "Pete and I rode horses together in Maine. We learned to ride very early; we grew up on horses. Pete was an especially great horseman. Mom and Dad loved riding and we had as many as five saddle horses at one time." On Sundays Abbott would take his kids to the Episcopal church. "Mom would spend Sunday morning in the house by herself," Carol muses. "I think she wanted time alone. She was always a spiritual person, but I think she was also a private person and Sunday was a good way to get some privacy."

On December 9, 1951, Rev. Everett W. Lord presented Pete with a Confirmation Bible, which stayed by his bedside. Carol re-members Pete's appreciation for the Bible, and for "ethereal things, like the sound of the night waves or the delicate flight of the shore-birds" and his love of the family dogs. "We had a dog named Tessie, half collie and half shepherd," Carol continues, "she was the finest and brightest dog we ever had."

Abbott's mother Ruth, Pete's grandmother, was an exceptional artist and adored Pete. Living in the artsy community of Bearskin Neck, Rockport, Massachusetts, everyone knew her as Smitty. "She was a character and a half. Pete and she were like 2 peas in a pod," Susie reflects. "He used to spend summers with her in Rockport. She was an artist. It was an artist's haven. Everybody who painted in the late 1800's and early 1900's went to Rockport to study art. She lived right on the neck of the Maltese #2, the most painted image in Rockport. There was a red lobster house on the end of the pier. She lived right at the street that went down to the pier. My grandmother smoked, swore, and she was Rockport's Number One character. She would go to Bermuda and be entertained royally by other artists, because the Rockport and Bermuda group kind of went back and forth. Granny Smith was right in the thick of all of that. Pete had to have been influenced by her. She was a free spirit. We still have some of her art and a portrait painted of her. It's a valuable painting. She was a big influence in Pete's attitude toward life. She adored him and he her."

Rockport artist and colleague Rutledge Bate painted Smitty's lifelike portrait, which now hangs in the Smith home. The oil on canvas depicts her in an every-day cucumber green cotton buttoned blouse. Her hair is short and silver, her right hand holding a lit cigarette. Her expression is contemplative; blue eyes looking through rimless glasses, pondering her next creative endeavor.

As a youth, Pete enjoyed spending summer months with his Grandma Smitty, eating lobster and enjoying the surf. On one of his summer vacations to Rockport, he asked his grandmother for egg-nog. Smitty was from a long-line of established people; she was raised in a well-to-do family that housed butlers, cooks, and maids. She never learned to cook. So, when Pete asked her to make eggnog, she asked him how to make it. Pete, with tilted eyebrows, naively explained that eggnog contained eggs. Smitty proudly presented Pete with an eggnog concocted with milk, ice cream, and hardboiled eggs.

Pete's maternal great-grandmother, Betty's mother, Louise Mumford Hix, was from a long line of American pioneers. At 94 years, she was celebrated with a write-up in the local newspaper. Originally from Nova Scotia, off the eastern coast of Canada, Louise was survived by 23 grandchildren and 34 great-grandchildren, including Pete.

Abbott and Betty kept the family educated, connected, and always loved. Carol, the eldest, remembers, "Dad gave us many things – things that serve us for a lifetime. Most notable for me is our collective desire to understand and use the English language correctly. We were never too old to be corrected if we erred! That's something that serves one well for the duration. I can't remember when I couldn't ride a horse and that too is a lifetime love. Dad was a great teacher."

"Pete was always doing daredevily things. He was fun. I worshiped him," Susie reflects. "He was my bigger brother. He could make me do anything. He made me put worms in my pocket, or a snake or frog. We all knew in the family that Pete knew what he wanted to do from the time he was four years old.

"Dad was a gentleman farmer," Susie continues. "He commuted to Portland for his work. We had cows and horses which mom had to take care of. By that time, Pete was milking cows and doing all the necessary stall mucking out. Dad and Mom were horse people. We all rode horses. Janet, of all of the three of us younger kids became an expert horseman. My mother was the best with horses. Jimmy was much more cerebral than we were. Jimmy and Dad were so much alike in IQ rating that they didn't get along. They fought like cats and dogs. Pete and Dad had issues, but mostly disciplinary issues. Mom and Dad would send us to play all over the farm, with all sorts of dangers, and told us to come back in time for dinner."

Susie recalls a story about her grandfather O'Brion, whom she never met, and her father. "In the '30s and '40s he was a salesman of Caterpillar tractors and agricultural equipment to the Soviet Union," she recounts. "Dad was on a Bank Board in Portland, Maine, and he had to approve a loan to his own father. That was really kind of turning the tables a little bit. He may have removed himself from the consideration, I don't know. It was odd; the son who did not have fond memories of his father had the opportunity to help his father. How he was treated as a child and that, his father, deserted his mother. If that didn't happen, Pete would not be Abbott Pete Smith, he would be somebody O'Brion."

Pete penned his childhood memories for his father's memorial booklet:

> It was bittersweet news that Dad's ordeal was finally over so he could move on. He definitely was a mover, and undoubtedly will continue to evolve on a more cosmic level. He always had a solid faith and involvement with the Episcopal Church. As a result, I have been able to draw comfort and inspiration from it, too. I am grateful to have been raised in Dad's chosen church. I always appreciated the opportunity to grow up in the rural environment of a large farm on the Maine Coast which he and Mom provided and which incidentally

remains virtually unchanged today as a sort of serendipitous memorial. Dad saw that I grew up imbued with classical music embellished by enough piano and trumpet lessons to at least understand that good music doesn't just happen. My home and life were filled with wonderful books, reference materials and suitable mythological heroes (as perfect heroes must be). I was also provided with lots of occasions to contemplate due to the isolation provided by the setting and Maine winters coupled with the focus and simplicity provided by poverty, albeit only poverty of the economic sort. Dad lived to see five children grow up tall and strong in body, mind and spirit – each unique and happy. It was a strong bow from which we were shot, and he deserves credit for our happiness today.

If God sends us on strong paths,
we are provided strong shoes.
Corrie ten Boom

---

3 MILLIRON

IN 1952, WHEN Pete was fourteen years old, the Smith family moved to Denver, Colorado. Pete's father, Abbott, suffered respiratory problems and his doctor recommended that he move to a drier climate, away from the seashore. He also suffered continual back problems from having broken his back playing college polo, and the cold, damp coastal region was not conducive to his health.

Moving to Colorado would change the course of Pete's life. At first the family lived in a lovely two-story home in the Capitol Hill area of Denver. Carol and Pete attended nearby South High School. One summer they moved to a mountain cabin, without plumbing or electric, that was lent to them by friends, the Keuts, rent free.

"We ate Chef Boyardee most of the time," sister Susie recalls, "sharing one can among the family. We had no money. Carol and Pete lived with us, but they went to different schools. Any money they earned during that time came back to help the family."

Abbott didn't really enjoy the move to Colorado, but found work at the Silas Dean Company selling sales training materials. "Dad was not easy on Pete and me," Carol says. "Dad thought nothing of whipping us. He was tough. Pete wanted to make his own way, and he did. They changed their parenting tactics with the little kids."

Betty secured work for the first time outside of the home as a secretary. As a skilled English major, she had no trouble finding work.

It once again became a time of upheaval and moving vans. Abbott, Betty, and the little kids - Susie, Janet, and Jim – returned to the East Coast. Pete and Carol stayed behind to pursue life in the west. Pete, then 15, decided to stay. He was smitten with the cowboy's life. He kept the family dog, a tall poodle named ZaZa. Pete would take ZaZa on roundups and to rodeos. Since Pete was underage, his parents signed a court document to have him legally emancipated from the family. Abbott and Betty could not support Pete; they were destitute. Penniless and eager to become solvent, his parents returned to Maine to regroup and look for work. Abbott eventually found employment with the International Harvester Corporation in Boston, and Betty became a secretary for the Polaroid Corporation. "We lived that summer on our old farm in Freeport as guests of our friends who had bought the farm," Susie explains. "We stayed in the little old hunter's cabin right down on the water, on the point. It had an outhouse. We lived there that whole summer while Dad was in Boston setting up a place for us to live. He was in charge of training salesmen."

"I remember when I babysat back in Denver, I would send money back to the family in Massachusetts to help buy groceries," Carol says. "We were that poor. That was quite a change, obviously, from the beginning. Dad went to Harvard and Bates with so much money in the depression from his Grandparents who raised him that he anonymously paid college tuition for kids who were in danger of not being able to finish college. It was a very unusual situation to come out of the depression and World War II in fairly good financial condition."

The Smith kids were growing up and tried to stay connected. Carol married her high school sweetheart, Hyle Otten; Pete was busy finishing high school, riding broncs in the rodeo in his spare time. Pete learned to use a lasso and how to manipulate a lariat, talents he would use in his future vetting as well as on his future farm. A mishap on a wild saddle bronc landed Pete on a rock, breaking his back and putting him off the rodeo circuit. He never had enough money to get his back fixed, an injury that would bother him throughout his life.

A well-liked high school sophomore, Pete became fast friends with the local ranchers and their horses. It was during these adolescent years that Pete learned the ways of the cowboy; the incredible journey of growing into a man. Living on a shoestring was tough, but Pete found work at a local veterinary clinic in Denver. The summer of his sophomore year, he took off for a ranch he had heard about in Laramie, Wyoming. The ranch was owned by Harvard graduate Frank Bosler and his wife Shirley. Pete's Dad had met Frank through the Denver Harvard Club. The Boslers took a shine to Pete and gave him as much guidance as anyone could.

Pete worked at Frank Bosler's ranch as a wrangler during the rest of high school, living in the bunkhouse with a burly bunch of cowboys. It was hard work at the ranch. Pete was paid partly in cattle and collected a herd of misfit Angus cattle – the lame, crippled, or just unwanted. Pete would buy cattle with eye cancer, surgically remove the cancer, and resell them. He rehabilitated each one and was able to establish a lucrative herd. He registered his own brand – the Milliron brand – and became the proprietor of the Milliron Land and Cattle Company. Fascinated with ranching, machinery and metal, Pete learned how to forge horseshoes and wield iron. The Milliron represented his future.

Riding bulls and broncs in the rodeo to supplement his meager income, Pete had his bad days. Sometimes he would come off everything he tried to ride. He began breaking horses for money. The first was a filly with a bad reputation. He got her going under saddle well enough, but she had one rule. You had to mount her with a loose rein or she'd blow up and dump you. Few people were brave enough to mount her with a loose rein. Soon, she ruined his reputation as a horse trainer.

Not only did he learn how to handle cattle and horses, but he learned the challenges of peer pressure and cowboy whiskey. The Bosler ranch cowboys made a lifetime impact on Pete; a man can build character and charisma while living in a bunkhouse. One

Saturday night, the bunkhouse party became rowdy, and teenage Pete was seduced by a one-quart bottle of Canadian Club whiskey. The cowboys smiled and drank along while Pete chugged the entire quart in no time flat, leaving him unconscious. Bunkhouse cowboys know the best thing for a first-time whiskey affair is to sleep it off. They let Pete lie where he fell, on the bunkhouse floor. Upon waking the next day, Pete experienced gut-wrenching stomach trouble, leaving a somber remembrance of Canadian Club whiskey.

"Pete somehow managed to support himself by doing ranch work in the summers – breaking horses, etc. One summer when he was hitchhiking he was picked up by some Hispanic tough guys," John Woolum, one of Pete's high school classmates, remembers. "They asked him if he had any money. He said he would not be hitchhiking if he did. One of the men sitting in the front seat next to him was swinging a knife around and began cutting up the dash and headliner in the car. Pete was quite worried. The others in the car kept trying to calm the man down saying, *'No Sweat Raton, no sweat Raton...'* This became a chant for the rest of us who heard the story. He managed to escape unharmed!"

Another school mate, Jerry Tiff, remembers, "Me and Pete Rinehart went to visit Pete when he was a wrangler at the Bosler ranch outside of Laramie. We ate with the ranch hands; antelope chicken-fried steak, the best fried steak in my life. Pete had to work, so socializing was cut kind of short."

In his junior year of high school, Pete broke his leg on a skiing trip. With the pain of a healing broken back, now a broken leg, he was unable to wrangle and work full-time. Money was scarce and food an option.

Besides the love of horses and the wild outdoors, of great importance and enjoyment to Pete was school; literature, the need to know how things work, the joy of reading and writing. A brown leather zippered three-ring notebook holds Pete's high school book reports, speeches, journals, essays, trigonometry and geometry homework. Now the white-lined school paper is faded, but it reveals Pete's commitment to education and his passion for writing. Sometimes signing Peter, sometimes Pete, his handwriting is readable cursive with a masculine flair.

The notebook contains a selection of book reports including *The Iliad of Homer, The Sea Around Us, Babushka,* and his favorite, Winston Churchill. There are essays of his battles with broncs, Senate Club Committee notes about religion, and other assignments for the Writer's Bureau. One teacher remarked on two of his book reports in red pencil cursive "Some very fine expressions here" and "You can write in an interesting manner." Leafing through the notebook, paging past detailed book reports with teacher edits and marks, the first essay is found. All of Pete's essays tell true-life experiences, which have been documented in another volume *The South High Horseman: Stories and Poems by a Teen Cowboy.* On May 17, 1956 Pete wrote a poem of his rodeo days:

Coyote Pete
>Behind the chutes the boys was crouched
>Their whole attention spent
>On drawin' straws and hopin' for
>A hoss as was hell-bent.
>
>Jick drawed a hoss named Coyote Pete
>Like in the comic strip
>And stretched his legs and waited for
>His turn to make the trip.
>
>The doggin' came, the barebacks went
>(The ropin' was plumb through.)
>And then at last came saddle broncs and
>One last swig 'o 'dew.
>
>The saddle – she was cinched up tight
>The flank strap was drawed down
>Jick eased onto that bronc's back
>And gave a look aroun'!
>
>He tucked his hat and stuck his spurs
>Into "Coyote's" shoulder blades
>Then he whispered "Let 'im out,"

And things began to blaze.

That hoss went ten feet in the air
An' crashed into the fences
He whirled and bucked and kicked and ran
Like 's if he'd lost 'is senses!

But ol' Jick hung to like a burr
An' never give an inch
For since the very first he had
Been hangin' to the fence.

In Pete's high school graduation picture, he radiates confidence, poise, and potential; a cowboy smile, handsome demeanor, olive complexion, hazel eyes, and wavy dark-brown hair. Wearing a horizontal striped tie, white shirt, and linen suit jacket, he was attractive. His copper colored high school yearbook, *The Johnny Reb*, celebrates his years amidst the Denver graduating class of 1956. Despite his financial adversities and lack of immediate family close by, Pete was active in high school extracurricular events and excelled in his studies. He was the Senate Club President and participated in Sophomore Track, Prom Club, French Club, Writer's Bureau, International Club Council, as well as the Annual Staff Sports Editor. The yearbook picture of the International Club Council shows Pete in the back row in a dark shirt, not smiling. His dark eyes look far away as if he is contemplating his next move. Restless, a dreamer, he doesn't look concerned about his demeanor, or the fact that he is not smiling.

Pete was the sports editor for his high school newspaper; but he really didn't have time for recreational main-stream sports and didn't make it to any of the games. He had very little interest in sports. He kept a long list of verbs that fit with sporting events, reviewed the game statistics, wrote the article, and submitted it to his editor.

Pete was well-liked in high school and the inscriptions in his senior yearbook confirm his fame. Here are a few:

19

Dear Pete,
Oh, there is a lot I could tell you and I'll try to just a little. You mean so very much to me with your quick easy-going personality. I probably would have lost my mind completely several times if you hadn't been around to tell my problems to. You probably didn't realize it, but you have really helped calm me down. Thanks. I know that I have sometimes treated you kind of cold, but I didn't mean to and I'm terribly sorry. I hope I can make it up to you. I know you'll be a great success as a rancher and I hope you'll allow me to share your sheep-wagon with you. Have fun at Aggies and don't forget me for those farm girls.
Love always,
Joanne (Junior Princess)

I'm going to write a book! Pete, I can't begin to tell you what a wonderful guy you are and how I feel about you. We've had some of the greatest times together and some good poker games. I surely hope our friendship won't end on the 8th of June as most friendships do. May I wish you the very, very best of everything always, Pete. You're a fabulous guy.
Much love and luck,
Glenda

Pete, Good luck and best wishes always to a real great guy. I hope that our friendship, which has developed in the past three years, will continue to prosper.
Good luck always,
Jim Morgan
Sr. Class President

This year has truly been a 'senior year'. I've met so many new kids what that will be friends forever. Pete, I consider you one of those friends. We've had so many fun times at I.R.C. and Inter-Club, etc. Best of luck and

happiness be with you always.
Mary Dee

'Cowboy Pete' I'll always remember you. You have a
fine personality, Pete; happy memories of your life at
South.
Harold Keables, Instructor, A.B., English

Colorado State University

In the fall of 1956, after high school graduation, Pete was just
getting by. Enrolled as a full-time student at Colorado Agricultural
& Mechanical (A&M) College (later, in 1958, it would become
Colorado State University), he was living out of his maroon Ford
ranch wagon, Henry, at the rodeo grounds, and eating canned dog
food and chicken noodle soup. It was hard-times that he would talk
about later in life. His connections finally moved him out of the
station wagon and into better housing. College professors said that
a veterinarian should not be living in his car.

Pete began his college studies with the required two years of
liberal arts, then, later, an additional four years in specialized study,
including chemistry, physiology, anatomy, surgery, feeding, and
breeding of animals. He found various jobs that would sustain him
physically and help to pay for college. He worked at Kraxberger's
Dairy in exchange for a room in a barely heated outbuilding. His
most dreaded job was at the local funeral home. One of his cowork-
ers at the funeral home stuffed him into a coffin one night as a joke,
but the worst of the job was being called to follow ambulances to
accidents and retrieving corpses. He saw people die. After that, he
didn't want anything to do with a funeral home.

For a time, Pete worked for the Denver Hunt Club. There he
met Topsail, an elegant Thoroughbred who jumped over his own
shadow instead of hurdles. Pete watched as Topsail hit the jump,
throwing and severely injuring his rider. The rider's father wanted
to destroy Topsail on the spot, but gave the horse to Pete on the
condition that he would never see the horse again. Pete jumped on
the horse and rode off, up the highway, all the way to Bosler's ranch
near Laramie, Wyoming. He counted the telephone poles by the side

of the highway, walking so many, trotting most, cantering a few. He'd saved the horse, though later, Frank Bosler accidentally hit Topsail with his pickup truck while herding horses, breaking Topsail's leg, ending Topsail's life.

"We made annual trips to Bosler Ranch just to see Pete," Susie continues. "It was fantastic. It was a typical ranch with a bunkhouse. I remember being on horseback and riding miles and miles all day, helping Pete check fences."

Pete's most memorable jobs were working as a houseboy at Sigma Kappa Sorority in exchange for his meals, as well as becoming a wrangler and cowboy for Burr and Lou Betts - Betts Circle Two Arabian Ranch, Parker, Colorado. Burr and Lou were helpful in getting Pete through college. While Pete was employed at the ranch, Burr and Lou stabled Witezar, son of historic Polish Arabian stallion Witez II, rescued by World War II General George Patton. Pete had the opportunity to purchase Witezar. He had earned enough money while wrangling for the Boslers and selling his herd of Angus cattle. Pete decided that his savings would be better spent on a more tangible item, so he passed the opportunity and instead purchased a boarding house at 917 Remington Street, Fort Collins, Colorado.

The boarding house was lucrative enough to help pay Pete's college tuition, books, and living expenses. He rented rooms to fellow college students. Living at the boarding house, he got to know his renters personally and a few became lifelong friends.

Life on Remington Street was full of surprises. When Pete bought the property, there was a horizontal garden of rhubarb on the west side of the house. An older local woman came and asked Pete if she could have some rhubarb. Pete said okay. The next day, when he arrived home from class, the entire rhubarb patch had been harvested. Turned out she was a cook from a nearby fraternity house and had made a dozen pies.

On the East Coast, Abbott, Pete's Dad, became the proprietor of his own executive consulting company, Abbott Smith Associates. He began writing, and published several books in his lifetime, including *How to Sell Intangibles*, Prentice-Hall Inc., 1958. He inscribed a copy to Pete "To my son Pete – even a Vet needs to be a salesman! Abbott P. Smith." In orange, black, and white graphics, the inside book jacket posts a portrait of Abbott's strong features; an extremely handsome suited man with dark hair, glasses, and a confident aura. About the Author (taken from the book jacket):

> Abbott P. Smith has been a professional salesman for a quarter of a century. In his outstanding career, he has trained and guided hundreds of salesmen and these salesmen's brilliant successes are living testimonials to Mr. Smith's unique insight and deep understanding of the problems which face the salesmen of intangibles day by day. Mr. Smith has earned an enviable reputation and sales record selling dozens of tangibles and intangibles lines...from sales training courses to microfilm...from radio time to real estate...from newspaper space to insurance. One of his many positions of responsibility was Supervisor of Sales Training and Sales Personnel for International Harvester Company.

Abbott's second book, *Complete Guide to Selling Intangibles*, was published in 1971 by Parker Publishing Company, Inc., New York. The book jacket notes that, by that time, he'd been a sales-training specialist and consultant for 18 years, developed training methods and programs at International Harvester, McGraw-Hill, Argyle Publishing Company, and the Silas Dean Organization before establishing his own firm in 1966. "Mr. Smith, now President of Abbott Smith Associates, Inc. and of ASA Training Consultants, Inc., has written three books for Prentice-Hall and numerous articles for various sales, management and training magazines," the bio continues. The book received great acclaim from various notable corporations throughout the United States.

Meanwhile, Betty pursued her secretarial career at Bobbs Merrill Publishing, then to Young & Rubicam Advertising. Her family news reports entitled *The New York Report* kept the family corresponding and informed. In 1962, the year Pete graduated from vet school, Betty and Abbott purchased a 90-acre farm in Millbrook, New York, they called The Last Resort. Betty and Abbott were avid bird watchers and enjoyed the milieu of farm life once again. The couple commuted to New York City for several years until settling in Millbrook full time in 1972. Betty was a long-time member of the Millbrook Garden Club. She wrote the Garden Club's newsletters for many years. She was also known for her column, *My Side of the Street*, for the Millbrook Round Table.

In 1996, the family moved Abbott, overtaken by Parkinson's disease and related medical conditions, to Farmington, Maine, to live at Edgewood Manor until his death in 1998. After selling their Millbrook home, in 1996, Betty moved to Kingfield to live with Pete's sister, Susan. In addition to a short stint writing a column for the local paper, *The Irregular*, Betty enjoyed reading, writing her monthly family newsletter, now *The Maine Report*, of nearly 50 years, rocking on the porch overlooking the Carrabassett River as it cascaded over the dam in front of the house, and keeping watch over the local traffic and neighbors.

Although occasionally on both sides some have
tried to break up this union, it's obvious that it ain't
gonna ever happen – it's too strong.
Pete Smith

---

3 PETE AND JODY

FROM MANSFIELD, OHIO, Virginia Joyann "Jody" Haley was
born on an April morning in Toledo, Ohio. Her Irish father was a
graduate of Ohio Northern University, a member of Sigma Phi
Epsilon fraternity, and was employed as a salesman. Her mother,
Virginia, was a 1929 graduate of Brenau College for Women,
Gainesville, Georgia, and a member of Zeta Tau Alpha. She was an
avid volunteer, housewife, and devoted mother.

Jody, a hazel-eyed brunette, was a horse enthusiast from the
start. She spent much of her youth riding horses, learning how to
connect with them, and knowing that if she forgave a horse's
mistake, they were forgiving of hers, too. "When I was about three
years old, my mother was shopping at a vegetable cart being pulled
by a draft horse," Jody says. "She looked around and I was
underneath the draft horse petting his belly. My mother practically
had a heart attack. She was trying to get me out of there. The owner
of the horse said, 'Oh, she's fine, don't worry about her.' But, my
mother was trying to tug me out and I held onto the horse's leg. This

wonderful old draft horse just stood there while this little kid was screaming on his leg – 'No!' Finally, the farmer disentangled me and I had to go home. That was my first encounter with a horse."

In her early teens, she traveled to Columbus to the Ohio State Fair just to see Wing Commander, a famous Saddlebred. "I would sit there and wait for Wing Commander to come out, time after time," she recalls. "I was crazy over him. He wasn't much to look at in the stall, but boy when he came in the ring you couldn't take your eyes off of him." Growing up, Jody was able to ride a friends Saddlebred. The horse had been shown, had only known life in the ring, and now was just standing in the barn. They said she could ride him. "Well, I didn't know anything, I just wanted to trail ride," Jody remembers. "That was the most willing horse I had ever seen. He didn't know what was going on, but he was so willing, so calm. He was just a wonderful horse. I don't think he ever had the chance to be a natural horse in his life, but he trusted me. Saddlebreds have a deep heart."

During her high school years, Jody attended a field trip with her Girl Scout mounted troop to Cheyenne Frontier Days, Wyoming. It was then that she became mesmerized by the West's natural beauty and equine offerings. Upon high school graduation Jody made her own pilgrimage to Fort Collins and began her college career at Colorado A&M. Majoring in literature, and an honor student, she was a member of Tri-Delta Sorority, quickly making lifetime friends. She was also a tomboy who didn't mind hanging out with the guys. There were plenty of them at Colorado A&M. The ratio was four guys to every woman. Finding a date was not difficult; finding the right date was a challenge.

In the fall of 1956, Jody met Pete the first day of class. Jody shines as she recalls the moment. "It was an Honors English Class. I remember what a good-looking guy he was. I noticed him right away. It was not love at first sight, it was attraction at first sight."

They became good friends, sharing horse stories and studying together. Pete was dating Jody's Tri-Delta roommate, Janet "Simmy" Simmons, a South High School classmate of Pete's. Jody was working at the college bookstore, earning extra cash to help pay for boarding her horse, Starboy. Pete would stop in the bookstore and ask Jody to give messages to Simmy, but he also liked to talk to Jody about horses. "One time he showed me a black and white 8 x 10 picture of him riding a beautiful horse. I said, 'Oh, that's the most gorgeous Morgan I've ever seen.' He archly explained that the stallion was Witezar, a son of one of the most famous Polish Arabians, Witez II, who had been rescued along with other Arabians and Lipizzans by General Patton near the end of World War II. Pete loved that horse. He spent a lot of time backing Witezar up in irrigation ditches to develop gaskin muscles."

As their friendship grew, Pete stopped dating Simmy and asked Jody out for a date. "Pete usually invited Simmy to the quarterly dance held by the veterinary school," Jody says. "This time he invited me to go with him. I said I couldn't until I checked with Simmy. He seemed to find that amusing but said to let him know what we decided. When I got off work and back to the sorority house, Simmy and I discussed the turn of events. Simmy said, 'He asked you. Go with him if you want.' He did and I did. To jump ahead a bit, Simmy was my maid of honor at our wedding. I chased Pete two years before I caught him. I had a lovely time at the vet dances as they somehow managed to get excellent country western artists, some of whom became well-known stars. Later I invited Pete to our sorority formals. They were quite the contrast, but also fun." Pete asked Jody for her hand in February 1959.

An April 1959 picture of Pete and Jody at a Tri-Delta dance captures them in the throes of infatuation. Jody, in a light blue formal evening gown, stands alongside Pete in his spiffy gray suit. They are the image of young love. It was at this point that Pete and Jody became a couple; horseback riding, nights under the Colorado stars, and occasional out-on-the-town dates as Pete could afford. Jody's short hair, easy demeanor, and horse-girl savvy kept Pete engaged and determined to keep Jody as his own. At Pete's request, Jody began growing her hair longer, eventually long enough for her signature braid that she would wear for many years.

Jody kept Starboy at Birky's ranch, the home of Dr. Birky and his wife Pauline. Dr. Birky was a professor at Colorado A&M and Pauline worked there for Maury Albertson, one of the founding architects of The Peace Corps. Pauline went on to author a book about her experience, including her work in Iran and in training overseas volunteers, and earned the title of Mother of the Peace Corps.

Starboy, a mild chestnut Quarter Horse gelding with a prominent forehead star, would remain a worthy companion. He was given to Jody by one of her sorority sister's parents. Jody trained Starboy to the cart, impressing the Birky's, who asked Jody to help train one of their Arabian horses, Saha, to the cart, too. Jody declined, knowing that Saha needed more training than she was able to provide.

"When we were dating we were walking across the dam on Birky's ranch and Starboy came running through the pasture," Jody smiles. "Pete and I were holding hands. Starboy was jealous. He put his head between us. One time when I was breaking Starboy to drive, he balked and I was babying Starboy along, and Pete said, 'No, you got to show him! Get down.' So, I got out of the cart, Pete got in, and whacked down on Starboy. In one swift movement, Starboy whistled his shod hind feet on each side of Pete's head. Pete turned white and said, 'Your horse.' Pete gave the reins back to me and I went driving. Anytime I gave the reins to Pete, Starboy would stop dead.

"Pete invited me to accompany him on a trip to Bosler's ranch near Laramie, Wyoming, to meet Frank and Shirley Bosler and Pete's best friends Les and Hope Rivers who worked on the ranch," Jody continues. "He also introduced me to a man, the Bosler's ranch foreman, Freddy Ferguson. Freddy lived in a small trailer. My memory of him is a gentleman with a lovely smile. His sense of humor showed when he asked me if I wanted to go into the corral with him, ostensibly, to 'try to catch his mare' Gypsy. Of course, I did and as we walked into the corral, Freddy said, 'Now where is that mare?' Suddenly a horse broke from the group, ran up and stuck her head in the halter Freddy was carrying. Freddy then stroked her, gave her some corn and fastened the halter. She followed him without a lead rope. Pete was sitting on the corral fence, laughing at the amazed look on my face."

Driving back to Fort Collins, Pete explained that Freddy "had a way with horses." He also extolled more of Freddy Ferguson's virtues, including rescuing several abandoned boys and helping them onto better paths in life. Pete didn't include himself in that group, but he obviously admired Freddy.

Driving in the moonlight, Pete invited Jody to sit close to him as he drove Henry, the Ford ranch wagon, named after Henry Ford, but he spelled it in the French way. "Of course, it had a bench seat so I could have just slid across from where I was sitting by the door," Jody remembers. "I said I was fine where I was. Pete then pulled off the road, stopped the car and said, 'You drive, then. I'm tired' and proceeded to get in the backseat and promptly fell asleep. I still remember driving back to the sorority house on that silent, moonlit trip. When we arrived, Pete walked me to the Tri-Delta door. On all of my dates in college I had developed what I thought was a clever strategy. I would slip inside the screen door and then say pleasant goodnights, thanking my date for a good time, etc. This had worked with Pete also after the vet dance, and study dates at the library, which was all he could afford. This time, however, I couldn't get the screen door to budge. I looked up to see Pete's hand firmly against the door, his cowboy hat blocking some of the moon and we had a lovely goodnight kiss, the first of many over the next fifty plus years."

While they were dating, working, and attending classes, Pete received a call that Carol, his older sister, who was living with her husband Hyle in Colorado Springs, was in the hospital with a brain hemorrhage. It was a time of concern; Carol would remain unconscious for over a month. Pete attempted to drive the long distance in Henry, his maroon Ford ranch wagon, but Henry was not running. Pete borrowed Jody's car, another Ford, known as "The Rattler." After a long hospital stay, Carol recovered and was dismissed from the hospital.

In 1959 Pete was among the youngest students in the Colorado A&M Veterinary College. Many of the other students were veterans, returning from the Korean War, finding their way through college. They mentored Pete and became a tight-knit group. The course of study for a veterinarian at Colorado A&M was intense and required long hours of study as well as field work, focusing on large animals, particularly equines.

"The vet school students would go to the Colorado hills on the weekends, or when they had free time," reminisces Dr. Ron Bell, one of Pete's vet school comrades and classmates. "Pete was one of the quieter ones in the class, a very definite entrepreneur type; had a goal more than the rest. Pete would tackle anything. We were all older; he was among the youngest in the class. Most of us had been in the military at the end of the Korean War. Most of us didn't have a goal set, we just wanted to graduate. We had keg parties in the mountains. We had a barrel set up between two trees to ride like a bull. The barrel had four ties, someone pulled on the ropes to make it go. Pete came up to ride more than to drink beer. I just had to drink his share. We just never got to the last beer. Pete would fall asleep after only two beers. He was not much of a drinker, but took his turn riding the wild bull barrel."

"Sometimes girls would like to hang out with the vet students," Jody remembers. "One girl wanted to be one of the guys. That day at school, the vet students had castrated a bunch of calves. They would fry up a bunch of Rocky Mountain Oysters (calf testicles) over an open fire, a delicacy for the hungry students. Watching the men eat the oysters, the girl said, 'Boy, this one is really big!' One of the guys said, 'Well, we put a Saint Bernard in; thought we would try something new.' The girl lost it. She got sick right there. She could have handled the calves, but not dogs. It was a little too much for her. The guys were just kidding; of course, all of the meat was bovine."

Pete continued his ambition to become a veterinarian. Rowen D. Frandson, D.V.M., one of Pete's professors at Colorado State, enjoyed Pete's whit and whimsy. They became fast friends and enjoyed riding on Dr. Frandson's ten-acre ranch outside of Loveland, Colorado.

Eric, Dr. Frandson's son, remembers Pete. "My sister and I were children when he would stop by to visit our house. We had a few horses. Pete and my father would ride. My sister and I thought that Pete was the comedian Bob Newhart. We would sneak out when my parents were having coffee or tea with Pete so we could listen to their conversation. I remember him being quite funny and looked just like Bob Newhart. It was exciting to think that my parents knew such a famous person. Later my mother told me that he enjoyed that we had confused him with Newhart. One time, Pete stopped by a week or so before Christmas. He left a beautifully wrapped Christmas box under the tree. My sister and I were unable to lift the heavy box. When my parents had company, they would take them to the tree, point out the present and my father or mother would say, 'A veterinarian student, Pete Smith, gave us this present, try and lift it.' Most would give up and smile, when they couldn't get a grip on the box, much less lift it even an inch. Almost everyone tried to guess what the present could possibly be, but none guessed correctly. Finally, Christmas day arrived, and we tore open our presents, but we wanted our father to open the box from Pete before he opened any others. He had to open the box in place under the tree, and when he got it open, there was a small solid metal anvil. I remember my Dad laughing after he discovered what the present was, and my mother's broad grin. While one would think the present would be quite the joke, it turns out we had my grandfather's forge, and this was a very useful present to my father. Pete would come over and use the forge and anvil for horseshoes. I used it too, as I got older. We still have the anvil."

Living in the Remington Street boarding house, Pete was known for his hard work and sense of humor. Working and going to school with little time left in a day, Pete knew how to get things done. There was a tree stump in front of the boarding house that Pete needed removed. He couldn't afford a tree service. Hearing of Pete's dilemma to remove the stump, Pete Matthews, a fellow vet student who was a demolition specialist during the Korean War, knew how to handle dynamite. Pete bought dynamite at Tolliver Kinny's Hardware Store in Ft. Collins. They drilled holes in the stump, placed the dynamite in the holes, placed a couple of mattresses on top to muffle the sound, and lit the charge. The stump lifted out of the hole just as planned. In the following weeks, the fraternity house across the street tried to copy Pete's process. They did not have an expert dynamite man, so they layered mattresses over the stump to muffle the sound, too. Their stumps remained unmoved and the mattresses landed in the telephone lines along the street. Pete found this amusing and would share this story throughout his lifetime.

Pete was always looking for ways to make money. He decided to buy 20 acres of land from Burr and Lou Betts, which he would later sell to Jody's parents. Jody and Pete continued seeing each other through their college years. Both diligently working and studying to finish college, there was no time for a lot of dating. However, Virginia, Jody's mother, in her own motherly way, attempted to persuade Jody to date other men. Virginia coaxed Jody to go on a trip overseas to forget about Pete. Jody conceded and traveled abroad, only to find that her love for Pete grew deeper. They were married two weeks after Jody returned from Europe.

The couple, at that time still in college, along with their families, congregated in Mansfield for the wedding. While wedding preparations were being made, Pete and Jody went to a nearby farm to pick up Jody's dog, Mertaugh's Mahogany Mike, a loveable Irish Setter that Jody had acquired as a high school teenager. With Jody away, her mother did not want to care for Mike and took him to the farm family for temporary keeping. "When we were getting ready to leave for Colorado, we went out to get Mike. I was excited that the rooming house where we were going to live had a big fenced in yard and I thought, *Wow*! I'll be able to have my dog! The young son of the farmer had his arms around the dog and crying at the thought of losing him. The boy was about nine years old. Pete was standing over to the side motioning to me. 'No, we couldn't take the dog.' Pete told the young boy that we were 'just visiting.' We just couldn't separate the two, so we left Mike with the boy."

The Wedding

The entire wedding was planned by Jody's mother, Virginia, who wrote the wedding announcement for the local paper. The announcement featured a picture of Jody in a navy-blue sweater and dainty pearl necklace:

Mr. and Mrs. Peter Franklin Haley, 692 West Andover Road, Mansfield, Ohio announce the engagement and approaching marriage of their only daughter, Miss Virginia Joyann Haley, to Mr. Abbott P. Smith, III, Englewood, Colorado, son of Mr. and Mrs.

Abbott P. Smith II, Natick, Massachusetts, and New York City. The double-ring ceremony will be solemnized at 3:30 p.m. September 4, 1959 at Grace Episcopal Church. The Reverend Canon Samuel U. J. Peard, rector of the church, and Dr. Calvin Winder, pastor of First United Presbyterian Church, will officiate. Miss Haley is a senior at Colorado State University and is a member of Delta Delta Delta Sorority. Her fiancé is studying veterinary medicine at the same university. The custom of open church will be observed for the couple's wedding.

Jody wanted to get married at The Chapel of Transfiguration in Jackson Hole, Wyoming. As a young girl Jody had been to Jackson Hole and visited the Chapel, a simple little log church. The entire back of the Chapel showcased a clear glass window, the mountains as a backdrop, behind the altar's large wooden cross. It was a breathtaking view. But, due to distance, Pete's family could not afford to travel to Wyoming. Abbott and Betty said they could make it to Ohio, so Jody agreed to change the wedding venue to Mansfield. Jody told Pete she didn't care where they got married, just as long as it was in an Episcopal Church, as they were now both Episcopalians. Jody's mother was hoping that the couple would never get married, so she did not send out wedding invitations.

The Mansfield Episcopalian priest requested a consultation with Pete and Jody prior to the wedding. Jody's mother, a longtime Presbyterian, insisted that both minsters be there. That really was not done in those days, but her mother insisted and the Episcopal priest and Presbyterian minister cooperated beautifully.

The happy couple shared a day of pomp and pageantry. *The Mansfield News Journal* reported the event:

Nuptial Vows Exchanged by Joyann Haley, A. P. Smith III

The Reverend Samuel U. J. Peard, rector of the Grace Episcopal Church and Dr. J. Calvin Winder, pastor of the First United Presbyterian Church, officiated at the September 4 nuptials of Miss Virginia Joyann Haley and Mr. Abbott P. Smith III, the latter of Englewood, Colorado. The double-ring wedding was solemnized at Grace Episcopal Church at 4:30 p.m.

Mr. and Mrs. Peter Franklin (Bart) Haley, 692 West Andover

Rd., are the parents of the bride. The bridegroom is the son of Mr. and Mrs. Abbott P. Smith II, of Natick, Massachusetts and New York City.

Mrs. Dean Eckert presented a half-hour program of nuptial music preceding the exchange of vows. Mr. Haley escorted his daughter to the altar.

The bride wore a floor-length gown of organza taffeta styled with a fitted bodice and a full skirt which was worn over a hoop. Iridescent sequins were embroidered on the Venetian lace trim at the scooped neckline.

A hand-made mantilla wedding veil, which she had purchased in Venice, Italy, was the bride's headdress. In her shoes were Irish and Australian sixpence coins, also brought back by the bride when she returned from a trip abroad this summer.

She carried a white prayer book topped with a corsage of white roses and stephanotis and tied with white ribbon lovers-knots.

Preceding the bride to the altar were her three attendants, Miss Janet Simmons, Denver, Colorado, maid of honor and Delta Delta Delta sorority sister; Miss Susan Smith, Natick, Massachusetts and New York City, sister of the bridegroom; and Mrs. Gary L. Haley, sister-in-law of the bride.

They wore like-styled gowns of organza taffeta, the honor attendant in royal blue and the others in cotillion blue. The dresses were styled with fitted bodices and ballerina-length skirts, the drape of the sweetheart necklines repeated in the draped effect at the hemlines.

Each wore a matching headpiece of taffeta and velvet petals with an attached circular veil of shoulder length, and carried an arm bouquet of white carnations tied with white taffeta ribbons.

The bridegroom's father attended him as best man. Mr. James Smith, Natick, Massachusetts and New York City, brother of the bridegroom, served as acolyte. Guests were ushered to their places by Dr. Gary L. Haley, brother of the bride, and Mr. Charles Keiper, Dunkirk.

Following the ceremony, members of and close friends of the families were entertained at a wedding supper in the Lincoln Room at The Loff. Miss Janet Smith, sister of the bridegroom, was in charge of the guest book.

A graduate of Mansfield Senior High School, the bride is a senior at Colorado State University, Fort Collins, Colorado. She served as chaplain of her sorority during the past year.

The bridegroom is a graduate of Denver schools and is studying veterinary medicine at Colorado State University. He owns the Milliron Land and Cattle Company.

Now honeymooning at a mountain retreat in Wyoming, the couple will be at home after September 15, at 917 Remington, Fort Collins, Colorado.

Mr. and Mrs. Hal Moore, Barberton, entertained the bridal party at dinner early last week. The rehearsal dinner was held at Westbrook Country Club.

The newspaper wedding announcement was written by Virginia and displayed a large photograph of Jody at the church in her striking organza taffeta wedding dress. A well-known local photographer presented the couple with an impressive keepsake wedding album. Due to Virginia's disapproval of the event, she did not smile in any of the photographs, which she would later regret. The remainder of the wedding party looked lovely as they enjoyed the special occasion. All through the dinner reception Pete kept telling Jody, "I'm not hungry; let's just go to the motel."

When the couple arrived at their honeymoon hotel room in Mansfield, there was a huge bouquet of beautiful red roses in the room from Burr and Lou Betts, friends from Colorado. Jody left the roses for the maid who cleaned the room the next day. After the wedding and upon their arrival in Colorado, Jody presented Pete with a lovely hand-carved chess set she brought from Switzerland as a wedding gift. Pete really liked chess. He didn't have a chess set, the only thing he owned was his car. "It doesn't say much for our honeymoon," Jody says. "When I was in Europe I bought a book *How to Play Chess*, so I could learn to play. A few days into our honeymoon, on one of the evenings he didn't work, we played chess, I beat him. I got to see a new side of Pete. He stomped up and said, 'Where's that *damn* book!' I went to bed at three or four a.m. Pete stayed up and read the whole book. When he was finished, he couldn't wait to play, 'We are going to play chess! Wake up! Wake up!'"

The honeymoon was in true cowhand style. Jody's mother had reported erroneously that the couple was honeymooning in a Wyoming mountain retreat. "We were both still in college. We couldn't afford a honeymoon. My mother felt a need to stretch the truth a bit in the wedding announcement," Jody says. "At the time, Pete owned few cattle and the land was limited to one lot in town below the rooming house. He did own the brands, Milliron and Milliron Half-Circle. The 'honeymoon at the mountain retreat in Wyoming' was actually Pete working on Frank and Shirley Bosler's cattle ranch while I remained in Fort Collins at my part-time job at the college bookstore."

After they were married, Pete and Jody pursued their college endeavors. Living on $10 a week was tough. Jody continued to stable Starboy at the Birky Ranch. One of Pete's vet school classmates, knowing Pete was pressed for money, asked, "Pete, why don't you sell Jody's horse?" Pete solemnly replied, "Well, If I live long enough for her to divorce me..."

When time allowed, Pete and Jody would spend outings together, riding and roaming the countryside. Once Pete persuaded Jody to go deer hunting at Bosler's ranch and they came upon a beautiful mule deer. Since Pete was riding a difficult horse called Badger, Jody carried the rifle in the scabbard of her saddle on a gentler horse.

Pete whispered as he quietly dismounted, "Give me the gun."

"No," Jody says. "He's too beautiful to kill."

A slow turn of his head in Jody's direction, Pete scratched his brow. A little perturbed, he quickly decided that Jody needed to return to the ranch house and wait while he set out alone. He came back later that day with a beautiful buck.

With Pete's graduation on the horizon, job opportunities were flowing in. "Pete wanted to go to Australia," Jody recalls. "He was offered a terrific job; they would pay all of our transportation over there, roundtrip. We would stay for a year, but they would not pay the fare for my Starboy. I told Pete that whenever he had the money all saved for Starboy's fare, we could go. Pete never saved the money. So, we didn't go to Australia."

The Remington Street Boarding House was a hub of activity. Pete rented to veterans returning from war and fellow Colorado A&M students, including a couple from India. The couple invited Pete and Jody for dinner one evening. The Indian cuisine was an exotic treat. "They served something like Cream of Wheat for dessert," Jody says. "Pete and I glanced at each other with raised eyebrows. We were surprised. We reminisced about it often."

The boarding house was noisy, with people coming and going all hours of the day and night. The newlyweds decided they needed their own space, so they moved to the Birky's ranch. That year, Pete and Jody were invited to the Betts' Circle 2 Ranch annual Christmas Party. The Betts were very wealthy, owning acreage, cattle, horses, and more. The Betts' daughter, Mona, announced that she and her husband were expecting a baby in July. Pete excitedly announced, "We are, too!" This was the first public announcement that Jody was pregnant. Mona gave birth to her daughter, Lisa, on the same day that Jessica was born.

A New Family

In June of 1960, Jody graduated from college. Jessica Lynne was born in July. Named for Jody's grandmother, Jesse, Jessica arrived on Pete's one day off. The couple was enjoying Sunday dinner with Roger and Barbara King. "My water broke while Barbara and I were doing dishes," Jody smiles. "I wanted to help finish the dishes, but Barbara, wiser in the ways of motherhood, insisted we leave for the hospital."

Jessica arrived at 9:30 p.m. on a sultry summer evening at Larimer County Hospital, Fort Collins, Colorado. After the delivery, and knowing that mother and baby were fine, Pete returned to Roger and Barbara's to finish dessert.

Jessica quickly became known as 'Jasper' to Pete. She was baptized the following October; Godmothers Velma Frandson and Nancy Sonneman, Godfather Rowan Frandson, D.V.M..

Residing at the Birky Ranch in Fort Collins, where Starboy was boarded, Jody took care of the Birky horses in exchange for rent. She kept busy with motherly duties and Pete's demanding schedule.

Pete's hunter-green coveralls had to be ironed every day, and Jody would sometimes nod off at the ironing board.

On one evening Pete was busy studying and Jessica was asleep. Jody decided it was a good time to drive to Kraxberger's Dairy, where Pete had worked, to buy some milk. Driving the aged Henry, now with an unreliable gas gauge, Jody ran out of gas. She walked the last mile to the dairy and called Pete to bring her some fuel. He borrowed a car from Birkys, got the gas and arrived in good time. Jody, looking into the car with great alarm asked, "Where's Jessica?" Pete exclaimed, "Oh, no! I forgot about her!" A quick phone to call to Birky's, and Ann, the Birky's teenage daughter, stayed with Jessica until the couple returned. Jessica slept through it all.

The Smiths remained friends with Burr and Lou Betts, Pete's former employer. Burr commissioned Pete to assemble a skeleton of one of his prized Arabians that had colic and died. Burr wanted to prove that Arabians had one less vertebrae, as the story went. It was extra money for Pete. Jody boiled the bones and Pete assembled the skeleton. Hauling the skeleton back to Betts' ranch was a memorable trip. "People were staring at the skeleton on the trailer," Jody remembers. "They yelled 'Feed your horse lady!' Burr kept the skeleton in his fancy tack room until another horse smashed it to pieces."

When Jessica was a baby, the Betts gifted Jessica with a baby Shetland Pony, Tinker Toy. "We stuffed Tinker Toy into Henry to take him back to Fort Collins. We folded the backseats down and fit him right in there," Jody says. "Tinker Toy was moving around in the back seat. He broke a window!"

The Birky ranch had a scenic view from all angles of the Colorado landscape. With sprawling pastures, exquisite trees, sturdy corrals and neat fences, the ranch was a perfect place for the Smith family. Alongside the Birky's barn was a Quonset hut that was used for storage. Due to a recent storm, a big dead tree branch was overhanging the hut and Pete assured Professor Birky that he could dynamite it. Pete climbed up the tree, set the charge and attempted to descend, only to find his boot had lodged in the fork of the tree. He hurriedly removed his boot and scrambled down the tree. Pete and Jody waited and waited for the charge to go off. Pete, wearing only one boot, was tired of waiting and began to go back up the tree to see if the fuse had gone out.

"No! I've had enough anxiety for one day!" Jody demanded.

Just then, the dynamite went off and the branch sailed over the Quonset hut. Pete's boot fell unharmed to the ground. After the dust had settled and his boot recovered, he took the chainsaw, sawed up the branch and stacked the wood by the lane for Professor Birky.

Still in veterinary school, Pete rented several corrals at a feedlot near the college. He continued the Milliron Land and Cattle Company, a lucrative venture. Pete purchased train cars of unwanted Hereford cattle from local ranchers. The white-faced cattle were sometimes thwarted by the blazing Colorado summers, developing cancer of the eye, and had been culled for slaughter. Pete removed the cow's infected eye, stitching it back up, and then taking the cow to the sale. Besides making money at this endeavor, he also profited from the surgical experience. He did all this while running the Remington rooming house and going to classes – a hectic schedule. Jody would ride Starboy out to the cattle corrals to help load the cattle into trucks after Pete had sold them. Pete had to get to class, so Jody drove him there in Henry. Jody hesitated to leave Starboy out in the corral alone all day until Pete finished with classes in the evening, so she immediately drove back to the now empty corral, tied Starboy to the back of the station wagon (on the right-hand side) and ponied him back several miles to the Birky ranch. A risky venture, "but one has to do what one has to do."

During Pete's many endeavors, plus classes, he lost his wedding ring vetting his Hereford cattle. He looked around for a few minutes for the ring, found nothing, and then continued with his work. Later that evening and back home with Jody, he told Jody that he had lost the ring. Jody cuddled Jessica to sleep and put her to bed. Knowing Pete would be studying through the night; she drove Henry to the cattle corral and searched for the missing wedding ring with a flashlight. She gave herself a limit of one hour to find the ring. She found the ring in 45 minutes, and returned home with Pete still studying and Jessica fast asleep.

In his second year of vet school, Pete worked with Dr.

Frandson at the Mile High Racetrack, a Greyhound track, making routine observations and collecting urine to test for illegal drugs. Pete enjoyed the company of the hounds. When Pete showed up for work at the track there would be new dogs, replacing the slower, less lucrative hounds. He worked at the track in the summer evenings, sometimes arriving home at one or two in the morning. He would tell Jody all of the dirty jokes that he had heard at the track that day. Living on a shoestring, he munched on the leftover popcorn at the dog track; he ate so much of it, his teeth suffered from the hard, stale kernels. A local dentist told him he would need to have all his teeth pulled, and be fitted with dentures. The whole affair would take some time and be quite costly. The rancher he worked for agreed to see to it the dentist was paid out of Pete's cattle. After the first tooth was pulled, it was so painful Pete never went back.

"I was working in the kitchen boiling the bones of a Greyhound Pete had brought home from the track," Jody smiles. "Pete was going to use the skeleton to explain to his clients the anatomy of a dog. The legs of the Greyhound were sticking out of the boiling water. The house reeked of formaldehyde. The doorbell rang and a salesman was at the door. "Do you want to stay for lunch?" I asked him. "Oh, no!" eyeing the pot of Greyhound bones. I never saw him again."

"I remember Pete put himself through A&M on a shoestring," sister Carol says, "and whenever he needed money he had a wealthy horse friend down in Denver that he could still work for. He had Arabian horses. Pete was very close to those horses and the gentleman who owned the place. Pete had no money, a wife, and now a baby."

With Pete still in vet school, Jody learned she was pregnant again. She continued to ride Starboy during her second pregnancy. Janet came to live with Pete and Jody to help with baby Jessica. Janet and Ann Birky became fast friends. Like Pete, Janet had been taught to ride early on and enjoyed riding in the foothills of the Colorado mountains. Jody and Janet would ride, even during Jody's false contractions.

As her pregnancy progressed, the western saddle horn made it difficult to ride, so she switched to an English saddle. Pete was concerned. He had seen Dr. Rumley on the street and she mentioned to Pete that the baby's head was down and that the baby could be born anytime. Concerned, Pete removed Starboy's horseshoes so that Jody could not ride long distances.

Abbott Pliny Smith IV came along in April of 1962. "The evening before Pat was born, I began having labor pains," Jody smiles. "I tried to talk Pete into delivering our baby since he had attended many different births, albeit of the four-footed variety. He was having none of it and sped through a snow storm to arrive at the hospital a little before midnight. I refused to get out of the car in spite of his pleadings because I didn't want to be charged for an extra day. We entered the hospital at 12:15 a.m. Pat was born at 1:51 a.m. at Larimer County Hospital, Fort Collins." He weighed 7 pounds, 6 ounces, a cuddly new cowboy. He was baptized the following June by Father Edwin L. Ostertag; Godmother Hope Rivers, Godfathers Les Rivers and Edward Kueck. Abbott IV was nicknamed 'Pat' after Jody's father.

Pete graduated vet school debt free in June. The graduation ceremony was eventful. He had worked long and hard to get his diploma. As he walked across the stage, he stopped, unrolled his diploma, and checked to make sure it was correct.

His little family stayed on at the Birky ranch briefly after Pete's graduation. The atmosphere at the Birky Ranch was family-oriented; positive, encouraging, and supportive. While Pete was studying in college, interning, and working part time, Jody was completely consumed with her handsome husband, her children, her horse, Jessica's pony, and their Australian Shepherd, Shep. Eventually, Shep had to be rehomed. He was a known biter, and with Jessica toddling, they couldn't take the risk. Dr. Voss, one of Pete's professors, suggested a new home for Shep with a couple without children.

Good friends Les and Hope Rivers were frequent visitors to the Birky Ranch, visiting Pete and Jody. Les was still working at the ranch in Wyoming where he first met Pete. On occasion, the bed of

Les and Hope's pickup truck was covered with bales of straw and Professor Birky remarked that it was a bit odd they hauled straw around. It hadn't occurred to him that under the straw was a mule deer all cut up and ready for Pete and Jody's freezer. "We couldn't afford baby food," Jody recalls. "When Jessica and Pat were ready for solid food they got a lot of government beef, ground up in my Foley food mill, a small hand-turned implement to make baby food."

Sniff and Smith

Pete accepted a position with Elmer Sniff, D.V.M., in Lamar, Colorado. The couple uprooted their menagerie of animals, which now included the pony, Tinker Toy, Jody's gelding, Starboy and a cat named Trefa. The house they moved into was owned by Dr. Sniff's brother-in-law, a hog farmer. "Those damn hogs," Pete would proclaim in the middle of the night. The noise of the hogs banging their feeders was annoying. *Bam! Bam!* Jody remembers, "Starboy got used to the hogs before we did. We lived there a whole two months. Too long! So, then Pete bought this little house that had some property, not *property*, but like two lots, in Lamar. We had good neighbors, including teenager Sammy Cowan, who would later prove to be a great babysitter. We could put up a corral; there was a shed for the horses. It was right on the edge of town. We didn't have a lot of money, but some money. So, Pete said, 'Well, we're going to buy this and live here.' So, we did. We didn't even bother going down the road. Well, down the road was the city dump. We found that out quickly that it was better than the hog farm. The only thing was the rattlesnakes. I would go out in the yard with a broom first thing in the morning and make sure there were no rattlesnakes before I let the dogs out, or the kids out. When we drove by the Lamar Golf Course, we'd see them slither across the road. Pete would say, 'I know they're going to need their clubs today!' We lived in Lamar for a year. It was 120 degrees in the summer. It was 30 degrees below in the winter. You couldn't even see the mountains from there."

Dr. Sniff really liked Pete and his enthusiast demeanor as well as his lust for life. The receptionist answered the phone "Dr. Sniff and Smith, may I help you?" This became a funny anecdote through the years; *Sniff and Smith*. Pete drove a yellow vet truck to outcalls. He was keen for chewing tobacco at the time, to Jody's dismay. The yellow truck showed signs of brown tobacco stains on the driver's side door. Pete had stopped smoking before they were married, began chewing tobacco instead, which he would finally give up. "Driving home from watching the movie *Butch Cassidy and the Sundance Kid* I was quite enthralled with the Sundance Kid as portrayed by Robert Redford. Pete stopped that talk by saying, 'You weren't complaining about the big wad of tobacco in his cheek like you did mine!' I had not noticed it."

As a new veterinarian, Pete worked long hours. Family outings were rare, but Pete enjoyed spending time with Jody and the kids. Jessica was running here and there; Pat was busy being cute. Pete would throw Pat in the air just to hear him giggle, and catch him in strong arms. "Pete was playing with Pat one day. He gently tossed Pat up in the air, stumbled, and Pat fell to the ground. Pat cried," Jody winces. "We took Pat to Dr. Sniff's hospital for an X-ray. It was after-hours at the clinic. Pete took the X-ray over an X-ray of a dog's leg to save money. The next day, we took Pat to the pediatrician along with the X-ray. The pediatrician said, 'I can't tell you much about the dog, but the kid's fine.'"

The Lamar, Colorado, weather leaves a lot to be desired. The summer of 1962, not one drop of rain fell. Pete would say, "When it's not raining, it's snowing; when it's not snowing its blowing." Sand blew everywhere, in the eyes, nose, and throat – all day. Everything was very arid and crusty, the year with no rain. Pete, from the ocean-spray coasts of Maine, and Jody, from the dense greenery of Ohio, realized it was more than they could bear. The couple thought they could find something better. They were tired of the unruly climate, rattlesnakes, sagebrush, and sand. They wanted lush, green pastures where a vet could have a large animal practice while raising healthy kids. "Wonderful people in Colorado, but terrible weather," Jody says. "When they learned that we were looking to move, the neighbors had already decided who would take our dogs Shane and Melody. They were quite surprised we had always planned to take them with us."

Pete liked the change of seasons, but was in favor of raising his family where it rained at least several times a year. He was looking for a lot of cheap farmland near a university town. He wanted culture and access to a quality life; that is what he dreamed of.

In August of 1963 the annual American Veterinary Medical Association (AMVA) meeting was held in New York City. Jody and Pete stayed with Pete's parents, Abbott and Betty, at their 771 West End Avenue apartment. Jessica and Pat were left behind to stay with Jody's parents in Mansfield.

Early in their marriage, Jody had complained to Pete about his frequent use of coarse language. At his first opportunity, walking with Jody and her father, Pete said, "Bart, what do you call that?" pointing to a small ant crawling along at their feet. Bart replied, "Why that's a piss ant, too small to piss on." "Daddy!" Jody exclaimed, "you never talked like that around me." "Oh, you're married now," Bart shrugged. Pete just smiled his mischievous grin.

"Betty, Pete's mother, worked for a publishing company, a very big publishing company in New York City," recalls Jody. "Abbott had his own business at that point. He was very successful in some ways. He had been bankrupt, but he was later successful. He just got carried away. So, we went back East. I tell you, it was like coming into the Garden of Eden after living with no water. It was so dry in Colorado. We pretty well decided we wanted to live toward the eastern seaboard."

While Pete was attending AVMA seminars during the day and evening, Jody bravely took the subway by herself to see Rosa Bonheur's famous painting *The Horse Fair* at the Metropolitan Museum of Art. She was frightened to travel the subway alone, but Pete persuaded her she would be all right to venture to see the larger than life, amazing painting.

During their stay in New York, the couple looked for veterinary practices for sale. AVMA and realtors posted clinics for sale throughout the United States. There were several that sparked inter-est – one in Upstate New York, and the other in Athens, Ohio. They looked at a clinic near Buffalo, the practice was beautiful, of course, but this was August and Pete asked the realtor, "How high does the snow get here?" Already he was thinking about doing outcalls and the drive through the deep snow. The winter snow in Buffalo can top as much as ten to twelve feet. The couple shied from the thought of bitter cold and harsh winters, and Pete decided he didn't want to be too close to his family in New York.

Pete, 22 years old, revisiting Maine

Leaving New York, they visited Pete's childhood home in Maine and connected with some of Pete's extended family and friends. The very wealthy LMC Smith family, who then owned Pete's childhood farm before it became a state park, and who are of no relation, congratulated Pete on his graduation from vet school and position with Dr. Sniff, and appropriately said, "The world is your oyster." Jody remembers. "It was a nice house, a mansion for a summer place in Maine. They were very, very wealthy. You had to follow a little path in the house. All over the place were first-edition books, paintings, and all this incredible stuff."

After their visit to Maine, Pete and Jody returned to Ohio. There were several practices for sale in Ohio that were intriguing, including Dr. Manly's practice in Athens. It was out on Route 56. Pete and Jody went to look at it. Pete was pretty astute, pretty observant, knew that it had flooded inside the building. The watermarks along the clinic wall were a tell-all. Being close to Margaret Creek, the clinic was in a flood zone. Then Pete heard that James Bratton, D.V.M. and Marvin Phillips, D.V.M., of Athens Veterinary Hospital on Pomeroy Road in Athens were looking for an employee. With Pete's excellent credentials and quality recommendations, they offered him a job. Pete accepted.

The farmland and the homes in Athens County were much cheaper than the dry, dusty offerings in Colorado. The beauty of the rolling hills, the climate, and the vicinity of Ohio University were exactly what the couple was looking for.

We all acquire each strand of warp and woof in unique
and wonderful ways according to our experiences.
Pete Smith

_____

4 OHIO

IN THE FALL of 1963, when Pete was 25 years old, he and Jody
packed up their family and animals and set out for Ohio. The sadness
of leaving good friends at Lamar was overshadowed by the
excitement of the new venture ahead. Jessica and Pat stayed in
Mansfield with Jody's parents while Pete and Jody drove the long-
distance cross-country. Pete drove the mid-size two-ton Hertz truck
containing all of their earthly possessions, and Jody drove the horse
trailer with Starboy and Tinker Toy. Melody, Pete's large black and
tan coonhound, rode shotgun with Pete, while Shane, the German
Shepherd, rode with Jody. "We started out that way," Jody says,
"but driving the horse trailer made me nervous, so we switched. Pete
said, 'Damn it, you drive the truck!' I drove the Hertz truck,
following Pete who was driving Henry, the Ford Ranch Wagon, with
the horse trailer so I could keep an eye on my horse. Of course,
Tinker Toy was in the trailer; too, you just couldn't see him. It was
a fun trip."

But the journey was slow and arduous. The couple made the
best of it. "Near Booneville, Missouri, Henry was pulling the horse

trailer and decided to break down," Jody says. "An unscrupulous and unpleasant auto repair mechanic came and hauled the Ranch Wagon off to his repair shop, only to be redeemed at an unreasonably high price, but he knew we had little choice. This was balanced by a friendly widow who saw us by the side of the road with the horse trailer grazing Starboy and Tinker Toy. She invited us to put them in her unused, nearby barn for the night so we could take the Hertz truck and the dogs to a motel. She kindly refused any payment; a more pleasant memory of Missouri."

At a gas station stop late the next night in the middle of St. Louis, they let the dogs out to stretch. Pete's curious coonhound stuck her cold nose into the buttocks of a short-skirted "lady of the night" as only a 100-pound coonhound could. The prostitute whirled around to hit Pete who was backing up and pointing at Melody. "It was the dog. It was the dog!" Pete cried. The woman started laughing and knelt down. She hugged and petted Melody, then Shane, and started telling Pete and Jody about the dog she had as a child.

Finally driving into Athens on Route 33, the old homemade horse trailer had a flat tire. Stopped on the side of the road with Starboy and Tinker Toy out of the trailer, Pete wearily grabbed the tire iron and spare tire. A car pulled up alongside to help.

"Need any help?" Tom, the Pomeroy postmaster grinned.

"Well, sure…thanks…" replied Pete.

"Where you headed?" Tom asked.

"Athens. I'll be working for two doctors, Dr. Bratton and Dr. Phillips, there on the corner, Athens Veterinary Hospital," Pete pointed.

"Oh, yeah. I know the place," Tom said, as he grabbed a lug nut.

Veterinarian Joins Staff
Press Release

A 1962 graduate of Colorado State University, Dr. Abbott P. Smith, has joined the staff of the Athens Veterinary Hospital, Pomeroy Road. The hospital has two other veterinarians, Dr. Marvin Phillips and Dr. James Bratton. Doctor Smith has been in private practice in Lamar, Colorado, and while in school worked for four years with the Colorado State Racing Commission with Dr. Frandson. Doctor Smith, who completed the six-year course at Colorado State, was born in Augusta, Maine. Married and the father of two children, Dr. Smith, 25, lives on Elliottsville Road, near Athens.

Arrangements had been made to rent a gracious farmhouse on Elliottsville Road, off State Route 56. Known as the "Taylor" property, the house was for sale, but out of their price range. It had very little land and only the ground floor was inhabitable; the second floor needed a complete remodel. In the meantime, Starboy and Tinker Toy found pasture at Dr. Phillips' place.

The family quietly settled at the Taylor property taking time to get used to the new territory. After work hours, Pete refinished his recent purchase of a roll-top desk and took care of the family nest. He strung an electric fence for pasture behind the Taylor property and moved Starboy and Tinker Toy from Dr. Phillips' temporary pasture. Working at Athens Veterinary Hospital kept Pete busy. People were intrigued with the new handsome vet in town who had graduated from Colorado State University. He was sought after by many local farmers for everything from routine inoculations to large animal ailments. Everyone liked Pete's demeanor. His friendliness and charismatic smile were captivating. A fresh vet, he knew all of the latest medical procedures, and had a few innovative "vetting" ideas of his own.

One afternoon, Dr. Phillips called Jody, "Just wanted to let you know that Pete's all right. Silver Bridge collapsed between Ohio and West Virginia. Pete got there just as the bridge went down. We knew he was in that area and wanted to make sure he was okay." Another time, Jody remembers Dr. Phillips pulling up in his truck and having to help Pete out. Pete had accidently injected himself in his hand with the Bangs Vaccine when he was inoculating cattle. "He was really ill," Jody recalls. "Nauseated, weak, sick, the whole bit. Pete, of course, wouldn't go to a hospital." And there were other hazards, too. Horse kicks, cow kicks, dog bites, and the rest.

Human interactions in Ohio's Appalachian region could be interesting as well. "In the Fall of 1963, living at the Taylor property, we were on our way home from church and run off the road by an aggressive driver," Jody says. "When we got home, Pete ordered us out of the car. He took off after the other car, returned home about a half hour later. I was relieved to see Pete and our car appear to be undamaged. I asked him, 'What happened?' He replied, 'Oh, further education.' He explained he found what he thought was the offending car parked in a driveway off Route 56. He ran up to the house and pounded on the door, shouting for the s.o.b. who ran his family off the road. A giant of a man appeared at the door and said, 'Okay, jackass, feel the hood of that car. You'll see it hasn't been driven today, but if you still want to fight, I'm ready.' Pete muttered an apology and came home, 'tail between his legs' as he described it."

Pete was excited about his work, meeting new clients, getting to know the flavor of the hill country, and the funky college-town aesthetics of Athens. Days and nights were busy and sleep came easy. Pete enjoyed his employment with Dr. Bratton and Dr. Phillips, but he wanted to build a large animal vet hospital of his own. And he wanted to focus on equines. Pete thought that Dr. Bratton and Dr. Phillip's idea of a vet hospital was maybe something in the garage, not the vision Pete had in mind. Pete steadily looked for a place to build his own clinic. Jody was too busy with kids to know what Pete was up to.

Gene Engle, a horseman and cattleman from Vinton County, found out that Pete was in the area and made Pete a very good offer to move to Vinton County and set up his practice. Since Gene would be backing Pete's practice, he would have priority over other clients. Pete was seriously thinking about it. He respected and liked Gene Engle. But after talking with other people in the area, decided to decline the offer. Pete, being such an independent guy, didn't want to be beholding to one person.

Finding a New Home

The Smiths lived at the Taylor property for six months. During that time, Pete hired realtor Carl Clifford to show them houses and farms in the area. Carl, a member of the Episcopalian Church where Pete and Jody attended, showed the couple a few places in the area that they might like. "I told the realtor that I didn't want to be close to a highway," Jody remembers. One farm was south of Athens on State Route 33, which would have been handy for Pete to drive, but it was on the corner of a road and the house was a few yards from the road. And at that time Route 33 was *swoosh-swoosh-swoosh* with traffic, not the best environment to raise kids and pets. Arriving at the farm, Jody refused to get out of the car.

"I already told you, we have to have enough room to fence in a yard for our kids and our dogs," she repeated to Pete.

"Oh, just look at it," Pete replied with a frown.

"Why would I waste your time and these people's time looking at it? I am not getting out of the car. I already told you, we can't have something that's close to a road."

Embarrassed, Pete got out of the car and looked around the farm, just for the sake of looking.

Carl took the couple to a farm over Dividing Ridge Hill. Jody was not impressed, at first. "This is a long drive from town," Jody said. "It's too far, Pete, too far from town and the Athens Vet Hospital. I think it's just too far." She had no clue that Pete had already cased the farm and liked it. Pete was envisioning an office with examination rooms, surgical tables and recovery rooms. Jody was looking for a kid-friendly home and a place to keep Starboy and Tinker Toy.

It was a dry, fall day when they drove across the cattleguard, over the McDougall Creek, up the hill to where the 1860s farmhouse lazily looks over the bank to the valley below. As they got out of the car, Carl explained that the house had once been a strategic stop in the Underground Railroad. He knew the history of the house would stir Jody's interest. They viewed the inside of the house, then the pastures. Carl drove the couple all the way back through the pasture to show them the property's great potential. They were sold. Pete liked the idea of the house on the hill with plenty of road frontage and farmland. He was secretly thinking about a clinic in the valley below. Jody liked the idea that the house had historical significance and her horse could be in the pasture by the house. The picture window overlooking the far meadow where horses could roam was the perfect vision of prosperity. They bought the house, barn, well, 250 acres and fenced road frontage, all on a state highway, for $17,500.

In his book, *The McDougal Story*, Harold O'Neal recorded the people and history of the area where Pete and Jody decided to live. He describes in detail the 1850 McDougal Community, its settlement and the underground railway system that was conducive to moving slaves through Ohio to the Canadian border. Pete and Jody's home was part of the underground railway, as well as the shallow hillside caverns that were once owned by pioneer William Donaldson.

One cave in particular continues to hold interest, even though now destroyed by a cave-in, as recorded by Harold O'Neal.

> Around the beginning of this century the thick stratum of sandstone which jutted out from the latter cave or caves, then weakened by widening cracks, one night broke away from the hill as great boulders which thundered down the short but steep incline, coming at the bottom to their final rest. Our father remembered as a boy of hearing the ominous sound. This is still a place of rugged scenic beauty, a sight well worth the short hike necessary to get there.

Harold O'Neal's initials, as well as many others, can still be seen on one of the fallen rocks.

A local newspaper reporter, Dan Linneman, of the *Athens Messenger* wrote the compelling article, "En route to freedom: Athens County played a role in the Underground Railroad." Linneman traveled to Milliron Farm to retrace the sophisticated trails of the Underground Railroad, indicating that there are so many tales and legends of the area's impact on the Underground Railroad that it is difficult to determine fact from fiction. The article includes a large photograph of Jody and dogs looking at a collapsed recess cave, also known as the Negro Den. With walking stick in her right hand and signature long braid, Jody tells the newspaper's photographer, Chad Stiles, the secrets and history of the surrounding underground caves, sandstone cliffs, frequent nooks, and dense woodlands.

Thirteen years before Pete and Jody moved into their new home, Mr. Fred Beasley and his wife Jenny had managed to get together the original 500-acre land grant that was given to Jenny's relatives during the Revolutionary War. Not long after Jenny died, Fred Beasley had put a portion of the original land grant up for sale: two farms, one of which was the Smith's new farm. Jody remembers, "The farm that we bought, I didn't realize at the time why Pete liked it so much better than the other farm Fred Beasley had for sale. Of course, the other farm had no road frontage. Not impressed by the significant history of the house, Fred restored the plumbing in our farmhouse and had the area where the slaves were hidden torn out. But Pete had his mind on building a vet hospital right down there by the road. He didn't mention that to me. He was always thinking ahead; way ahead of me."

Pete bought out of the Athens Veterinary Hospital practice. Local resident George Guthrie helped with moving the Smith family from Elliottsville Road to State Route 550, just outside of Amesville. Pete named the place Milliron Farm and worked out of the farmhouse, mostly farm calls to the clients he had acquired the few years he had been in Athens County. His dream was coming true and he was enjoying the result of hard work and determination.

"The first year before the clinic was built, my God, that was a nightmare," Jody says. "I had to answer the phone 24 hours a day. And with two little kids, having to go to the barn. We didn't have answering machines back then. It was not like you could say 'call me back in an hour.' The kids were too young to answer the phone. Pete was always on outcalls."

Before the clinic, the pasture went right up to the road, to Route 550 and was fenced for livestock. The cattleguard, that would later become a signature rumble into the Smith sanctuary, was already in place when the property was purchased. The Smith's horses loved to race up the hill to the farmhouse and barnyard. "One time," Jody remembers, "I foolishly jumped on Starboy bareback and bareheaded without really thinking first, and all the horses raced up the hill. Fortunately, I clung to his mane and he stopped when we got to the barn. Definitely one of my wildest rides."

A young mother, Jody stayed busy taking care of kids, livestock, and Pete's schedule. Weary from the day's events, she was startled when a deputy sheriff drove his car up the hill to the farmhouse, lights blazing. "Ma'am," the deputy said through the screen door, "do you have black cattle? Well, they're out on the highway. Looks like the cows plowed through the fence." Jody went with the deputy to find the pasture fence down and the cattle out. The deputy helped her herd the Angus back into the pasture, but had to race off to an emergency. Pete was down in Meigs County on a calving case. A neighbor, Joe Lucas, wise in the ways of cattle, drove the cattle up the hill to the barn. Then, in a heavy rain, he helped Jody try to repair the post and rail fence that came with the farm. "We practically had the whole thing dismantled before we got it reassembled," Jody laughs. The cattle were then banished to the upper pasture.

May 1969

Pictures of Pete illustrate "Spring Check Up: Horse Saver" in a horse magazine; however, Pete is not mentioned in the article or picture captions. The article praises veterinarians for their care and encourages horse owners to have their horses vet checked regularly, including for up-to-date vaccinations. In the four pictures connected to this article is Pete in vet attire, at work. The first picture is of a young Pete, in his white lab coat, talking with Mrs. Martha Bratton and her son. Martha's son is sitting on a stool intently looking through a microscope.

The second picture of Pete is at a family farm in summertime. He is wearing his customary gumboots and short-sleeved work coveralls. The picture depicts Pete injecting a pinned-eared buckskin horse in its left chest muscle. A young girl with long braids holds the lead-rope as she leans against Pete's white Ford truck. The truck bed's outer compartments were used as Pete's dispensary. The compartments were opened and contained everything Pete needed for farm calls.

The third picture shows Pete at a large stable yard completing a thorough examination of a horse's feet, pasterns, cannons, hocks, and knees. Pete is kneeling on his left knee, swabbing the horse's cannon. The horse is blanketed from head to tail, being held by a fellow with a long rope. Pete's portable surgical table and medicine bag is nearby.

The final picture shows Pete floating a horse's teeth. Client Sherry Indestadt is holding a dark bay horse and a speculum, a device veterinarians use to float a horse's teeth. Pete is intently peering in the horse's agape mouth with a rasp held tightly in both hands.

The New Clinic

In 1969 while working for Dr. Bratton and Dr. Phillips, Pete was busy planning his new clinic - the reception area, examination rooms, surgery area, and livestock barn. Pete had plans to replicate his new clinic after one of the top equine facilities in Kentucky. He would name the new clinic Milliron after the cattle brand he began in Colorado. Pete hired an architect to help with the clinic design. A barn was built first, then the clinic. Once the clinic and barn were in place, the state inspector said that the barn and the clinic were too close together and would not meet state fire code. One of the buildings had to be moved. Of course, being on the edge financially, Pete and Jody couldn't see how this could be possible. The architect refused to go to the regulatory board in Columbus to appeal, so Pete traveled to Columbus by himself, still in his green coveralls and boots from farm calls. Wiser, more practical "suits" decided that if Pete would join the two buildings by building a roof to join them together, it would meet the code by qualifying as one building.

A roof soon joined the barn and the clinic, which provided a covered area for transporting the large animal surgery table from the prep area to the surgery room, then back to the padded, straw filled recovery stall after surgery. On non-large animal surgery days, it made a useful carport for Pete's current vehicle, which could be quickly backed out of the way if a large animal emergency requiring surgery arrived.

Milliron Clinic Only Part of Area Vet's Plans
Press Release, November 9, 1969

Two related events may become increasingly important to the eastern section of Athens County's Ames Township and might eventually have some impact on a wider area of Southeastern Ohio.

One is the completion of Milliron Clinic. The other is the purchase by Dr. Abbott Smith, the clinic's founder, of the Fred Phillips farm.

The Milliron Clinic is along Route 50A [later to become Route 550] opposite the entrance to Windy Hills Farm. It has been under construction for some time, and it is among the most complete hospitals for the treatment of sick or injured animals to be found in the state. Dr. Smith says that his clinic has some modern facilities which are not yet available by the Veterinary School of Ohio State University.

The clinic facilities are housed in two adjacent buildings. The offices are in a brick building which is entered from the parking lot which is on the opposite side of the building from Route 50A.

Besides the office, this building has two consultation rooms for examination of small animals, a dispensary, a darkroom and storage areas.

Larger animals, such as horses, have their own quarters in an adjacent frame building. It contains stalls and an indoor corral equipped with a mechanical exerciser. Facilities for X-raying and administering anesthetics are available here.

They are near a unique hydraulically-controlled operating table. This table can be put into a vertical position and a patient walked to its side. After the animal has been fastened to it and anesthetized, the table is rotated to a horizontal position. Casters are placed under it, and it is rolled to the operating room in the main building.

Following an operation, the table is rolled to a recovery room in the frame building. Here the patient is deposited on a clay floor which has been covered with fresh hay. Foam rubber covers the sides of this room to prevent the possibility of an animal injuring itself.

When he named his clinic, Dr. Smith was not aware that Milliron is a family name that is part of the county. He explained that a milliron is a piece of metal which holds a lathe shaft to a pillow block. He adopted the shape of this as a brand design for his livestock when he lived in Colorado.

The clinic occupies a small portion of the 280-acre farm. They have cattle, riding horses, dogs, sheep, goats, burros and ducks on the premises. From this, the conclusion that they are an outdoor oriented family is fairly obvious.

Just as the Clinic was being completed the Smiths were able to acquire the 760-acre Fred Phillips farm which stretches across Route 50A and extends along a part of Athens Route 3 near the intersection with Routes 690 and 50A. W.P. "Bill" Clark of Strout Realty negotiated the transaction which he says involved one of the largest tracts of land to change ownership in Athens County recently.

Dr. Smith hopes to develop gradually his combined holdings into a recreational area. He views this as a gradual transformation to be accomplished over a number of years.

Meanwhile, persons who wish to ride or hike over the area are welcome to do so, as long as they close gates and refrain from leaving litter behind. Because of the frequent presence of horseback riders and hikers, the 1,040-acre tract has been declared a game preserve and no hunting is permitted.

Among Smith's long-range plans is laying out restricted five to ten-acre home sites on the part of his tract roughly north of Route 50A. These sites will be so planned as to appeal to buyers who would like to live in the country with enough land around them so they can own pleasure horses.

One of the first things Smith hopes to do is start a cow and calf raising operation which can utilize corn grown on his bottom lands as well as the grass which grows abundantly on many of the acres. Smith also has some sheep grazing on his farm, accompanied by goats to keep dogs away.

There is possibility that Smith may eventually be able to construct a lake on part of his property which is adjacent to 690. All the land which comprises the watershed of two creeks which would feed the lake is located on the property.

The countryside in the vicinity of the proposed lake offers a variety of interesting visual experiences to the hiker or rider. There are sandstone cliffs and several huge chunks of sandstone which have fallen from them so long ago that they have been split by the roots of good size trees.

Development of this area probably will take years, because it must be cleared of thorn bearing locust trees. However, it might be attractive to some campers in its present wild state.

It is the location closest to Athens which has been suggested for development of this type of recreational facility. Service station employees and others in the Athens vicinity say they have frequent inquiries about camping facilities in the area. They usually direct those who ask about such facilities either to the Burr Oak region near Glouster or to Royal Oak Park off Route 7 north of Pomeroy. Smith's projected camp sites would be considerably closer than either of these.

The 1969 article includes a large picture of Pete performing horse surgery on his state-of-the-art hydraulic operating table. James Keirns is assisting Pete during the surgery. The horse is fastened vertically to the table by large straps, anesthetized, X-rayed, and then while still on the table, wheeled into the operating room in the adjoining building.

On February 1, 1971, Milliron Clinic officially opened. Pete scheduled farm calls two weekdays and Saturdays, appointments and small animal surgeries were scheduled for the rest of the week. Jody kept the appointment and financial books, and answered the phone, all while caring for Jessica, Pat, and the family's pets.

Pete wanted to have a Grand Opening. Jody remembers, "A wealthy Ohio client, E.E. Davis, was politically connected and planned to get Ohio's Governor Rhodes there. But Pete got too busy." The Grand Opening notion melted away. "Pete always had great plans for it, but then he'd be off to West Virginia trying to make money," explains Jody. "E.E. Davis and his wife treated Pete like royalty when we went down there to their Royal Oaks farm. They couldn't have been nicer."

My Dad thought his call on earth
was to take care of animals.
That was his way of serving God.
Jessica Smith Fox

------

5 SERVING GOD

TRAVELING TO MILLIRON Clinic from US Route 33 South to the State Route 550 exit, you will encounter rolling foothills fanning from the Appalachian Mountains. Sedimentary rocks jut out from low cliffs lined with deciduous trees, stately evergreens, and thick underbrush. Driving along the two-lane road, several small burghs snuggle parallel to the banks of Sugar Creek and what used to be the 50A Inn, later called Sweet Water Station, then Silver Saddle Bar, currently Mel's Roadhouse. The country road twists and turns, ascending and dipping, spying important landmarks and venues. The McDougal Church stands reverently to the right, a hub of community activity. Cattle, horses, barns, old farmhouses, and a Volkswagen buried halfway in the ground, are some of the sights. Finally, on the right-hand side of the road, the iconic sign "Milliron Clinic: Abbott P. Smith, D.V.M." comes into view.

Turning south, the rumble of the cattleguard signifies that you have officially entered Milliron Farm and Clinic. To the left flies the Milliron flag. Created by employee and artist Kelly Lincoln, the flag's blue background is offset by the Milliron Brand. Sycamore trees grove to the right of the clinic, just beyond the bridge over the McDougal Branch of Federal Creek. The road to the farmhouse is just ahead, up the steep hill, beyond the oak plank fence that surrounds the facility.

The clinic stands to the left of the bridge; regal with its variegated orange ombre` brick, proprietary stables, and surgical facilities. Clicker-training dog agility articles can be seen to the side of the barn, as well as the vast supply of firewood for the clinic's woodstove.

Entering the clinic through the glass door, you'll find the art of Shary B. Akers, a former Ohio University student who painted the large mural of Milliron Farm. Depicted in the mural are the animals Pete and Jody brought with them from Colorado, and some acquired after their arrival; Persimmon, the grey jenny; Lollipop, the black jenny; Silver Dollar, the pony; Poo 2, the seal-point Siamese cat; Jody's German shepherd, Shane; Melody, Pete's coonhound; Tinker Toy, Jessica's Shetland pony; Cricket, Pete's mare; and Jody's beloved gelding Starboy. The local McDougal Church stands in the background amidst the rolling hills. The floor to ceiling mural captures the essence of the Smith family; their love of animals, their passion for art, and their commitment to community.

The smell of combiotic mingled with Clorox bleach fill the reception area. Sitting on ochre tile floors are church pews for clients and pets to wait. Across from the church pews is the counter where the receptionist greets clients, answers questions, and keeps the daily schedule. Behind the reception desk are drawers upon drawers of client's files.

Through the years, several adopted felines have sat regally on the counter; listening and watching. Hairball was the most notorious. She was a calico feline that had been dropped off with a serious illness and her owners requested her to be euthanized. Pete decided to operate on Hairball, and, with the owner's permission, he would keep her at the clinic. In her variegated grey, orange, and tan coat, she graced advertisements, postcards, and clinic correspondence. She was the Milliron Clinic icon for many years. Her portrait was on this advertisement that Dr. Smith placed in local phonebooks and newspapers:

At the heart of critical care

Abbott (Pete) Smith, D.V.M.
Equine & Small Animals
14025 State Rte. 550 Athens
Dentistry Arthroscopy Ultrasound
Computerized EKG * 2 Fiber optic Scopes
3 X-ray Machines
w/Automatic Processing
Automated Blood & Chemistry Lab
Complete Orthopedic Layout
"…to allow our staff of 12 to better
Serve your animal friends."

The reception counter wraps around to the animal scale, where animals are weighed upon arrival. To the left of the scale is the woodstove, two examination rooms, and another seating area. On the knotty pine wall proudly hangs the Moravian Creed along with Dr. Smith's trade-mark, the Milliron Brand.

The aquarium that is encased in the reception counter holds the interest of children and adults alike as they wait in the reception area. Through the years, the tank contained several species of fish, including goldfish, catfish, and alligator gar.

The door to the kennels is to the left of the reception desk. Barking dogs and mewing cats greet your entrance into the belly of the clinic. Kennels are arranged from floor to ceiling and contain animals recovering from surgery and those awaiting treatment. A nearby table is where animals are prepped for surgery and sedation. A few of the tables came from Army surplus, while others are high-dollar surgical steel. There are shelves of bandages, syringes, and other important vetting instruments. Vet techs are busy working on small dogs and cats; cleaning teeth, clipping nails, and replacing soiled bandages. Down the hall is what used to be the furnace room, but is now the laundry room. Next is the darkroom for developing X-rays, and then forward to the large surgical area, leading to the surgical preparation room, the clinic stables, and more kennels.

Outside, the parking lot sometimes fills completely, with no room to turn around. Mega horse trailers, lowboys, stock trailers, shabby trailers, and many more, all have made a mark amidst the gravel and square drainage outlets that dot the parking lot. Parking lot obstacles came in the form of cats (Simon) who liked to jump in car windows and pee in the interior, but the peacocks remain the most memorable. They were the guardians of the outer limits. Pete had acquired peacock chicks as barter for vet services. "I had nothing to do with the peacocks," Jody makes clear. "One time Gil Whalen's killer turkey attacked a peacock. The peacock went away for a while. It came back and would tromp around on the roof of our house. Our metal roof. You could imagine the noise. The peacock flew off the hill to the clinic parking lot one day, swooping and calling. Pete was working on a paint mare that was being a real jerk, jumping around, being difficult. When the peacock swooped down into the parking lot where the horse was, that horse just froze. The horse never moved again until Pete was finished vetting it. The last peacock was stolen when someone broke into the clinic and lifted eleven dollars, some rabies vaccine, and J.B., short for Jaunty Bird, the last of the peacocks. The night of the robbery, we could see the tire tracks up our hill. We could also see by the scratches on the inside of our kitchen door that Puff, my Belgian sheepdog, had greeted them with growls and barking. J.B. had already cost Pete plenty when he decided to roost on top of a client's car and scratched it, requiring Pete to pay for a new paint job. After that, I said, '*No more peacocks.*'"

Press Release February 8, 1972

Being a veterinarian isn't just an occupation for Abbott P. Smith; it's his life.

"I've always had a rapport with animals because they can sense my love for them. It's surprising how much they behave like little kids when they enter my office. A horse or cow who knows he's healthy gets a shot and then feels abused. You have to show love to make them realize it's for their own good," Smith said.

Smith was graduated from Colorado State University in 1962 with a Doctor of Veterinary Medicine degree and then moved to Athens with his wife, Jody, his son, Pat, and his daughter, Jessica because he said he enjoyed the four seasons and liked to see rain occasionally.

"When I got to Athens, I worked for Athens Veterinary Hospital, but I left to strike it out on my own. I enjoy being my own boss and I wanted to build a huge veterinary hospital," Smith explained.

Smith said his working area of 8000 square feet is still unfinished.

"My large and small animal operating rooms allow me to perform surgery on any animal of any size," Smith added, "and I also have an indoor corral for cattle."

Although Smith admitted never treating large elephants or giraffes in his large animal operating room he has worked with other strange pets such as boa constrictors, turkey buzzards and vultures.

"I am personal veterinarian to the Royal Lipizzan Stallions, the grey Austrian horses that Patton kept the Russians from eating during World War II," Smith mused. "I never know when a sick one will be sent to me, but it's always an honor, they're so beautiful and so highly trained."

Smith said he once operated on one of the horses, "Neil," who starred in a Walt Disney movie.

Long working hours are a part of Smith's life. "I start at 8 a.m. every day and usually finish up between 10 or 11 p.m. or whenever the people stop coming in. After that, I may stay and do some surgery.

"My wife has a great sense of humor and she loves animals as much as I do. She has an obedience school for dogs which opens up in April every year," Smith said.

Smith cannot always be found at Milliron Clinic, located six miles east of Athens on Route 50A, though.

"On Tuesdays, Thursdays and Saturdays I make house calls to the farms in the area. Plus, 20 percent of my time is spent furthering my education through out-of-town veterinarian meetings which brief me on the latest breakthroughs. I recently returned from one in Switzerland," Smith explained.

Noting the animals running around the clinic, Smith admitted his family didn't consist only of his wife, son and daughter.

"To this moment, I have six adopted dogs, 14 adopted cats and 30 sheep, 13 horses, geese, ducks, goats, "Milkshake" the milk snake and an iguana which are my own," Smith added.

The impact of a veterinarian's assessment of an ill pet ripples throughout a lifetime. Pete assured his clients that, usually, there is no one to blame for genetic predispositions, environmental triggers, ailments, disease, or accidents. Pete knew that being a vet was more than a scalpel and medicine; he was a teacher, a lifelong student of medical procedures, a member of the veterinarian community, and a part of the community. He knew that medicine was constantly evolving, challenged and bolstered by daily advances in science and technology. He knew that miracles happened when the law of medicine was challenged, tweaked, and bent.

The vocabulary of veterinarians is foreign to most people. As a pet owner, you may need to learn the meaning of palpate, colostrum, dystocia, and more. Pete was determined that each of his clients understood, in layman's terms, veterinary procedures and protocol. The client was as important to Pete as the pet. He went to great lengths explaining surgeries, medicines, and the what-ifs. Some clients understood the importance of animal nutrition, care, and safety; while others had a difficult time grasping the animal-human connection.

Sidney, the Greyhound skeleton that traveled with Pete and Jody from Colorado, a souvenir of Pete's racetrack vetting, stands in the clinic operating room. Pete used Sidney to show clients the infrastructure of canines. Sidney would become the project of a local artist who created intricate designs and quotes on Sidney's skeleton in exchange for vet services.

The fully-assembled horse skeleton in the surgery preparation room gives an inside view to a horse. Pete used the skeleton to explain broken bones, fractures, head injuries, tooth problems, and much more.

It was this hands-on approach that drew people to Milliron Clinic. People really liked Pete. He was charismatic, charming, funny, and intriguing. He could draw you in with a smile and a twinkle of his eye; forever friends. Or, you may disagree with his beliefs on certain theologies, practices, doctrines, and responsibilities. Either way, Pete was a person who was unforgettable.

"He was a skilled surgeon," Jody says, "and he liked to do bone plating, especially. When someone would bring their pet in, mostly dogs who had been hit by a car that needed bone plating, Pete was like 'Oh, boy!' I often told him not to look so eager in front of clients."

People are in complete awe of veterinarians. It seems like an exciting, fascinating job. A lot of little kids want to grow up to become veterinarians, but once they become older and find out that the job may require at least six years of college, and a twenty-four-hour-a-day, seven-day-a-week work schedule, they opt for another job. Most of the time the work is routine, and perhaps mundane; repetitive surgeries like neutering cats and dogs, castrating horses, and giving periodic inoculations. However, there is always the eventful moment which reminds veterinarians that they are an important part of the circle of life.

Pete stayed on top of his schedule, usually taking more time with clients than the schedule allowed, running him late into the evening for other appointments. He realized the discord and uncertainty that an animal's illness can bring upon a family. Inevitability, some clients were forced to make a hard decision to operate or euthanize. Weighing the cost of surgery vs. the pain of euthanizing is finally the client's. Pete, in his guiding role, led clients through a sea of uncertainty and helped them through the decision-making process. He listened. He was a skilled surgeon with a big personality and a penetrating laugh. He hired people who were willing to learn, willing to work long hours, and shared his vision of a top-notch clinic. Beyond all of the daily animal care and interactions with clients, Pete embraced every opportunity to excel as a vet.

The clinic now built and Pete well underway with his new venture, Jessica and Pat found their way down the big hill from the farmhouse to the new clinic. As farm kids, they had daily chores; as veterinarian's kids, they had more chores than average. Pete expected a lot; the mindset that dedication to hard work at a young age builds character, stamina, and the desire to achieve. Jessica and Pat were part of the work crew; cleaning kennels, helping vet techs, going on outcalls, answering the phone, connecting with clients, nurturing animals, and accommodating a busy dad.

"I've been watching my Dad vetting since I was a little kid," Jessica says. "Farmers pulling a calf with a tractor; the ingenuity of farm vetting. He made it up as he went. Some people waited until the last minute to pull a calf. People would wait until the last minute to call the vet; by the time they called the vet, everybody tried every remedy there was."

"It wasn't until he was in his early to mid-60's before he figured out that not everybody had the same level of commitment to the cause that he did," Pat explains. "I said to him one day, 'You know Dad, none of these people are going to starve to death or lose their farm if they don't work tomorrow,'" Pat explains. "You can't expect them to have the same level of commitment to the cause. And he's like, 'Really? What the...' He was a lot better after that. He expected you to share it."

The Staff
The receptionist maintains a vet's schedule and is the hub of activity. Vet techs keep busy, too, helping with surgeries, cleaning

kennels, scrubbing surgical tools, consoling disgruntled pets and people, making sure Pete stayed on task.

Rose Keirns was the first receptionist at Milliron Clinic, followed by Joanne Hanson, then Christy McDonald, who also kept books, billed, and helped with surgeries; finally iconic redhead Karen Miller. Christy worked alongside Jody and Jan Crall, who was a volunteer. "She was such a God send," Jody says. The staff likes to reminisce about working for Pete.

Jan remembers first meeting Pete when she was in college and brought her dog to him. Soon she was working for him, after classes. "Pete would call about 8 o'clock pm, just when I was ready to leave the house for night school," Jan says. "He was putting a horse on the table with a colic surgery. We would prep the horse, and Pete would come back about 10 o'clock to perform the surgery. During surgery, you would be standing there with guts in your hands. If you didn't have a sense of humor, doing the work that you did, then you would not have survived ten to fifteen years with Pete. I always had this spot for Pete."

Pete's ambitions and impatience sometimes outran his income, and his staff learned to compensate. Christy explains, "I would always hide the checkbook from Pete, and tell Jan where it was, but he'd find it."

"When I used to work on the books, I always made the balance $2,000 less than what it actually was," Jan confesses. One day he wanted to buy an automated blood analyzer for the clinic vs. sending blood away to a lab for analysis. Beckman Coulter manufactured the machine Pete wanted. With the Beckman Coulter catalog in hand, Pete, in his orotund voice, asked Jan, "Can we afford this?" Jan replied, "*No*, we can't!" Pete bought it the next day.

Soon, "the Coulter lady" was calling from California" about the overdue invoice. But Christy also remembers that Pete's acquisition was a "big deal" that helped put him and his clinic on the map. "It could do CBC's and analyze blood," Christy says. "It was huge and black and it sat there and we were all excited about it. Pete was all excited about it. We were the first in the area to have a CBC machine. When I told my mother, who worked for the state sanitarium as a medical technologist, she couldn't believe it."

Everything Pete did, he did big. He outfitted the lab to do blood chemistry panels. He purchased several large pieces of human hospital equipment and tried to use them for veterinary medicine, including an infant incubator, fluoroscope, C-arm, and ultrasound.

A skilled surgeon, Pete exuded confidence, knowledge, and wit. The behind the scenes preparation of a surgeon are lost to the general public; scrubbing and washing of hands, relying on the integrity of staff for disinfecting the workspace, laying out appropriate surgical tools for the surgery at hand, prepping the animal, making sure that the dispensary had the drugs and supplies needed to run the clinic, the wherewithal to assist during the surgery, and much more. Before beginning a difficult surgery, Pete would say, "We need to do this like porcupines make love, very carefully."

Everyone was amazed by Pete's constant work. "He began working, then go out on calls, and then come back to the clinic," says Jan. "He began drinking coffee to keep him going; he liked it, but it didn't like him. Coffee made him ill. He'd drink it, and then he'd come back and say, 'Why did you let me drink that?' He'd bitch at you if you brought coffee, and he'd bitch at you if you didn't. Food was important. We would clear off the surgery table and it would be covered with food for lunch, and then cleared it off again for surgery.

"Oh! The day I told Pete I was pregnant," Jan remembers. "I walked into work and I started yelling, 'If you can't make coffee right, I'll make it.' He looked me quizzically and said, 'What is wrong with you?' I said, 'I walk in here every morning and the coffee smells burnt. I'll make the coffee.'

"Pete knew something was up. We actually did the pregnancy test through the clinic. We sent it off to the lab and wrote on the form my name as the dog. The lab called and they said, 'We have the results for Jan Crall.' I said, 'And…?' The lab said, 'The bitch is pregnant.' We had a good laugh. As soon as Pete found out I was pregnant, he took care of me. After I had my brain surgery, he stopped in the barn and people were here to pick up their horses and he said, 'Just look at her. Doesn't she look amazing? She just had brain surgery.' Pete would always say things like that."

The staff came and went; however, a few of the original staff are still there to this day. After working with Pete for many years, relationships became solid and there was a bond that would last lifetimes. Jody recalls one that didn't last, "I just happened to walk around the back, and she was throwing a cat out back. I mean she threw it. She had lost her temper. I told Pete and that was the end of that. That is the thing – if you don't respect animals then it isn't a good place to work." And then, she allows, some workers couldn't take Pete's stressed-out temperament and occasional outbursts. "We have a list of people who only made it a few hours, mostly from being unable to endure the *blue air* surrounding one of Pete's brief but memorable fits. We had a lot of employees come and go. Pete hired this young guy; maybe Pete was doing him a favor by hiring him," Jody continues. "The guy helped plant a thousand pine tree seedlings. It was on a Friday. He came back to work on Monday, after being infatuated with wonder weed most of the weekend. The guy mowed all the trees down he had planted the Friday before. Pete was not happy."

From 1972 to 1975, then college student Betsy Hammer remembers working for Pete as educational and exciting. "My duties included cleaning all the cages for the animals, cleaning stalls, helping Dr. Smith during surgery, running the anesthesia machine, walking the animals, greeting patients at the front desk, answering phones, scrubbing the floors, and doing anything and everything that anyone who assisted Dr. Smith had to do; dealing with horses, pigs, and cows, dogs, birds, and cats and everything.

"One Saturday night, it was around 11 p.m., I was still working and Pete looked at me and said, 'Do you want to go on one of the most exciting experiences of your whole life? Come on. Grab your purse, let's go.' So, I grab my purse, we hop into his truck, drove up the road and pull into a long driveway. At the top of the driveway was a farmer who escorted us to his barn where a cow was lying in a stall about to give birth, but she had was having a breach birth and she had to have a C-section. The farmer went for some boiling hot water. I held the lantern for Dr. Smith while he injected the animal, then opened the cow, and pulled out a calf.

"I had to be the farmer because Pete said to me, 'Grab a leg!' I had to grab both legs. Pete grabbed the other two legs, and we began swinging it and swinging the calf in the middle of the barn. Moments later the calf stood up, as calves do, and it truly was one of the most memorable experiences of my life helping Pete Smith deliver and bring to life that beautiful young calf."

Employee Kitty Peterson multitasked as needed throughout the clinic. Kitty smiles, "We were all just like family. I did sewing for Pete. I created a pattern from one of his old smocks and made five or six for him. He wore them for years. I worked for Pete for about a year in the back doing lab stuff, X-rays, and helping Pete when he whistled. His whistle could go right through you. If you didn't get to where he was when he you heard the whistle, *whoa*. He wanted you there immediately. He could go for four or five hours without communicating with me. I loved helping with surgeries. Pete put me to the test once. There was a stallion that wasn't feeling well. Pete told me to hold onto the stallion's rope. He said to not let go of the rope and to not tie the stallion up. The stallion began raring up and down. Pete left me out there for twenty minutes. I know he was behind the door laughing at me. Pete was ornery that way. I knew it was a test." When Kitty was three months pregnant, Pete had to let her go because she was not allowed around the chemicals and X-ray.

The summer of 1980, Pete hired Jelea Bookman, a local young woman, to work at the clinic. She was responsible for cleaning cages, mowing grass, prepping and assisting with minor and major surgeries, and any other duty that Pete needed help with. It was an ordinary day when Jelea had to stand for an hour in McDougal Creek with a horse who had laminitis, then meet Pete for a chainsaw lesson. "I remember, Pete was the first one who taught me to use a chainsaw," Jelea says. "We didn't always have vet work to do. Every Tuesday and Thursday were farm calls, so while Pete was away, we played catch up on those days."

"He never expected anybody to do any more than what he did," Jody adds. "Craig Higgins worked here for a short while. He was a good worker. The funniest thing about Craig is the comment he made about a client's Rottweiler. The client requested a total post-mortem on her dog. She wanted everything sent in. Everything. So, Pete had the dog spread out all over, taking samples. Craig comes around the corner, points his finger at the dog's carcass, and says, 'Bad dog, bad dog.' When I would tell Craig, 'Surely it's all right.' Craig would always say, 'Quit calling me Shirley.'"

Long-time employee Dana Gardner remembers how things like putting a dead animal in a freezer, or burying spare animal parts a group at a time in a big hole, were a daily task. "It's just like working in a hospital throwing chunky bits away. We had to deal with what we call our 'chunky bits bucket' which is what's left over after surgeries. Whether it's a leg or a heart, or they went to the freezer first. Then they got buried."

"He would do things for the staff," former employee Will Tevis remembers, "like take us to the upscale Century House in Athens to eat. There would be about twenty or thirty of us from the clinic. Pete would buy, well he was trading the restaurant owner for vet services, but it would be about $500 for all of our meals. Pete shared in a big way with all of us."

Dana likewise remembers his generosity: "Pete would always pay if we wanted to take a course to advance our skills. We went to Kentucky and Ohio State University conferences. I went to the conference for birds and snakes. He also sent me to a vet lab at Ohio State; I thought it was going to be for cats. We had to pair up, turns out they were all veterinarians. One time Pete took us to the Ohio

Veterinary Medical Association (OVMA) meeting, and then to The Wilds in northern Ohio after the meeting."

David Barger was an employee at the clinic. "The first time I met Pete is when Jan (Crall) brought an animal to the clinic," David says. "It was in the early 70s. As far as I knew, Pete was just another vet. I wasn't raised with animals. I was a city boy. I got to work for Pete because Jan worked for Pete and Pete was hiring. I lived with Jan for a while and she got tired of me leaching off of her; she got me a job working for Pete. I had been an English major for three and a half years at Ohio University, because my girlfriend (Jan) was an English major. That's how 19-year-old kids think. I quit college because I thought *what am I going to do with this except go on to get a Masters and a Doctorate.* I wanted to become more of me. I needed to find something to do because my parents cut me off. I worked for Pete for nine to ten months. I was a laborer, doing whatever Pete needed done; cleaning stalls, digging ditches, mowing grass, putting up hay. I didn't know about the stuff he told me to do. We didn't know how to do it. We had to figure it out. Pete got rid of the guys that knew how to do it. I painted the lettering on the mural as you walk into the clinic *The Earth is the Lord's and the fullness thereof.*

"I figured Pete was instrumental for me going back to college," David says. "Because I thought after being in college for three and a half years in English (thinking *what the hell am I going to do with a degree in English*), I thought I would be a farmer. Then, after being a farmer for a while, I thought, shit, I don't want to do this for the rest of my life. So, I went back to school. Jan and I got married so we could get a loan so I could go back to school. Pete was instrumental for me going back to school, instrumental for me getting married. Jan and I stayed at the Phillips' place, Pete's property, which was the first house on Route 690. It sits way back in the woods; which was a wonderful place to be. We were there because Pete couldn't give Jan a raise. He said there was this empty house that we could live in. That was part of her pay, living at that house.

"We had to keep rugs on the floor of the house to keep the cold air from coming up through the cracks. Po folks have po ways,"

David grins. "After I put a new furnace in the Phillips place, Pete sold it out from under us. We didn't know that he was selling it, so we had to move. Pete was probably three months' arrears on his mortgage. He was under all kind of pressure financially; life on the edge. Pete had no problem incurring debt. He'd bitch when he had to pay it. In fact, when I worked here, he came down the hill once…he was always coming down the hill…he said, 'I had a friend in college that said if I owed a million dollars by the time I was twenty-two it would be the same as being a millionaire because no bank could let me go under.' There's a problem with Pete's theory. When you die they call the mortgage in. That's what you do to your family. Of course he didn't because of all that stupid shit he would do all the time. When he got his first 350 bulldozer, the guy who sold it to him stood on the back of the hitch. Pete went straight up the hill towards the house. When he got all the way to the top, he turned around and looked at the guy. The guy said, 'What's wrong with you? You can roll those things over! It will roll right over on itself!' It didn't. He'd do crap like that all the time. He had an old blue Dodge. He put it on the lowboy and told me to take it down the road. If I hit a bump, the front end came up. I had to go 5 mph all the way down the road. Then there was the Gravely tractor. When he first got it, he mowed the front yard with the plow on it. Great little tractor, but it's the remnants of a Studebaker. The first thing, Pete bought dually wheels for it. *Mow the lawn.* I always had to use the freakin' Gravely that would beat me half to death."

One day Pete came down the hill from the farmhouse. David was working under Pete's truck and rust was falling in his eyes. David said, "Jesus Christ."

Pete said, "Did you want me?"

David said, "No, I was talking to your son."

"Everything Pete did was big; sheep, farming, landowner, sawmill, stove – just to name a few," says former employee Will

Tevis. "He did many things well. I remember Pete's dog, Ruffian and how he would feed her scraps. Pete was the not the type of guy that I wanted to be friends with. I was too young to be friends with him. I would have been in my late twenties. We didn't chum around or anything. But he always did nice things for me and I always respected and admired him. I was hired to build the woodshed that's out front of the clinic. Pete liked the work I did, so I wound up doing a lot of stuff; we remodeled the apartment above the recovery stall. There are a series of horse stalls, too, those are the ones I worked on. They were torn up from years of abuse.

"I would spend time at the farmhouse because Pete was kind of infatuated with me," Will laughs. "We would play chess together. He called me Sire Tevis. I only lived about five or six miles from the clinic. My Dad was an English professor at Ohio University in Athens. He wrote *The Hustler* when I was about six. Then he wrote *The Man Who Fell to Earth* when I was about seven or eight. Because of my background, I don't come from a place like a mechanical person or carpenter would come from. I made the choice to do that. I am sure that my personality had something to do with why Pete liked me. I don't know much about vets, but Pete was a good one. He had a good reputation, especially as a horse vet. Pete liked to build things, or garden; he and I had the same interests, but he couldn't do it because he was working at the clinic. I think at that time, it was a hard time too, because that's when interest rates ballooned; he had to work a lot then to pay the bills.

"Pete had a lariat," Will remembers. "I had never seen one before. It was made from woven rawhide leather, like a lasso. It wasn't very long, maybe twenty feet long. Pete could rope stuff. I remember the dog he roped. He would throw it down at their feet while they were walking. Pretty cool. And he tried to do rope tricks that he didn't do very well, but I think at one time he could have. Pete also had ideas on how to do stuff. Like, for instance, I have some artistic flair. So, this one time a couple came out, their cat had died. They were upset. Pete asked me, 'Can you make a coffin for this cat.' I said, 'Sure, I can do that.' I made a coffin for a cat, carved its name in it and sanded it off. After that, Pete offered coffins to clients. I made a few after that. It is kind of an interesting thing; you have to deal with the dying also. Farm animals, with pets anyway, it was an emotional thing. You heard how he unloaded animals. He had a big red pickup truck, in the wintertime he would just throw dead animals in it. And then, this is a terrible story, you might not want to include it; we dug this waterline out to this building I was working on. It had like a three-foot-wide trench by 100-foot long. We just unloaded the truck of dead animals into the ditch. I guess the only problem I had with it is, well, I didn't have an emotional attachment, but if you had a dead dog and drove by and saw it being tossed into the ditch; I guess a dead dog is a dead dog.

"There's another thing about Pete," Will continues. "I don't harbor any resentment about it. He sold me some property, which I still live on. He gave me a fair deal. He had multiple oil wells around and I wanted a certain oil well. I had never bought any land, never had bought a house. The way I remember the deal is that he was going to sell me this ten acres of ground for $5,000, and as it was, have it surveyed off, it would include that well and the mineral rights. We are walking up to the courthouse and he said, 'Let's go with this deal, $10,000 for the property and rights to the well.' And I said, 'I thought it was $5,000 and rights to the well.' As we were walking by the church on College Avenue, on the way to the courthouse, Pete said, '$7,500 and no rights to the well.' I said, 'OK.' I look back at that and think what a weird deal it was. I don't think Pete was trying to bait me, or steal anything from me. There was nothing in writing. I could buy the well, but I didn't have the money. The way I built my house was I built a woodstove and put an electric furnace in because I didn't have the gas. I lived there and had correspondence with Pete to get this well. This took place over five or six years. After living on the property for about ten years, I got a call from Paul Garrett. He said, 'Do you live on Eddy Road?' I said, 'Yes.' He said, 'There's a well on that property. Would you like to own it?' He says, 'I'll give it to you.' He explains that it is easier for him to give it to me than it is for him to cap the well off. I said, 'Okay, but I thought Pete Smith owned it.' And the guy says, 'I hate to rain on your parade, but Pete Smith has never owned that well.'

"Pete was not a dishonest man, but there were deals like that that happened," Will explains. "He was never into details. He was always move on, move on. If I had it written out when we first made the deal, and if he had changed the plans when we went to the courthouse, and I showed him the paper, he would honor it. I am not being mean or anything, it's just the way it happened. This is important for me to say about Pete. He was likeable and generous. He made emotional decisions. I say that if I was going to rewrite Pete Smith's life, the thing I would say is to pay a little more attention to detail.

"I hit it off really well with Pat. He was probably about 16 or 17 at the time. I don't know what it would be like to have Pete for a dad. When I was at there, Pete and Pat were always around. They always seemed to get along pretty good."

Surgical nurse, Annette Anderson was one of Pete's favorites. An instrumental part of Pete's staff, she had the opportunity to talk with Pete during the silence of surgical procedures. He told Annette that he so disliked his middle name Pliny, that, as a kid, he carved the name on the back of a box turtle and hoped the creature would carry it away. Annette smiles as she remembers her first encounter with Pete. "I started working for Dr. Smith in October 1991. He gave us specific instructions to make his morning hot chocolate; a scoop of cocoa, powdered milk, Cosequin, and a scoop of MSM (organic Sulphur). The Cosequin and MSM were both horse-strength. He felt that they helped him deal with his arthritis. He would fast two or three days a week. He could be grouchy on those days. I worked on his eating days, fortunately."

Soon veterinarians throughout the region were sending their difficult surgeries and confounding cases to Milliron. In the ultimate show of respect, many veterinarians sent their own pets and horses to Pete. He developed a reputation as a veterinarian willing to take on the most unlikely cases. Sometimes this made him a hero, other times his unconventional attempts went awry.

Never having forgotten his own struggles making ends meet, he agreed to work for postdated checks, and other forms of credit. He would barter for services, taking in stereos, guns, auto titles, and driving licenses to hold until payment could be made. In time, other clinics were sending their hard luck cases to him, much to his chagrin.

Even with dedicated assistants and passionate volunteers, the weight of responsibility hangs on the veterinarian heaviest of all. Every now and then the staff felt the pressure of the unwavering responsibility. "Angry outbursts from a frustrated Dr. Smith were common," Annette says. "As were the angry outbursts from frustrated clients battling against economic hardships, scheduling and transportation restraints, anything keeping their animal from getting timely care. Not to mention, the anger felt toward anyone showing callousness toward a suffering animal."

On top of that, Annette remembers, the hours were long and unpredictable. Emergency calls came at the most inopportune times. Sundays could include a St. Bernard that was having difficulty birthing puppies, on top of hit-by-car-dogs, and colic surgeries, compounding an afternoon of horse surgeries for clients who could only get their animals in on the weekend. "I remember working exhausted, in the early hours of the morning, cleaning up after a full day of bloody surgeries, when Dr. Smith came down off the hill with the severed foreleg of a horse," Annette says. "The skin and tendons of the cannon bone were gone, revealing four long surgical plates, each held in place with a dozen screws. He wanted the plates removed, and the screws cleaned and sterilized, that night. Compared to today's specialized and compartmentalized medicine, we had been practicing in the 'Wild West' of medicine. The focus was on treatment, not documentation; skill and experience, not certification; sincere diligence, not conventional treatment or standard of care. Dr. Smith wanted everybody to be able to do everything. I was able to handle, foxes, bear cubs, deer, various birds, lion and leopard cubs, iguanas, snakes, turtles, llamas, sheep, cattle, camels, potbellied pigs, cats and dogs of every breed, wolves and wolf hybrids, and, of course, horses and ponies of every size and discipline. No, the job wasn't for everyone. Looking back, I liken it to veterans reminiscing about war. We all invested our blood, sweat, and tears. Only someone who was there can truly appreciate what it could be like. But I'm proud of the good we accomplished, and glad to have been part of it."

A country veterinarian must be prepared for any situation and every hazard that may befall the local fauna or the family down the road who ran over their cat "Lucky." As the adage confirms, a good vet is always on call. And Pete was.

Withstanding the obligatory emergency, the schedule was solid. Surgeries and small animals in the morning, lunch at noon, a couple more appointments after lunch, then back up the hill to the farmhouse for a nap.

Early to rise, Pete arrived at the clinic after breakfast. He liked to jokingly say, "I'd have some ham and eggs, if we had ham and eggs." Milk toast was one of his favorite breakfasts. Naps were important to Pete. He would enter the kitchen, remove his boots, pants, and shirt, and go to bed. He was on a tight schedule and napped exactly forty-five minutes. He awoke without prompting; dressed and ready for the afternoon and into evening appointments.

Another day, another castration, inoculation, incision, and on and on. The number of sutures he placed in living and dying animals is countless. In the words of his clients, Dr. Smith was "fearless, eager, passionate, and a bag of boundless energy." People liked to be around him and he enjoyed the company of people.

The clinic drew normal vetting as well as the unusual. Sometimes the events that happened were beyond anyone's belief; people were amazing, and adding an animal to the equation sometimes equaled a dramatic problem.

"He vetted cougars," Pat says. "He had just finished giving a cougar its yearly shots and was looking out the clinic window and there was this guy who had coonhounds, he was real obnoxious, never made appointments, just dropped in unexpectedly to be treated like royalty. The guy came in with his hounds bragging about how fabulous they were and how fearless they were and all that. Pete told the cougar owner, 'If you wait here just a few minutes, everything I've done for you today will be free.' The guy agreed. Pete said to him, 'Okay, you can go out to the waiting room now.' This guy takes his cougar out of the exam room past the coonhounds. The coonhounds pissed on the floor and I think the guy did too. The coonhounds and the guy ran out the door and never came back. That was one of his ways of firing clients. He fired other clients, too, but more directly."

"Somebody gave Dad giant roosters that were fighting cocks," Jessica says, "I had this little black rooster that a friend had given me, it didn't weigh much, maybe two pounds. Dad said, 'Hey, Jessica, would you take these roosters; I don't have a place for them?' My little black rooster killed both of those giant fighting cocks. Dad always thought that was so funny because this guy traded $500 worth of a vet bill for these two fighting cocks that were so valuable."

Farm Calls

In the beginning, farm calls were Pete's main source of income. Pete enjoyed traveling, meeting new people, connecting with familiar clients, and the challenge of being a veterinarian. Despite being nailed by a cow, chased by a bull, or bitten by a barn cat, he was living the dream.

Jody explains, "Farm calls were usually scheduled for after-noons or evenings, unless it was an emergency. Pete would often-times run late at the clinic and be late to a farm call. He may have had a scheduled appointment for 2:00 p.m. in West Virginia, but, due to emergencies, wasn't able to arrive until 3:00 a.m. Clients didn't mind Pete's lateness because he was such an outstanding vet-erinarian. Sometimes a client would ask what it took to get on Pete's dayshift schedule. It didn't bother Pete. He would just laugh and go about his work. We had disagreements about his long hours away on farm calls. He had just gone to Racine in Meigs County for a calving case, arriving home at one or two in the am. I asked him how much money he made on the project. He said, 'Oh, just the going rate.' Which wasn't much, it seemed to me. The next day I called a taxi company to see how much they would charge to take me to Racine and wait an hour there for me and bring me home. It was more than what Pete had gotten for the calving case. I teased him and told him that the next time I wanted to go somewhere and I didn't have transportation, I would call a large animal vet and have them take me."

A few longtime clients revered Pete as a family member as well as a talented surgeon and respected veterinarian. He explained procedures to clients prior to surgeries and procedures, if time allowed. Emergencies were always considered just that, and animals were handled in the order that suited their situation. When Pete was on farm calls, he would eat with the family at dinnertime, or late evenings. If he was driving by a client's place in route to another, he would feel welcome enough to stop and visit and have dinner.

Working up an appetite, always accepting, Pete enjoyed food and knew that he would be well-fed. He could travel anywhere in the tristate area and always find a place to sit, eat, or just to rest with one of his many clients. Pauline Kercheval knew Pete had a love affair with food. She remembers how he always dined with her family when he came to their farm. She always made Pete's favorite blueberry cream pie. Jody was with Pete on one farm call to the Kercheval's farm. Pauline served Jody a large piece of pie. At that instant, Pete reached across the table, grabbed Jody's pie, and said, "Go get your smaller piece!"

"Pete really had a sense of humor and loved his work," Pauline says. "We had a disabled neighbor who had a collie that was down. The neighbor was unable to get to a vet. It so happened that Pete was on his way to our farm to take care of our horses and dogs. I asked Pete if he would look at our neighbor's dog. As soon as Pete was finished at our farm, he vetted our neighbor's dog. She was so grateful. Pete would go out of his way to help people."

"Pete saved farm calls for evening hours and usually showed up after dark," remembers Virgil, a Hereford cattle farmer from Hocking County. "I had called Pete to come and inoculate my herd for foot rot. It was in April, and we had had a lot of rain. It was after 8 p.m. before Pete came to our farmhouse. Jody was with him. My wife had made blackberry pie. She knew Pete enjoyed pie. Jody stayed at the farmhouse while Pete, my son, daughter, and I went to the barn.

"The cattle were in the corral and waiting. I had 75 Herefords that needed vaccinated. The weather took a turn, and as we were walking to the barn, dark clouds rolled in, along with lightning and torrential rain. The rain on the barn roof was deafening. Voices were muted and the cattle were fidgety. As Pete prepared syringes, my

son and I brought a group of cows into the barn. It was raining too hard to vet the cattle in the corral. Pete, in his green coveralls, gumboots, and with complete confidence, yelled, 'Pack them in tight, so they can't move!' He placed a syringe between each finger and two syringes between his teeth. Climbing into the large cattle-filled stall,

Pete went to work. He was like Tinker Bell stepping from cow to cow, landing on their sturdy hindquarters, injecting each cow and throwing empty syringes into the aisle way. 'Bring in the next group,' Pete yelled, as apocalyptic lightning and thunder came through the valley. When the last cow was vaccinated, Pete told one of his ornery jokes and we all had a good laugh. We all walked back to the farmhouse for a piece of blackberry pine. Pete enjoyed his work; he knew how to handle cattle. In all my years of farming, I have never seen anything like Pete. We still talk about the night Pete walked on cattle in the thunderstorm."

"Sometimes when Pete would go on farm calls, he would run into unintentional situations," Jody says. "One time he was driving to a farm call and the owner's dog met him in their driveway. Pete was tired and in his usual hurry and wham! He accidently hit the dog with his car. Pete felt really bad about it, but the dog had run right into him."

Citroën, Doris, and Shirley

Farm calls lead us to Pete's vehicles. Each vehicle had a name, an identity, a profound purpose, an assigned dog (or two), and, of course, a story behind it. Ann Howland, PhD, Doctor of Psychology, neighbor and fellow horse lover, rider and good friend, once jumped into Pete's truck only to rest on a recently removed horse testicle which Ruffian, Pete's Border Collie sidekick, had secreted there. Ann exclaimed, "Dr. Smith! You have the grossest profession!"
Pete was fascinated with his Citroën. Jody's brother, Gary, while in the US Navy, had a Citroën, and Pete was impressed that the car could travel in deep snow. The car had five levels of carriage hydraulics, lifting the car when necessary, settling down on a street curb, or dodging flood waters. Parking the car at a Pennsylvania Turnpike on a trip to visit Pete's folks, Pete turned the ignition off and the car began setting down as usual. "We were heading into a restaurant," Jody says, "when we heard someone yelling 'give me my broom!!!' The boy had been sweeping the street in front of the restaurant and now the Citroën was sitting on the end of his broom. Pete went back to the car, started the engine, and lifted the car off the boy's broom. The boy just kept sweeping as if nothing had happened."
Pete liked the Citroën because it could easily go 120 mph in any kind of weather. "He was on his way to a foaling case in Meigs County," Jody remembers, "and his Citroën had a flat tire, but the car automatically leveled itself and Pete continued driving. When at

his destination, Pete changed the tire. The car was front wheel drive and got 30 miles per gallon."

Once, driving a flooded road near Darwin, Ohio, as usual Pete was in a hurry to get to a farm call. Pete stopped in front of a deep spot, and a pickup pulled up behind him and honked. Pete slowly raised the Citroën as he drove through water then gradually lowered it down as he came out the other side. The pickup driver roared into the water and stalled. Pete told the story time and again with an ornery smile.

Jerry Hartley, a local horseman, client and good friend of Pete's, would occasionally travel with Pete to farm calls throughout Ohio and West Virginia. Pete was known for his expert equine care, from small stables to large stud farms. "We would go to West Virginia for three or four days at a time. We would live in the truck or the Citroën. The Citroën was more comfortable to sleep in, and, of course, we had Ruffian, Pete's dog, with us, too," Jerry explains. "Pete and I would be working on horses at three or four o'clock in the morning. Maybe we would get a call and set up an appointment for six am. We would sleep in the truck and be there at six a.m. the next morning. We would work all night; twenty-four hours. I used to go into the barn first and all the horses would have their heads stuck out the stall doors. Then Pete would walk in the barn and there wouldn't be a horse to be seen; a clear view all the way down the aisle."

Jerry remembers the time he and Pete were working on a man's horses, and the owner said, "What are you guys doing later?"

"Well, we have a few more calls," Pete replied.

"I got six steaks in the refrigerator, why don't you get caught up and come back to the house. The keys are under the mat. You get some potatoes and things and we will have a feast tonight!"

Pete and Jerry made their scheduled rounds. They stopped and got some potatoes and things and went back to the man's house. Jerry put the potatoes in the sink, washing and peeling them. They had dinner and the man invited them to stay the night.

The next morning, Pete and Jerry bid the guy farewell and set back out for Ohio; but, first, breakfast. Pete loved food. Almost every farm call involved food. If you were traveling with Pete, you got your plate and ate because Pete had already eaten and was going out the door.

"I never saw anybody in better shape than Pete, to eat like he did!" Jerry says. "One time we were working in a round pen with stallions. We were there to castrate the lot of them. Pete would rope a horse, castrate it, then let it go, all while the other horses were running around in the pen. I kept a needle ready, and had one sticking in between my teeth. There was so much commotion that the needle got me and numbed my mouth. We laughed and went on with our work."

Finally, Pete's Citroën, having seen many miles of country road, was no longer reliable enough for farm calls. Pete had a buyer for the car, his first cousin Marshall Adams, who was living on Milliron Farm in a tent. Marshall told Pete that if he ever wanted to sell it, he wanted to have first chance to buy it. Pete had one of the clinic workers hose it out and try to remove the imprinted odors of manure, medicines, sheep, and the worst.

When the car was somewhat clean, Pete called Marshall.

"I am going to have to have $250 for the Citroën," Pete said.

"I won't pay more than $275," Marshall replied.

Pete was confused, but couldn't convince Marshall that his price was higher. Marshall didn't listen and stubbornly held to his price, was pleased with his purchase and confident that the car would be worth every penny.

Jody used her white Citroën station wagon for household errands and repairs. She loaded her ailing dishwasher in it to take into Athens for repair. She finally had to give up her beloved car after they could no longer get parts for it. The Cleveland dealership where they had been getting parts had closed. The next-door neighbor, who was a mechanical genius, kept it running for the family as long as possible. The era of the Citroën's came to an end in the late '70's when Pete purchased Doris, a black Cadillac. Sylvia Snabl recalls Doris sported, "a Rottweiler emblem on the hood, leather seats, and the springs were all gone." When Doris could no longer make the grade, *she* was replaced by Shirley, a very-used yellow Lincoln.

Farmhand and clinic employee, Jerry Sullivan, remembers traveling with Pete. "Gumboots and barn muck. The car smelled like manure. He kept all of his instruments in the trunk; meds in a cooler, buckets, syringes, everything he needed. There was barely room for me in that car."

There were the standard farm calls, vaccinations, inoculations, deworming, castrating, etc., and emergency farm calls. Sometimes farm calls would last through the night, especially on trips to West Virginia. John Leslie, a well-known horse breeder and client of Pete's, often asked, "How long do I have to be a client before I can get off the midnight shift?" or "When am I going to see Dr. Smith?" Sometimes Pete would do the vetting through the night while the client slept.

God forbid that I should go to any heaven
in which there are no horses.
Robert Graham

---

6 HORSE STORIES

A HORSE ENTHUSIAST, Pete knew horses - inside and out. He was known for his ability to complete intricate equine surgeries with great results. Horse owners trailered their disabled horses to Milliron Clinic, knowing Pete would make his best attempt to save their horse. Veterinarians would send their clients to Pete, as well their own family horses.

Milliron Clinic's stables stand to the right of the main clinic. Each stall is designed from different timber from the farm. Pete never used sawdust for stall bedding at the clinic because of associated problems. "We paid through the nose for straw," Jody says.

Pete was a prominent figure in the Athens and surrounding area horse groups: Ohio Horse Council, 4H, County Fairs, horse races, and more. "People came to Dad," Jessica explains, "and said 'I'm going to raise a foal.' Dad would say, 'You're going to spend $10,000 raising a foal and you don't even know what you're going to get! Why don't you take that $10,000 and go and buy something that you know is already a fit!'"

Equines and horse-folk were seen at 7 p.m., unless, of course, there was an emergency. Tuesday and Thursday were the days scheduled for horse surgeries. There would be a long line of horse trailers in the parking lot. Sometimes there would be six or eight horse surgeries a day, which was all day, sometimes until two or three a.m. People brought horses from everywhere.

Sometimes the staff had to work in small animal emergencies during scheduled horse surgeries. For instance, there was a Saint Bernard who needed an emergency C-section, or a dog that got hit by a car, or a laceration. Pete always said, "Bring it in and we will work on it."

Horse people usually flock together. Usually, everyone is acquainted, or anxious to be acquainted, if you are a congenial horse owner. There are horse owner snobs, who know everything, but don't know anything. Then there are those who are humble enough to let the vet tell them what is wrong and move forward with the plan for treatment. Sometimes it was the owner who needed sedation vs. the horse; a simple wound can bring out extreme emotions. Pete learned how to deal with both.

Surgical nurse Annette Anderson was on the frontline. "We had some interesting times rolling over giant draft horses for surgeries," Annette says. "We had to get the farmhands to help us. It was a dance; putting a horse on the surgery table was very choreographed. It was difficult to roll a full-size horse over onto it's back, let alone a draft horse. You had to be at the right spot at the right time to go smoothly. Through the years, Dr. Smith trained multiple crews to put horses on the surgical table; employees came and went. Eventually, Dr. Smith installed a pulley system to help move giant horses onto the table. We did a lot of surgeries on horses with throat obstructions or breathing issues. As it turns out, it's a common problem in some draft horses. When people found out that Dr. Smith could treat and perform surgery to improve respiratory function, he acquired a lot of new clients."

Pete treated every horse ailment known to man. He treated each equine – from the homeless mule to the fancy stud – the same. He loved them all. Longtime client and riding pal Steve Shingler says, "Pete was favorably impressed by a Podunk horse just as much as $1 million horse. He gave his full attention to whomever." Pete would reply, "I treat every animal to the best of my debility."

"I remember one time at a stable in West Virginia, a young horse trampled him in the corner and broke a bunch of his ribs,"

Jody recalls. "Another time, he broke bones in his left hand while vaccinating Black Angus cattle. Good thing he was right-handed. As he became experienced, he knew his limitations, and when to avoid some animals. He was called to deworm a large stable of Quarter Horses one time. There were rows of horses on either side. He walked to each stall, tube-worming each horse. As he came to the next stall, he looked at the horse and, just by looking at the mare, said that he wasn't going to deworm that mare because she looked pregnant. The stable owner was skeptical. Pete continued vetting the remaining horses. The next morning, the stable owner called and said that the mare was indeed pregnant, and that she had aborted during the night. If Pete dewormed the mare and she had aborted, the stable owner could have come back on Pete and sued. That would have been a million-dollar foal. I spent a lot of time making yogurt in big containers. Fortunately, our oven has a pilot light, which would keep the oven at a constant temperature. I would turn the oven on low, then turn the oven off. One little thing of yogurt would make a gallon of yogurt culture. He used the whole batch along with charcoal to save a horse."

People brought horses from Ohio, West Virginia, Michigan, Pennsylvania, and Kentucky. Pete even had one client bring his horse all the way from Texas. He had invested heavily in outfitting his clinic, and was one of the few places set up to do equine surgery. He was also cheaper and faster. Pete trained his own crew, a crack team that could put a horse on the surgery table with maximum efficiency. He pioneered a surgical technique for removing a testicle retained in a horse's abdomen, through the flank, that reduced complications and healing time. He learned to improve the period of relief garnered by cutting the nerve servicing the heel portion of the hoof in the treatment of navicular disease, and began using the surgery to help horses with other conditions as well. He was on the cutting edge of using a less invasive surgery to straighten crooked legs in foals. He had a higher than average survival rate after equine abdominal surgery. Toward the end of his life, he was working to find a more efficient way to surgically help draft horses with breathing problems.

90

Once, a horse owner called in the morning, frantic to get her injured mare in immediately. The mare had injured her leg. The horse owner had been urged to hurry. It takes time to arrange transport, load a horse, and drive to the clinic. By late afternoon, the horse had still not arrived. The owner had not contacted the clinic, and the clinic staff was unable to contact her. Everyone assumed the horse had passed away, or she'd opted to put it down. She finally arrived in the middle of evening appointments, demanding immediate service. She had been late, she said, because it was hot. She decided to stop and have an air-conditioned break and some dinner on their way, all while her injured mare waited in the trailer. When they opened the trailer door, several inches of blood that had accumulated on the trailer floor poured out. Needing extra hands, Pete called his surgical nurse, Annette, in to help put the horse on the surgery table, and perform anesthesia. "By the time I arrived," Annette says, "the poor animal had been moved to a stall and was down. It was too weak to rise. Dr. Smith had explained to the owner, that the horse was a poor surgical candidate, and it was unlikely to survive. The owner refused to have the mare euthanized. She insisted that Dr. Smith do everything he could to save her. I'll always remember the feel of that shattered leg. It felt like a bag of wet rocks. We did all we could, but the mare succumbed to her injuries. The owner refused to pay, and threatened to sue for the inflated value of the horse, on the ground of 'lack of timely care.' Nobody was happy.

"We had an unusual case one time. A horse came to us that had been treated unsuccessfully by another veterinarian. The horse had been on antibiotics, but continued to have respiratory problems and a discharge," Annette continues. "The owners were very frustrated, so they brought the horse to Dr. Smith. He scoped the horse and found something in the horse's trachea. We put the horse on the surgery table and found an 18-inch piece of briar, like a blackberry bramble, all the way down the trachea. The briar was beginning to rot. Dr. Smith was able to remove the briar intact."

Before Pete performed surgery, he would almost always say, "Just for fun, let's put this horse on the table." Sometimes he would have horses, like a colic horse, where the client didn't have the money to cover the cost. The client would say, "Well, we can't afford the surgery, so let's put him down." With the client's consent, Pete would say, "Just for fun, let's see if we can fix him." Pete wanted the experience, but, more importantly, he wanted to save the horse. If the horse did survive, he would let the owners know and if they wanted the horse back, he would negotiate the cost of the surgery. Annette says, "I always told him that he had a funny idea of fun because the colic surgeries were big messy affairs. You didn't always know what you were getting into. Dr. Smith enjoyed the work, he enjoyed the surgeries and being able to make a difference in helping animals. He was willing to take a risk. We were often in competition with Ohio State as far as surgeries. Competition may not be the best word, but there were not a lot of places where you could take a horse and put it on the surgery table and do the kind of surgeries that Dr. Smith performed. People would tell us there were three things that made us stand out from Ohio State. One would be Dr. Smith's customer service; he was easy to talk to and deal with. Clients said that when they went to Ohio State, the first thing they wanted to know was how they were going to pay for the surgery. It was expensive. They didn't want to do the work until they would be guaranteed that they would be paid. Price was the second thing; Ohio State was a lot more expensive than we were. But, one of the things that we had as an advantage was that we had a crack team to put the horse on the table. We had trained personnel on hand. Ohio State didn't have the experienced personnel that we had. We were able to get horses on the table quickly. We found out that the horses Dr. Smith performed surgery on were on the operating table for a fraction of the time than at Ohio State. That is important to the horse's health and recovery. We had better outcomes."

The surgery table was a big deal for the employees who were trained to operate it. The original footboard that was on the table had been broken. Working on big animals, Pete broke a couple of them. He finally had a footboard custom made. It was heavy. Employees dreaded putting the foot board on the table. Each time there was a surgery, they had to put the footboard on, and then take it off. If anyone slipped or fell, the table would collapse.

Horse clients were so thankful that Pete could save, or attempt to save, their horse that they would go the extra mile to show their appreciation. Equestrian and author Dick Pieper brought his Quarter Horse to Pete for surgery. The horse went on to win his class at the Ohio Quarter Horse Congress. He was so thrilled with Pete's skills and that his horse won the class, he took Pete and Jody to dinner afterward.

In the early '90's, Pete was delving into artificial insemination (AI), for both horses and cattle, but primarily horses. He bought all the expensive equipment needed to house the semen. He had a large AI clientele. He was well-known for his AI practice and was given many referrals by other veterinarians. At the time, he was the only AI facility in southeastern Ohio and northern West Virginia. He would order the semen as requested by the client; the client would give Pete the phone number of the stud farm and he would order the semen, shipping it directly to the clinic. Jerry Sullivan, a clinic employee, rode his Yamaha motorcycle to transport petri dishes of frozen semen that he kept in his backpack. Sometimes semen deliveries to the clinic would be on the weekend, interfering with family and social events.

"Pete, I want to go to a concert," Jody said.

"No, we can't go to a concert, semen's coming in," Pete said.

Tom Wagner, Ph.D.

Besides his day-to-day vetting, maintaining Milliron Farm, and raising children, somewhere in between Pete found time to connect with Dr. Tom Wagner, a pioneer scientist from Ohio University. Dr. Wagner explains, "This story is a serious contribution Pete made to the history of science. Pete arranged and made possible the collection of vast quantities of stallion sperm which were used in my laboratory to produce artificially generated male pronuclei allowing me to discover that the chromosomes in sperm cells were extensively damaged by breaks in their DNA. Knowing that such damage could not be allowed into the developing embryo I was able to discover that DNA repair enzymes in the egg could repair such DNA breaks just after fertilization. This knowledge led me to wonder what would happen if I inserted small fragments of DNA encoding a gene into the egg while this repair was taking place. The result of experiments to answer this question showed that these added gene fragments were 'repaired' into the egg's chromosomes resulting in the world's first transgenic animals. This technology has now led to the production of tens of thousands of 'transgenic animals' that have allowed scientists to better understand many, many diseases including cancer and perhaps will allow for the effective treatment of these diseases as well.

"Pete's waiting room was always an interesting place. I overheard a conversation between two horsemen who had come up from Kentucky. It was just a few months after the tragic death of the great race mare Ruffian. They went on and on about the tragic situation that occurred with her post surgery. After a while they both stopped talking for a few minutes and then one of them said, 'I believe if it had been Pete operating on that mare she would have been fine.' The other guy nodded and said, 'Yeah, me, too.'

"Ruffian was Pete's Border collie and I learned a great deal about her personality and fierce protective character regarding Pete or any of his possessions from a particular incident. Again, I was at Pete's clinic where I had driven in my old pickup truck that incidentally looked a lot like Pete's pickup. I had my daughter's Border collie Mugs with me and I left her in the truck while I went into the clinic to pick up a prescription for one of my horses. Well, I came out of the clinic in a hurry, passing Pete as he rushed into the clinic, late as usual. I pulled open the door of the pickup and started to swing into the seat greeting Mugs. But, it was not Mugs! I had mistakenly jumped into Pete's truck and Ruffian was on me like white on rice. Pete's staff saw the episode and sent him out front to intercede if things got worse. He asked me if I was OK and when I said that I was fine he kind of winced, looked at Ruffian and scolded her saying, 'I'd expect you to do a bit more damage to someone trying to steal my truck!' Every time after that, whenever I came near that dog, she would growl and bare her teeth trying to make up for not killing me the first time.

"Once when I was visiting with Pete in his clinic we got to talking about farms and farming and I started telling him some story about my grandfather. One story led to another and somewhere in the conversation I mentioned how my mom kept trying to get my Granddad to downsize his operation after he was 80, but he would not. I told Pete that after my Granddad bought another farm next to his during his 83rd year my Mom asked him why he would not stop buying land. My Granddad had replied by saying, 'I only want to buy what adjoins me, that's all.' Pete looked at me as serious as can be and said, 'That sounds reasonable to me.'

"Once and only once I was able to outwit Pete about equine behavior and physiology. One of my Belgian mares, Lady, was quite overdue to deliver. I asked Pete to come around the corner to check on her. He came over, looked her over, and determined that she was due to foal right now. I said no, she is not quite ready, because when she is ready and I come into the barn, she always circles and acts like she wants to lay down but lets me lead her out into the barnyard when she lies down and delivers. It's always like that I told him. 'Nonsense,' says Pete. 'Mares always wait until you leave to deliver. Let's just go in the house and wait awhile, when we come out she will be foaling.' So, we went into the kitchen and my wife made a quick dinner. After dinner, we went out to the barn and there stood the mare, just as before. Pete said, 'We did not wait long enough.' 'Nonsense,' says I. 'Just go around the back of the barn and wait a moment.' As soon as Pete left, Lady started circling and I led her out into the barnyard where she lay down and delivered a beautiful blond filly foal on the clean spring grass. While she was foaling, Pete came out from behind the barn shaking his head and said, 'That mare likes you.'

Ohio University Alumni Journal
> May-June 1976 (reprinted with permission)
> Collaborative Research

> Some people say that important medical research is best done in big city universities and research centers.
> Ohio University associate professor of chemistry Thomas Wagner, a former researcher at the Sloan-Kettering Institute, refutes this, saying that in some

cases, the rural setting is better, particularly when the research is being done initially on large animals.

To prove it, Wagner and a collaborator, local veterinarian Abbott P. Smith, successfully sought a grant from the National Institutes of Health (NIH) – at a time when medical grant money was scarce – and are now engaged in research which could lead to more knowledge of human birth defects.

Dr. Smith's standing as a leader in the development of equine surgical techniques and practices was a major factor in attracting the NIH funds, Wagner said. Equally impressive to the NIH team that did an on-site visit was Smith's well-equipped veterinary clinic which contains certain pieces of equipment that even some veterinary colleges don't have.

Together the men are studying the initial events in fertilization. Horses are being used in the research because of their large size. The researchers contend that if they can determine exactly what happens when sperm meets ovum, they might also be able to tell something about irregular fertilization and the causes of birth defects.

Wagner points to a number of advantages of the rural setting for such medical study. A major one is the relative ease of maintaining herds of large test animals in an agricultural area as opposed to a city. He cited the example of one major urban university medical center which has to hire a sheep herder to transport a flock of eight sheep by elevator to an eighth-floor test laboratory each day from ground floor stalls.

The cost of maintaining the animals is also less in rural Southeastern Ohio because grazing land is plentiful and grain can be raised right here rather than shipped in.

Most important to this particular project, Wagner said, is the availability of a private practicing vet with the skill to handle the surgery part of the research. Such collaboration is unique in the country because usually a scientist is teamed up with a medical doctor for medical research.

Wagner says a veterinarian is actually preferable since MDs only know about one species – humans – and yet are required to conduct their research on animals. "Veterinarians are really more qualified to do such research and probably are more sensitive to their best subjects," he said.

The actual research involves Wagner examining the detailed molecular changes in the chromosomal material of the male sperm cell during and after fertilization, which he simulates in a chemical environment. In the meantime, Smith is perfecting a surgical technique so that a just fertilized egg can quickly and easily be removed from a horse and examined microscopically.

Wagner said both researchers share an interest in the basic sciences, and that with this project comes the opportunity to take a whole animal down to the molecular level to see how it reproduces.

Wagner is examining the detailed molecular changes in the chromosomal material of the male sperm cell during and after fertilization which he simulates in a chemical environment.

In the meantime, Smith is perfecting a surgical technique so that a just-fertilized egg can quickly be removed from a horse and examined microscopically to see how it compares to the simulation.

The meeting point for the two men will be when they can jointly study the chromosomal event in a fertilized ovum under the microscope. But that point is still a long way down the road, with the project funding of $84,000 to last until June of 1978.

Wagner noted the team is restricted to doing the surgery refinement in the summer because of the specific breeding period horses have. And it will take a lot more trial and error before the men are able to systematize the breeding and the surgery in order to get the fertilized ovum out in time to see the molecular changes that take place.

Certainly the potential of learning about birth defects which occur in early pregnancy of humans is the major thrust of the research. Smith points out, however, that a side benefit will be a much-increased understanding of horse fertilization which could improve breeding in the species. "This kind of thing has never been done on horses before," he said.

"Never a day goes by that some interesting quirk in our research doesn't pop up. We also have the possibility of being in on the ground floor of what may be something very big. And there's bound to other kinds of fallout from any research project," Smith said.

Asked why a veterinarian with a very busy practice would be interested in devoting so much time to medical research, Smith cited the 'serendipity' of the thing.

Royal Lipizzan Stallions

In the early 70s, the Wonderful World of Horses toured the Charleston, West Virginia area. The horses were the Royal Lipizzan Stallions, the grey Austrian horses that Patton kept the Russians from eating during World War II. They had heard of Dr. Pete Smith from Pete's West Virginia clients. While performing in Charleston, the head trainer called Pete for assistance with one of their stallions. One of the magnificent stallions had a mysterious illness that no other veterinarian could diagnose. Pete was able to diagnose and cure the stallion, becoming a personal veterinarian to the royal breed. Wherever they were touring in the world, they called Pete with horse-related problems, seeking diagnosis and means of treatment. In an interview, Pete said "I never know when a sick one will be sent to me, but it's always an honor, they're so beautiful and so highly trained."

After leaving the United States, the horse troop continued with a South American tour, stopping in Brazil. Several of the horses had uncontrollable diarrhea. The veterinarian for the Lipizzans called Pete and asked if he would come to Brazil to diagnosis and medicate the horses. Pete agreed, only if they paid for his roundtrip ticket, incidental expenses, and vet fee. "It was very distractive at the clinic," Christy McDonald, Pete's receptionist at the time remembers. "They said it was an emergency and Pete had to go to Brazil right away. We had clients with appointments."

"They wouldn't take a vet in Brazil; they wanted Pete because Pete had always worked on their horses. The company was in trouble at the time due to bad management," Jan Crall, longtime clinic employee says.

Arriving at the Brazil airport, Pete hailed a cab.

"Please take me to the stables of the Royal Lipizzan horses," Pete said in his deep North American voice. The driver looked quizzically at Pete, unable to understand his English accent.

"To the Royal Lipizzan stables, okay?" Pete made the gesture for what he thought was the international sign for *okay*, holding his thumb and forefinger together, creating an *O* circle while holding his other fingers in the presumable *kay*. Gesturing the okay sign was Pete's signature trademark back at the clinic. Everyone knew what it meant.

"*Merda,*" cursed the irritated cab driver.

"Okay. Comprehenda?" Pete insisted and made the symbol once more. This time the driver motioned Pete to get out of the cab.

"*Dar o for a,*" yelled the now angry cab driver, telling Pete to get the hell out as he pointed to the cab door. Pete got out. He hailed another cab, only to be thrown out of another cab. Finally, three cabs later, Pete realized that he was going nowhere with his accent and gestures. He couldn't understand the Brazilians' Portuguese and they certainly did not want him in their cab.

Four cabs later, Pete finally arrived at the Lipizzan Stables. He told the stable manager his dilemma with the airport cab drivers. With a perplexed expression, Pete made the okay sign. The stable manager threw back his head with a hearty laugh. "Oh, that means *asshole* in Brazil!" smiled the stable manager. "No, no. Don't do that in Brazil! You pull your earlobe for 'okay' in Brazil."

Charles Black
Sometimes driving to farm calls could be relaxing, entertaining,

and thoroughly enjoyable. The stables of national equestrian Charles Black of Chillicothe, Ohio, was one of those places. Charles was well known throughout the United States for his exquisite saddle horses. Driving up the tree-lined driveway to the big white house with grand pillars and porch, Pete enjoyed vetting here. He relished the time spent with Charles in the homey kitchen that was covered with knotty pine from walls to ceiling. Silver and gold trophies, majestic paintings of his horses, and horse show memorabilia line Charles' walls. Pete envied the large stables with twenty stalls and top-drawer facilities; a lot of living, a lot of horse stories. Charles and Pete were great friends. They loved horses, knew the integrity, loyalty, and dedication to be able to spend your whole life with horses. Charles encountered his first horse when he was seven years old. He was a small man, but looked big on a horse. He had served under General Patton in the Louisiana Maneuvers, then working with the Army's horses and mules, helping to send over 10,000 mules to Europe in 90 days. Charles was known for training Saddlebreds, three and five gaited horses.

"The first time I met Pete was down at Mr. E.E. Davis' stables," recalls Charles. "He had Morgan horses. He was an industrialist, a good friend of Jim Rhodes, the then Governor of Ohio. He had a most famous Morgan - Waseka's Skylark - that he took all over the country. That's where I met Pete. We got in a conversation about horses. Then we got into wormers and the veterinary things. He wanted to know how much time I had in. Well, I had not been out of the Army too long, and I had run into veterinarians that I had regular business with. It kind of developed. I took my horses to see him. I was having a lot of vet trouble at the time. The vets here didn't want to work on them; they wanted to send them to Columbus for vetting. I said, 'No, I have been through that course.' I had been to Ohio State before, where all the students sit in. I held horses there to have their throat worked on, with breathers; so many of them couldn't breathe.

"I took several horses to Pete. He operated on them. I told other horse owners, such as John Galbraith, who had high dollar horses, to take their horses to Pete Smith. Johnny, my prize stallion, had intestinal problems. They locked on him. He had a twisted gut. Pete operated on him and fixed him up. I owed Pete $750 for fixing him and I remember Jody said, 'Well, if you don't want him, I'll just keep him.' I said, 'No. I am going to take him home. I think too much of the horse to sell him right now.' I brought him home, kept him around here for a long time. He finally had a heart attack and died. We had a lot of those things. I was up at the car auction with John Galbreath, he had a Thoroughbred. That horse could only pass one biscuit at a time. One biscuit. Pete said, 'Bring him over, we'll look at him.' We took him over and Pete fixed that old horse. Pete said, 'Well, he'll be all right, but I'd better keep him here for a few more days, he doesn't act just right.' I said, 'Well, Pete there's one thing about it, I can't do anything with him at my place.' Pete said, 'Well, I'll keep him.' A few days' later peritonitis set in. It was all over. He was a nice high-priced horse.

"Pete and I had a lot with foundered horses, down in the coffin joint. Me and Pete got into that pretty deep. This horse I am going to tell you about, this horse's hooves dropped down, all four feet. Dr. Proctor, he was 90, had planes and flew from farm to farm to doctor horses. When Dr. Proctor saw the mare, he said he couldn't do anything for her. That was when Pete was coming on. Pete was there. They set that big horse there in the yard. Puss was running out of her feet. They didn't know the word for it. I let her lay there in the yard all night. They said that she would die before morning. The mare was in foal. I was trying to figure out what to do. I thought if we could get her in the barn, then we could work on her. After a long time, and a long story, the mare was able to walk again. She had her colt and got along all right. The best thing to do for a foundered horse is to tie it in a stream. A small stream.

"Pete did all my doctoring here as soon as I met him. Pete was right out of college and had all the new things. I got along with Pete. Me and him went on about the bones in his office in his barn. You could call Pete anytime you had a problem. It could be in the middle of the night. He always got back to you right away. People are serious about their horses. It's like a sick child. Pete would always call his clients and tell them if their horse was worse or going to be all right.

"I was going to Huntington once. Daisy, my wife, and I pulled into a restaurant, down there where the big iron mills were, in Portsmouth, going up Route 52 to Huntington. Pete had been to Huntington to doctor a horse and come back and stopped there to eat. Pete said, 'Wait a minute, we're going to eat together.' He got out of this truck, the one he used when he went to West Virginia to doctor. We had a long conversation. He said, "Well, I got to go down the road here. I got one on the way home; I'm going to have to catch it." He came up Route 93 out of there going to Jackson.

"The biggest story I have, and, of course, I had served under veterinarians quite a bit, is about Johnny's half-brother. I brought him to Pete in the truck. He was a working stallion and I had bred many mares to him. One leg was absolutely stiff. The vets here always wanted me to take him to Columbus and have him operated on. But, I said, 'I am going to take him to Pete.' I called Pete and he said, 'Bring him over, we'll look at it.' The horse walked all right, but he couldn't move only one little step. He couldn't let it lose in his stifle, in the stifle joint. Pete said, 'Get him off the truck.' Pete was busy, so I waited, and then I let him out. Pete said, 'Take him over and lead him up the hill.' Pete looked down at the ground a little bit and said, 'I haven't seen any like that for a long time. Put him back on the truck. Nobody can do anything for him.' I kept the horse until he had a heart attack and died. Saddlebreds never die with their tails on. I sold a horse's tail for $1,000 once. It was ten feet long. It went to California to make wigs. Horsetail wigs. That's a big business."

Bob Evans Farm

Bill Wells, Bob Evans' former wrangler and trail boss, has fond memories of Pete. Bill and Pete worked many a night on ailing horses. Bill remembers the off-duty times, too. "Bob (Evans) sent me out west to get Mustangs. They had an adoption program at the time. Every time we returned with the Mustangs, we would have a big hog roast and BBQ at my place. Pete was there. He worked hard that day. He had too many beers, grabbed a horse blanket from the barn and sat down by a tree out back; went to sleep."

Once Pete found Bill reading a book in the stall of a little Mustang stud they had gotten out West.

"What are you doing? Reading to that horse?" Pete asked.

"Well, he likes someone around," Bill answered as he continued quietly reading to himself.

"Pete really helped me a lot," Bill says. "Before I started working for Bob Evans, I was looking for work. Pete would come to my place when I lived in Middleport. He liked the strawberry ice cream my wife made. Pete knew I wanted to have a riding stable. One day, he said, 'Bill, I'll tell you what; you go over and see Horace Carr. Horace Carr owns a stable, but he doesn't know anything about it. Why don't you go over there and tell him you're laid off? Tell Horace that I sent you over.' That was in 1969. I went over, and the rest is history."

Bill was present on one memorable occasion when Pete came down to see a stud that belonged to someone else and had somehow jumped over the fence and was hit on the highway. The stallion had a broken neck and appeared to have colic, too. Pete looked at the horse and said, "You've got a dead horse standing there. He's full of stomach fluid; it's leaking through his stomach cavity." Pete lanced him and ran the fluid out, but said, because of the rupture, the only thing that you can do was to put him down. They took him around a hill and Pete put him down. Pete had all the necessary saws, axes, and knives. When he cut the stallion open, he saw that his stomach was eaten clear through from ulcers. That's from not feeding it enough hay. This guy, a dentist, would take a five-gallon bucket of feed and dump it in the feeder once a day. Pete was upset," Bill says. "People think that all horses do is walk and eat. They shut them up in a tiny stall and they wonder why they're climbing the wall."

Fred Vollburn, the former horse manager at Hidden Valley Ranch, in Rio Grande, Bob Evans' personal horse farm, knew Pete, too. Fred met the colorful veterinarian in 1968 when Fred started working for Evans. "I got married and my wife had never met Pete," Fred recalls. "Pete was supposed to be at the barn one afternoon, but he was running late. He had more work down the road than he thought. I had come in for supper and I told Linda I was going back out to work until dark. It was in the spring of the year. We had about 20 ponds on the ranch, but at the time, we only had two that we didn't let anybody fish in. Those were the two everybody wanted to fish in, especially that time of year. Linda was used to the welfare bunch coming and wanting to fish in the pond. So, she saw this old dirty black Cadillac pull up in the driveway. There were two dogs hanging out the window. She was prepared to send him on. He rolls down his window and says, 'I'm Dr. Smith.' She about fainted. "

One year, as soon as the weather got good, Evans wanted a mare and colt in the field where the farm's annual festival takes place. Fred recalls, "We brought a mare and foal over here from Hidden Valley. Of course, this was the main drag, and something had spooked that colt one night. It jumped the fence and a semi-truck hit it; broke its front leg or shoulder. That was the first time we used Pete. We took the mare and colt in the big cattle truck. The next day Pete called and said it was too much stress and the colt didn't make it. Pete said there would be no bill. I think it was four or five years before we did any business with him again. I called him one day and asked him something about the horses, or had something that needed fixed. He said, 'I thought Evans was mad at me!' I said, 'No, we just hadn't had anything major to do.'

"There was a time when we had a lot of horses in training and we had a lot of full-time trainers. Pete did a lot of work for us during that period of time. We had a lot of cattle, too, but any major horse work Pete did. We had registered cutting and reining horses. Rio Grande had a lot of tourist attractions and riding stables here. It was fast paced job. It was a lot of hard working hours for Pete and me. Pete would be out before dark and he would still be working into the night.

"We had a filly in Pennsylvania for reining training for the Futurity. She broke her front leg. They took her into a high-powered vet clinic in Pennsylvania. They put her through X-rays and called us and told us what it was going to cost to put that leg back together and get her going again. It was a shocking figure. I don't remember what it was, but it was big. The horse trainer and I decided to call Pete to see what he had to say. Pete said, 'Well, if you boys want to go get her bring her over. I'll see what I can do. I can't make any promises. Be sure to stop up here and get some pads and slings that you'll need to transport her.' We hauled her in there. It was a pretty good trip. Pete set her leg and everything looked like it was going to work. Three weeks later, Pete called and said that the mare was in a lot of pain and had gone downhill in the night. Pete wanted to know what we thought and if it was all right to put her down. We told Pete that he knew what to do. We just assumed he put her down. Two months later he called and said, 'That mare is ready to pick up.' I said, 'What mare?' He said, 'The one that I told you I was going to put down!' We just assumed Pete put her down. We brought her back for brood mare and raised four or five foals off her.

"Pete was always telling jokes and reciting limericks. He read a lot of cartoons, too. He was always quoting his favorite cartoon character Snuffy Smith."

The Athens County Fair

For many years, Pete was the official vet of the Athens County Fair. Held the first week in August, the fair was a demanding venue that required a lot of time away from the practice as well as interaction with fair participants.

"One day Pete shows up at the fairgrounds to castrate a colt," Rick Bowen remembers. "It had been raining and a huge mud puddle had developed in the center of the lot. Pete asked me to bring out the colt. I asked where he wanted to perform the task. Pete looked around and replied, 'After I give him the cocktail, just lead him in a circle around the puddle.' Pete administered the 'cocktail' and I began leading the colt around the puddle. When the drug hit, the colt jumped straight in the air and landed perfectly in the middle of the huge puddle. Pete looked at me, laughed and said, "Bullseye!" He then went to work. As usual, anytime you have Pete work in a public venue, you will have spectators. There were a few people and one dog. When finished, Pete threw the colt's testicles to the dog. The dog, of course, loved it. The people, well, the crowd dispersed."

Dr. Stifles

Laird Gassan, a favored client, is the former proprietor of Terrapin Farms, a horse farm where Jessica took riding lessons and Pete treated many horses. Laird's husband, Ohio University Professor Arnold Gassan, had designed a novel and well-functioning, smooth indoor arena with posts on the outside of the riding arena. Laird christened Pete *Dr. Stifles* as she made many a trip to the clinic with horses that 'hitched' coming down the slight grade in the lower driveway from the farmhouse to the clinic, also known as the 'stifles slope.'

Before the great strides in stifle surgeries, horses were usually euthanized with stifle problems. Pete was a pioneer in repairing stifles. Bud, the Quarter Horse-Arabian Pete had bought from fellow veterinarian Bud Strouss, was a candidate for stifle and navicular surgeries. Bud completely recovered and was one of Pete's favorite horses.

Cryptorchidism was one of Pete's surgical specialties. Statistically, cryptorchidism in horses is common. Usually, cryptorchid males are gelded since the condition is 25% inheritable and pre-cancerous. In rare cases, the testicle can be released without injury, securing a functional stallion. Pete had perfected cryptorchid surgery and was well-known throughout Ohio, Kentucky, Pennsylvania, and West Virginia for his innovative approach to cryptorchids.

Arnold Gassan, one of Pete's clients and friends, penned this poem in honor of Pete in his 1979 personal anthology, *A Diary of Poems…*

XXVII: HORSES
San was insane, we were told,
Stood quivering as we hammered
Together his stall around him.
March was bull-stubborn, bending
The stall door, leaning on us to
Get supper sooner; he died at David's
Standing sullen in the tracks, defying
The C&O. Tristan was half-cut, bugling
And herding his mares. Pete cut
Him fully, reaching deep inside for
His maleness: torn open in his stall,
Survived his tumbling guts pushed back,
Sewn together quickly like a sack of grain.
"Sold to Laird on a sunny day in June,"

Read his bill of sale. Half starved, half-
Cut he grew sleek, had a comforting canter.
Mulligan was our first full stallion, took
Command of barn and mares, trumpeted and
Kicked, watched puppy-eyed from his pen
As riders and mares passed. Jim bought him,
Half-starved him, sold him to a woman who
Cut his balls when he didn't fit her image.

Steve Sawchuk, D.V.M.

Amputating a dog's leg requires skill and finesse. Dr. Sawchuk is in the middle of surgery, while reminiscing about Pete. Talking while operating seems to be like rubbing your tummy while patting your head; requiring a lot of patience. Dr. Sawchuk smiles through his surgical mask, thinking of Pete. "Pete's most successful year financially was his last year, and he did the least amount of horses," Dr. Sawchuk says. "It had nothing to do with Pete, it was just a shift in the horse business, and people are not into horses as they were. Pete saw it coming. People just don't invest a lot of money into horses right now; $1,000 in vetting a horse - you can buy a horse for less. The economy went bad and horses were worth a lot more money, but not now.

"When I worked at the clinic, I'd do all the small animals for Pete," Dr. Sawchuk continues. "I'd come in, there might be a few horses come in, but basically we would do spays, neuters, tumor removals, etc., with dogs and cats; I just started with them. I would cover many breaks for Pete. He would go to meetings, etc. Pete really loved going out into the woods and cutting lumber. He wanted to get the sawmill up and running. A lot of times, anything routine, I would do all that.

"If there was something hard, like extreme surgeries or broken bones, Pete would do it and I would assist him for those harder things. He had confidence in me, I guess. I did those for a while, but I was kind of slow. I graduated in 1999 and I began working for Pete in 2006. When I met Pete, he'd been a vet for a very long time.

"When I graduated, and I began my practice in Perry County, I didn't have that much horse experience, and here I was working on horses. I didn't have anybody to rely on. I accidently found out about

107

Pete Smith. If you had a real serious horse problem in Perry County, everybody brought their horses to Pete. So, that's how I knew about Pete. Everybody talked about him," Dr. Sawchuk says. "So, eventually, I ended up talking to him. It got so that if I had a question or problem or something I couldn't figure out; I would just call him. Year after year, after year. They probably hated me here because I was always bothering him. 'Oh, that one vet is on the phone again, asking for free advice.'

"I was a student, he was the mentor, it seemed. So, that's just the way it was. He was just the person I admired the most; somebody that I was in awe of. When I left where I was working, I started working here; Pete thought I was slow. He called me slowpoke. Milliron Clinic was a hospital. It was a referral center. Other veterinarians sent horses to Pete. I would look at a horse and say, 'Oh my God, there's nothing I can do with this. You had better go to Pete Smith.' He was like Ohio State South."

Steve will never forget the first time he called Pete in an emergency, he had been a vet for two weeks, "didn't know a lot of anything," but had heard of Pete's horse expertise. "My boss at the time told me I was going to be the Perry County fair vet," Steve recalls. "My boss said he was scheduled to be the fair vet, but that he didn't do large animals. He told me that since I do large animals that I was going to be the new fair vet. I am like…*Um, all right*. I am not a fair person, didn't know much about it. So, there I was, suffering through my first fair. Someone called on my walkie-talkie and said that one of the draft horses in the pulling competition was colicing. I got in my truck and drive over to where the horse was. The horse was in a parking lot with all these guys and all their draft horses in a big ring. They all were watching. The one in the middle had colic. These guys all know everything. They were giving me free advice as to what was wrong with the horse. This big Percheron was very uncomfortable, stomping the ground, swinging his tail. It looked like a serious colic. It was certainly freaking me out. I had a huge audience of all these horse people, and I had been a vet for about a month.

"I had a lot of interest in colic when I was in school, so I had a little experience. I gave the horse a sedative just so I could manage him and see what was going on with him. I gave him his dose, the horse is sedated, but his heart rate is too close to 100. For a draft horse his heart rate should be one digit. His heart rate was very high. I was confused as to what was going on this case. Obviously, it was colic, but I am not sure I can manage in the parking lot, because nothing is making sense to me. I say to myself, 'I've heard of this Pete Smith, maybe I'll call him and ask his advice'. That's the first time I called the Milliron Clinic. That was in 1999. I called in and said, 'This is Dr. Sawchuk, I am at the Perry County Fair and I would like to talk with Pete Smith.' I described the horse and that I was confused; didn't know what was going on. Pete got on the phone and said, 'Well, hell, ask them how much caffeine they've given it.' The guy who owned the horse was standing with me, so I said, 'Dr. Smith wants to know how much caffeine you've given your horse.' The guy seemed all defensive and he said, 'I gave the horse only a spoonful of caffeine, and, oh, by the way, I gave him some Lasix.' The guy had given the horse Lasix all day to meet the weight requirement. So, in the end, Pete diagnosed it over the phone, from the history, just from his experience, and what the situation was. Of course, the horse was completely dehydrated and just a little constipated. The horse's heart rate didn't go down after sedation because of the caffeine. They had given it caffeine to make the horse perky for the fair. In the end, Pete gave me some other advice like to stick a hose up its butt and give it IV fluids. After the IV fluids, enema, etc., the horse was fine.

"I do lots and lots of surgeries. That's all I ever do. There were a lot of surgeries that Pete did that I won't do," Dr. Sawchuk continues. "Some surgeries I don't have the aptitude for, I guess. But you have to understand Pete had a different kind of attitude. An attitude of a true servant, which is - he was willing to try anything to save an animal. Not everything that Pete did surgery on lived, but the animal would have died anyway, or they were freakin' miracles and lived. A lot would be beyond hope, but Pete would always be willing to try. The nice thing we had when we had Pete was that he did so many surgeries, he was an expert. He would do them cheap, too. People could afford it. Back in the old days, before I knew how to do certain things, I sent clients to Pete. One case I remember was about a horse. The whole lower part of its leg was blown apart. At first, Pete didn't want to do the surgery, I don't know why; maybe he didn't think he could fix it. Pete told the owner that the surgery would be about $5,000, at that time that was a lot of money. Pete put in plates and screws. When a horse has that many screws with that much instability, a lot of times it's not going to be good. They always founder on that type of leg. It was the same time the horse Barbaro had almost the same kind of fracture. Pete went to the vet center in Pennsylvania and found out how the horse had to be repaired; I just remember seeing that horse and remembering that it had the same fracture as Barbaro. It just healed perfectly. What saved the horse was the large plate in the leg with screws all the way through it. There was no way that should have worked. But it did. The horse walked away.

"People can get really angry and pissy with the receptionists and vet techs, but when they talk to the vet, they're all nice and sweet. That's the hardest part about being a vet. It's not the animals or the surgeries, its dealing with the people, because you can imagine, there's all kinds of people. When I started working at Milliron Clinic, Pete was mellow towards patients. Sometimes he would get angry, but the good thing about Pete was, he could bullshit with people, especially horse people. He was definitely different with horse people than with small animal people. Horse people loved him. He just had an air of authority with them. They didn't question him as much. Pete had been a vet for so long that he had the weight of experience and authority that someone new wouldn't have. I don't know what he was like when he first started, but he'd been doing it for so long that he had so much confidence. With horse people, he'd say 'This is the way it is.' The horse people have the type of personality that what Pete said carried through, and that's what you have to have with horse people. I'd pull up to the clinic, horses were Tuesdays and Thursdays; there would be three or four horse trailers and they'd all say, 'West Virginia, West Virginia, West Virginia.' And all these people would come around who had horses with colic, or needed castrated or cryptorchid surgery. That was the three surgeries that he did most. He was so good at them, and he had been doing them for so long. I went with Pete to West

Virginia once. We went to one stable and all these people would come out with all their horses, kind of in the middle of nowhere. We stopped at a client's house. We walked in and nobody said anything. Pete didn't say anything, we just walked in, and there's all this food. Pete sits down and starts eating. I couldn't believe how much food this lady had prepared. I tried to eat as much as I could. Pete just ate all of it. It was amazing. Afterward, we went to look at the horses."

Eric and Rhonda Curfman

Andalusian horse owners Eric and Rhonda Curfman live in West Virginia. They heard of Pete's miraculous surgeries. "The first time we meet Pete, we had a couple of horses," Eric remembers. "I came home from work one day and Rhonda had a Saddlebred gelding out in the yard and she was crying. I thought, *Oh my God.* I looked at him, he had cut his leg. I didn't say anything to her, but his left front leg, he had cut it this way and all the way up here. I could see tendons. We think he got cut on the barn down there, but we never found any blood or hair. At the time, we were dealing with a vet out of Belpre. A very nice man. I called him, of course it was a Sunday. This stuff always happens on a weekend. I called Doc Barrett, he said that he couldn't do anything for him, it was that bad. He said to try Dr. Spindler in Marietta. We called Dr. Spindler. He finally got back with me and he said he could fix it but it wouldn't be right. I thought why would I go there. He said our only choices were to go to Ohio State or Dr. Smith in Athens. I was thinking that Athens was closer than Ohio State and I knew Ohio State would be outrageous. So, I call up to Athens and get a hold of one of the girls. He wasn't there, but they were going to have him call me. Finally, he called and I told him the tendon was cut clear in two. He said, 'Bring him up, we'll take care of him.' Like it was no big deal. Everyone else was doom and gloom.

"We get up there, drop him off, and Pete's out riding. Anyway, we drop him off, put him in a stall. Pete called me late that night, about 11 pm that night. Pete said, 'You're right. He cut the tendon in two.' He operated next thing in the morning. He had to wear a cast for 3 months. He was supposed to wear it for 3 months, but in 6 weeks he had the bottom of it pawed off. We had to take him back.

So, we took him back and Pete looked at him and said, 'Man, that is healing really good.' He didn't even put the cast back on. So, that was the beginning of a wonderful relationship. It started out a little rocky. After that, no matter what we had, we took them up there because if it's ever bad, this is where they are going to end up, so why not just take them there for everything. The only time he ever came here is when we had that one mare that we couldn't get loaded. That mare was wild. That's the one that kicked me in the back of the leg. He brought his horse and trailer and the next morning we went to Cave Run Lake to ride.

"Pete was always telling jokes. The one he liked to tell is about this guy who was going to die. He wanted to pass on the family bejeweled chalice to his son. Pete went on and on that this diamond was added in this century, this diamond added in that century… He embellished it in the telling. Pete always had a glass in his hand when he was telling it. He would tell about all the jewels on the side of it. He said, 'Just remember, always drink from this side.' The son said, 'Why father? Are all the other parts highly poisonous?' He said, 'No, you jackass.' He drank from the wrong side and Pete would pour whatever he had right down the front of his shirt. You get sucked into the story and everything, and all it was that he poured it down the front of his shirt by drinking from the wrong side of the cup."

Last Chance Corral

Victoria Goss is a horsewoman. She is the proprietor of Last Chance Corral, a horse rescue and rehoming facility in Athens, saving horses for over 20 years. A fun personality, Victoria is an equestrian and horse trainer. She has trained horses as well as camels and zebras. Pete admired Victoria and was instrumental in helping her in her efforts to save horses, particularly abandoned foals. She has helped as many as 270 foals in one year.

"I know that I can't save the horses if I don't get along with the people. I think we all have to find the place within our temperament, what it is that we can do.

"We imprint babies all the time here. All our foals, people are like, "Oh my God. I never had a horse that I never had to train. It's like I think things and it just happens." We couldn't do here what we do here if not for Pete. He always insisted that I know how to do it, that I was totally capable; there were no excuses for me not do it and learn to do it so he didn't have to get up in the middle of the night. Pete would say, "Well, what are you going to do when I am not here? I am not going to be here forever. So, you need to learn all of this."

It wasn't necessarily that he was thinking anything else, but that he went off to vet meetings and other events. He forced me to know how to do all the things and to *get out your book.* He would have me read and then tell me to call back with questions." Victoria's foal facility is state-of-the-art. She writes of Pete...

> Pete:
> I could write a million words,
> and write a million more,
> but none could do what I need them to,
> and bring you to my door.

"In our own way we were very much in love," Victoria writes. "We shared a deep and abiding understanding of each other. In some ways we were very much alike (though certainly not in all ways). Out of this understanding we forged a comradery, a love. Not the love a man shares with his wife, or children; the love a man shares with his true friends. Like brothers in arms slogging through the matter of life... we were able to see each other's difficulties, goodness and flaws. We could be honest with each other. We were able to appreciate each other and accurately predict how the other would react to certain situations. Then, make each other laugh at our own folly... still finding that true, resounding beauty in those crystalline moments that make life wonderful. I guess maybe we were both in love with the same thing – the madness that is life.

"Early in my dealings with Doctor Smith, and this was way back in those Dark Ages, just around the time that they invented mud, back when he did farm calls. I had made an appointment with Pete but found that I had the occasion to be "off campus" (somehow it made me feel erudite if I called my farm that). I had completely forgotten. I returned to find my bill attached to my door by means of a dirty syringe and needle stabbed through it. Now it is true that one should always be about when the vet comes to call, being as you summoned the presence of the doctor to work on your large animals, you ought to be present to hold said animals steady for the vet to work on. I had committed the greatest sin there was in the vet-farmer relationship. The manner in which he presented my bill indicated his displeasure, it *was* my warning, and I fully understood the gravity of my mistake. It was also pretty flippin' funny! I will carry that image with a smile forever. To convey so very much with the strike of such a tiny dagger is priceless!

"At the time I owned a stallion. A *Morgan* stallion. An old-style Morgan stallion. Having grown up in New Hampshire on the Vermont border, these rugged little versatile horses were highly prized. You could log with them, drive, ride, fox hunt, and any other equestrian skill you could come up with.

"I was standing this stallion and had five mares all wanting to be bred on the same weekend. He was a hell of a horse, but I was thinking by the time he got to the last mare he would either be dead or she wasn't going to get much of a honeymoon. I conferred with Pete, in regard to my breeding quandary, and he said that he had a great idea... that we should gather all involved parties on that Saturday morning. He had everybody converge on the arena of Windy Hills Farm (directly across the street from the clinic). Well, quite a few folks heard that Dr. Smith was going to pull off some sort of breeding miracle (of course, *this* had to be some form of terrific entertainment if Pete was involved). There were lawn chairs (with coolers) pulled into a half circle in the designated area. Dr. Smith checked the mares – sure enough; each and every one was at the absolute apex of 'concept ability.'

"Four of the mares stood side by each on the opposite (from the spectators) side of the circle. The fifth mare, a brood mare who, shall we say, displayed the most "willing" and randy behavior (she was a regular whore) stood in the center. I went to the barn to get my stallion; Pete went to his car to retrieve the "necessary" equipment. When I returned to the breeding circle the laughter and guffaws were almost too much. Folks had actually fallen out of their lawn chairs and were on their knees laughing, holding stomachs and opening beers! There stood Dr. Smith, looking altogether like the conquering hero, tall, proud, brave, somber…wearing over his shoulder and across his chest – not a sash filled with medals, but…*the artificial vagina*!

"Pete stops the laughter (only temporarily) to tell everyone a story about how at one time he had been audited. The auditor, after many long days of going over Dr. Smith's books and receipts, of course had a list of questionable items, but right there at the tippy top, the first item on his agenda was this, "Dr. Smith you can't claim marital aids as a business expense on your taxes." Pete says, "Marital aids?" and the auditor says, "Yes, right here it says you paid $752 for an artificial vagina." Pete flashes a broad, crooked, shit-eating grin of a smile and says, "wait right here. I really want to show it to you, and if you think it's something I might actually find useful in the way you're thinking, we've got bigger problems than taxes to deal with!" A roar goes through our audience. Now you really need to try to visualize this apparatus. It sort of resembles a quiver – for arrows. It is made of heavy brown leather with an inner rubber sleeve that holds warm water – the amount of which is determined by the type of horse. It has a strap that the administrator wears over their shoulder, and here's the icing on the cake, it has a mason jar screwed on the end for "collection" purposes. All in all it's about three to three and a half feet long. I'm sure upon visual inspection that the auditor no longer considered this item to be of any meaningful personal use for Dr. Smith.

"So here's the set up. The mare is being held by its owner; Pete is standing at the current business end of the mare, at the ready to fool the stallion with the artificial vagina, when the stallion mounts the mare. I'm leading the stallion. The onlookers have quieted down to a respectful whisper. As the stallion mounts the mare, Pete directs him into the A.V. and all seems to be going perfectly well, then something goes terribly wrong.

"My stallion's eyes roll back into his head; he goes stiff all over and falls to the ground like he's been shot in the head. His lead rope was ripped from my hand when this happened. I ran to my now prone, useless husk of a horse and screamed at Pete, *"your god-damned artificial vagina killed my horse!"* The crowd was as silent as Sunday. Pete lifts up the A.V. to show a successful collection in the Mason jar, takes a step over and kicks my horse's forehead. As my bewildered horse lifted his head, eyes blinking with wonder, Pete says, "Naw…jus showed him a good time." Once again people were on their knees as my stallion made his way to his feet. His legs spread akimbo at the four corners like a newborn foal, gathering his wits. He then shook a mighty shake, picked up his head and whinnied – perfectly restored! "Maybe I shoulda put a little less water in there" – Pete's epilogue. After all the semen was divided up, all five mares were happily pregnant and Athens had a new tale to tell of how Pete killed my horse.

"When Pete saved one of my animals he would say, '*You can't kill 'em all.*' On most Saturday mornings you could find me at the clinic," Victoria grins. "Mostly because the nature of my business (taking in abused, neglected, misunderstood and otherwise unwanted equine, addressing their needs and finding them appropriate homes) meant that I had a never-ending parade of crazy sicknesses and injuries. Pete once said, 'If I'd known you were going to start something like this, I'd have had a couple more kids to put through college!' Needless to say, I became one of Milliron Clinic's most prolific customers. When Pete held his Saturday morning horse clinic, as often as not, my trailer was in the rotation, but being there was much more than simply having him inspect my most recent catastrophic acquisitions. It was like going back to school. I'd pitch in and help hold horses, pass equipment, anything so I could be in the thick of the action, asking questions or simply listening for answers in his conversations with other 'client's owners.'

"'None of my clients pay their bills, but occasionally their owners do,' Pete would say. As a matter of fact, one day when I was stopping by the clinic to pay my rather hefty bill, I walked in the door with a hundred-dollar bill plastered across my forehead, and my timing couldn't have been better, a deep thoughtful, weary-looking Pete was actually caught off guard! He glanced, and then lowered his head slightly to see over his bifocals on the double-take. I just stood there and watched him slowly smile, then crack up clear 'till he slapped his hands on his knees. 'I always knew that sooner or later you'd come up with a likeable characteristic.'

"There was a wealth of knowledge, ripe for the picking at those clinics; all you had to do was clean out your ears. There was also a great deal of emotions floating around, from jubilant to morose, depending upon why people had brought their animals and what the outcome had in store. When things get heavy, it's good to maintain that 'ole cheery disposition and Pete did. Let's face it, he was a joker and a merry prankster, and on occasion, without a word uttered between us, a situation would present itself and we would roll with it like a well-oiled machine or a couple of seasoned performers. I once brought a two-month old foal that had an abscess on his chest, most likely caused by a splinter from reaching through a wooden fence. There was a crowd at the clinic that morning. Pete got ready to lance the abscess and then we were going to pack it with gauze and strong iodine. We both looked at the big 'ole bottle of strong iodine and light bulbs above our heads snapped on in unison, we are creatures of habit: opportunists! He cracked it and we immediately started to tear. Tears streaming down our cheeks, we both broke out all our acting skills during the proceed (simple and straight-forward though this procedure was). Victoria: 'Do you think (sob) he'll make it (sob, sob) Doc?' Pete: '(Sob) I, (sob) just (sob) don't know (sob)' Together: 'It's just (sob) too early to tell (sob).' We went on and on while all these people stood by watching in complete silences, awestruck by Pete's sensitive, vulnerable nature. I'm sure some were thinking, *hell, if a little abscess does that to him, I better not show him my horse, he'll break down!*

"When he finished Pete offered to help me through the waterfall of tears and horrible acting to put my colt in the trailer. We walked around to the back parking lot laughing and drying tears for five minutes. We couldn't even talk; it was priceless. I waited for months for some probable acting award or citation to arrive; it never did."

I remember loading sheep and I tore a nail.
We stopped at a gas station to get some
gas on the way to the sale barn.
I asked the guy if he sold nail files.
He looked at me like why in the world
would I care about my nails since I was
dressed in old barn boots and coveralls!
Jody Smith

---

7 MILLIRON FARM

ABOUT A MILE or so from Milliron Farm is Pete Smith Road. The road is not eponymous; Pete Smith did not give his name for this road. The road was named for another Pete Smith, son of Lew Smith. The road existed before Jody and Pete purchased Milliron Farm, although they later owned the land bordering the road.

The Smith home was the hub of human and animal activity, including kids, dogs, sheep, cats, horses, goats, donkeys, chickens, snakes, visitors, and friends. The historic two-story farmhouse looked down over the clinic, sawmill, and highway. The large picture window in the living room of the Smith's farmhouse overlooks the hilltop meadow and has a panoramic view of the alley. It is where Jody placed her grandmother's rocking chair to sit and watch the living interplay of local flora and fauna. It is a family area, one that continues to hold many memories for the Smith family.

The farmhouse was always available for orphans from the clinic, most of the time. "Pete and I went with friends to see *The Man from Snowy River*," Jody says. "When we returned to the clinic, someone had stuck two baby raccoons in the back of our friend's truck. Pete took them in.

"Another time," Jody continues, "Pete was reading a book written by a veterinarian about how, to relocate a raccoon, and you can catch them up a tree and give it an anesthetic in the muscle. Then, once the raccoon is sedated, you can pull the raccoon out of the tree and relocate it. That worked for a couple of them. This time he grabbed the tail of a raccoon and *roar*, it came right down on his head. Pete fell out of the tree and the raccoon, too. It was a mommy raccoon with a baby. You don't mess with mommy raccoons. Pete had a pistol on his side in case things didn't go well. *Bam. Bam.* Pete brought the baby home. We named him Rowdy. Rowdy had the run of the farmhouse for a while," Jody sighed. "He shredded my curtains and all kinds of things before we found him another home. We didn't try that again."

Rick Bowen, a longtime friend and client was telling Pete one day about his upcoming frog gigging party, but that all of his gigging spots had been depleted. Rick says, "I asked Pete if he knew of any ponds that I might go to. He said he knew of some, but he would have to go with me. This shocked me because I assumed he would be too busy, but at the same time delighted as I always enjoyed spending time with Pete. We set out to some ponds, and after a couple of stops, we still needed more frogs. Pete said he knew of another spot to go to, but we would have to be sneaky. We decided to go to his 'secret' spot, which turned out to be Pete and Jody's farm pond. We put the boat into the pond and began looking for frogs. I couldn't believe my eyes, not only were there frogs everywhere, they were huge! We had a blast. We gigged our limit (and a few more) and started to take the boat out of the pond, when it hit me. 'Pete,' I whispered, 'why do we have to sneak on your property?' Pete turned around and quietly said, 'Jody likes to hear the frogs.'"

Farm Kids

As a pre-teen, Jessica was precocious, inquisitive, knowledge-able, and informative. Once her cousins were visiting from Mans-field and had rarely been on a farm. Jessica felt it her responsibility to explain to them the interaction between the farm animals. Black Angus could be seen grazing in the meadow from the large picture window. They were complacent in their hillside retreat, unknowing that they were being watched and monitored by Jessica and her cousins. Jessica pointed out the bull. "Sometimes he even sniffs their butts if he has to," she explained. The cousins, Tina and Gary Franklin, nodded with wide eyes and raised eyebrows.

Several years later at Tina's wedding, Pat was checking out the wedding party as they proceeded down the aisle. He suddenly exclaimed, "Wow! That's my sister and she's beautiful!"

Many times, family situations intertwined with Pete's work. As Jessica grew into her teenage years, she sometimes accompanied Pete on farm calls. Pete was happy to have Jessica tag along and help with vetting. As any father, he was ever-watchful, territorial, and proud of his daughter. Once, enroute to a farm call, Jessica had to use the restroom. Pete pulled into the Peanut Bar, a small hole-in-the-wall-dive where the locals gathered. Pete was sitting quietly at the bar as Larry Smith, Pete's friend and client, walked into the bar. Larry sat down on the stool beside Pete as Jessica sashays out of the restroom. "Oh, whoa, look at that!" the friend said to Pete as he ogled Jessica. "I'm in love!" Pete looks at Larry, and then glances at Jessica. When he realizes Jessica is the one Larry is in instant love with, Pete raises an eyebrow and proclaims, "That's my daughter!" Larry hurriedly replies, "Oh! I'm out of love, out of love…"

"Dad would say that anyone who married me would get a lifetime of free worming," Jessica says. Jessica met Rich Fox, her husband, while they were working for the same employer. "I will tell a story that I haven't told many people before," Rich says. "When I first moved in and was living with Jessica, she acquired a dog named Brewster. I don't know why, but Jessica was away for a couple of days. I really wasn't a farm boy. Brewster injured his hind leg and I didn't know what to do. I took the dog over to the clinic in the pickup. They were able to get him in right away. Turned out the dog was fine. Pete was very welcoming. I watched him write out the ticket. 'Owner afflicted, devastating injuries' to dog's hind leg, and I am waiting for him to add 'dumb owner'. I thought, *God, that's real insensitive.* I survived my first Pete encounter. Jessica and Pete are very much alike; both frequently wrong, but never in doubt."

Jessica and Pat saw a side of their dad that most children never see - their dad at work, during unusual circumstances relating to the life or death of an animal, how that scenario relates to the human condition, and the gamut of emotions that follow. Outward looking in, there were James Herriot moments. But at the end of the day, when Pete was tired, you found a quiet spot to do your homework, read a book, and be a kid.

The Smith kids were active in 4-H and other animal-related events, such as dog shows, horse clinics, and much more. At a young age, Jessica announced her desire to raise rabbits for 4-H. Pete told her that she could raise rabbits, but she couldn't keep them all, that the time would come when some of the rabbits would have to be butchered. Jessica understood. When the time came, Pete butchered some of the bunnies while Jessica was away at school. Jody made a nice meal of roasted rabbit for dinner. Jessica came home from school and asked, "What's for dinner?" Pete said, "We're having fried meat." Jessica was skeptical, and not to be out-smarted, looked at Pete and said, "I want a wing."

"One time we were coming back from town, just over Dividing Ridge Hill, from an event," Pat remembers. "Somebody had hit a deer and it was still lying in the middle of the road. A state highway patrolman had just shot this deer. He was starting to reload his gun. Dad says, 'Do you want me to shoot this deer? I am a veterinarian.' The state trooper had gone to 'I am a state trooper, I am from Asshole School' and he's telling Dad to get out of the way and I'll take care of this, get back in your truck. Dad doesn't take the 'I am an Asshole' thing very well. So, this young state highway patrolman shoots the deer three more times. Dad walks over with his .22 pistol that he carried in his back pocket. He pushes the trooper out of the way, walks over, shoots the deer and it just went *pppfff*. Dad walked away and the trooper started to say something to him. Dad said something really mean, 'You need to get your shit together' Dad got back in the truck and we drove home. Dad never said a word about it."

Just turning 16, Pat was a sophomore at Federal Hocking High School. He was crossing Court Street in Athens when he was hit by an oncoming car. As the driver hit Pat, breaking his hip, he was flipped onto the car hood. The driver then pumped the brakes until Pat fell back onto the pavement. The driver ran over him, crushing his chest. It was a hit and run.

They rushed Pat to the local hospital, finally transporting him to the emergency room at Ohio State Hospital, Columbus. Pat's heart was in peril. He underwent emergency heart surgery and was placed in intensive care.

Scheduling his clinic appointments so that he could travel to Columbus, about a two-hour drive, Pete was attentive to Pat during the recovery process, initiating an unspoken bond between father and son. Jody, sitting by Pat's bedside, remained in constant prayer.

"When they thought Pat was brain damaged, well, the high possibility that he could be, I was sitting by his bedside in intensive care. I was only allowed to sit with him for half an hour. When Pat woke up, I was trying not to cry. Pat said, 'Don't cry, Mom, your number one son is still here.' Pat would tease me that Puff, my Belgian sheepdog, was my number one son. I reassured Pat that he was my number one son."

Later, the surgeon who was prepping for Pat's surgery to repair his shattered hip recognized Pete from a bone plating conference they both attended in Switzerland. Pete was invited to observe. "They allowed him to operate the X-ray machine since surgery was taking longer than anticipated and the technician's shift ended. After hours of surgery, Pat slowly recovered. Several miracles helped him survive," Jody says.

Pat continued through months of rest and therapy. Relationships became different after the accident; Pete was grateful for Pat's courage and tenacity throughout. The accident was a harrowing experience for Pat. He with was left with many internal plates, screws and a Dacron aorta. The Smith family will be forever thankful for all of the well-wishers and prayer warriors.

Farm Animals

Rarely do you see veterinarians without pets of their own. Pete enjoyed geese in the yard, buzzards on the rooftops, cows in the pasture, dogs at his feet, and horses on the ready. Geese were special to him since childhood when his goose won a blue ribbon at the rural County Fair in Maine. "Why did you buy all these geese?" Jody asked Pete one day as they were driving through Sugar Creek, which was a coal mining town at the time. There was a pen of very thin geese alongside the road. He would drive by the pen every day, until finally he stopped and purchased, or rather rescued, the geese. They were Toulouse grey geese; two ganders and four geese. "The geese could fly," Jody says, "but after Pete fattened them up a little, they would only fly on the breeze off the hill to the clinic, walking up the hill back to the farmhouse."

The geese multiplied and became part of the Smith family. One day, they flew too high and instead of landing in the clinic parking lot, they landed on the highway in front of the clinic, causing a semi-truck to veer off the road. The driver managed to avoid injuring the geese, and the truck. "I saw the truck veer," Jody says. "The geese were startled. They managed to walk back up the hill to the farmhouse. They never went off the hill again. One year one of the females built a nest right by our kitchen door. They are very protective of their nests. They will reach out and pinch you if you get too close. I wanted Pete to move the nest. Pete wouldn't move it and said that we couldn't disturb her. We couldn't go out the back door, we had to go out the front door and go around. Pete's mom, Betty, was visiting us at the time. I warned Betty about going out the kitchen door. She assured me that she loved geese and they loved her. She got nailed big time. She had a big bruise mark on her leg. I told Pete that we had too many geese; that the gaggle was getting out of hand. I asked him if we could have one of the young ones for Christmas, a Christmas Goose. He took a young goose down the hill to butcher it. It wasn't very long before the goose comes walking back up the hill, with Pete walking alongside. He said he just couldn't do it. I figured he couldn't do it."

Jody reminisces about the Milliron Farm collection of pets. "A young vet was working for Pete, Dr. Nick Neutzling, Rosemary was

123

his wife. He was from Meigs County. When Pete was off to vet meetings, Dr. Neutzling filled in. Our neighbor, Joanne Hanson, had beautiful Muscovy ducks. They were colorful, black and white; drakes have an ugly red head, but the dillies are beautiful and petite and feminine. Pete admired Joanne's ducks, so I got a pair for Pete. Eventually, we have eighty ducks causing a mess. They would get into everything. They were very aggressive. I told Pete that that was enough and that all the drakes had to go, a few dillies were ok. That worked. Pete agreed, then went off to a vet meeting. I could catch a bunch with the herding dogs and put them in a crate and take them to the Athens Livestock Sale and sell them. Dr. Neutzling shot the drakes that retreated to the pond. We retrieved them with my canoe. They were headed for the freezer. When Pete got back, they were gone.

"Our friend Gil Whalen was moving and couldn't take her pet turkey with her, so we ended up with him. The tom turkey was strutting around the barnyard and being difficult. Pete had to go off to a vet meeting. He told Pat that he was the man of house and that he had to keep track of things. Pat strutted around giving me and Jessica orders. He was about five years old and he took it very seriously. We started up toward the barn and the turkey came running at us. I had a rake to ward off the turkey. Pat promptly got behind me and said he was 'man of the house, but he wasn't man of the barn.'

"Gil was a really good client. She used to come and ride Pete's Morgan mare Cricket. She was visiting one time and our Muscovy ducks were breeding in the pond. Jill came running, 'Pete! Pete! Stop them! They are trying to kill each other!' Pete raised a brow and said, 'No, actually that's the way ducks breed.'"

Family Horses

Pete would eagerly tell you that moments spent with a horse were well spent. Always equestrians, for Pete and Jody, spare time was riding time. "I would take the kids riding," she remembers. "I would put Jessica behind, hanging onto the Western saddle, and Pat in front of me, never thinking the horse might fall. I would never do that with my grandkids. I took the grandkids out riding, but I always had another adult with me."

Pete and Jody went riding often by themselves. A ride through McDougal Creek was a favorite. On one ride, Pete stopped and asked Jody to hold his horse while he went skinny dipping. After a leisurely swim, a leach stuck to his foot. Pete took off his sock and showed Jody, who was still mounted, the blood on his foot. Rolling her eyes, she shook her head and reminded Pete that that was the same spot where Jimmy Bonnett rode in and lost his glasses.

Other times, Pete and Jody would set out for a moonlight ride across their ridges and valleys. "We used to ride a lot during a full moon," Jody says. "We would ride to our cabin and back, just Pete and I. In the summertime, we rode in the mornings before daybreak when it was cool, before the clinic opened. Sometimes we would ride back through the stream to cool the horses off, and then turn them out to pasture. In the wintertime, Pete would ride upstream, breaking weak ice."

Usually, Pete wore his chaps while riding to avoid a rogue branch or multi-flora rose bramble. The woods could be a hazardous place if not prepared. He had a saddle scabbard for a 30.30 rifle that he sometimes carried.

"People always thought that Pete ran or raced, he rarely even galloped," Jody says. "He just trotted straight out and never stopped. If you've ever been on trail rides, there are some people that have to stop and adjust their saddle. They spend a lot of time adjusting this that and the other. But, he would just start straight out at a trot and he wouldn't have to stop!"

Horses are a Smith family icon. For years, Jody tended Tinker Toy, Jessica's Shetland Pony who traveled from Colorado to Ohio. Jessica outgrew Tinker Toy and she gave him to Pat, who would ride him alongside Pete through the Milliron Farm trails. "Tinker Toy was rotten with adults, but good with children," Jody recalls. "Pat came crying into our bedroom one summer night. He could hear the horses galloping in the pasture by the farmhouse. He had asked the day before why Tinker Toy's mane had a 'hole' in the tangled mane. I told him it was the *witches handhold*. Pat didn't want the witches riding his pony! I explained that I untangled Tinker's mane and no witch would be riding. Pat finally went back to bed, comforted in knowing that Tinker Toy was okay."

Starboy traveled with the Smith's from Colorado to Ohio. He was given to Jody as a gift while in college at Colorado A&M by the parents of one of her sorority sisters. One fateful night in 1970, Cricket and Starboy managed to get into the grain room by opening the unlatched lever of the tack room. They feasted on soybean meal and corn all night long. The next morning, both horses were at the clinic. They had foundered on grain and were in danger. Pete managed to save Cricket and her unborn foal, Apple, but Starboy, being the dominant horse, had eaten more of the grain. Pete treated him, operated on his feet, had him in a sling, and gave Starboy the best attention. Pete called a prominent Thoroughbred veterinarian in Kentucky, Dr. Copeland, who he sometimes consulted and knew from previous equine seminars and vet meetings. As Pete was telling Dr. Copeland what he had been doing to save Starboy, Dr. Copeland was amazed at all the effort and treatment that Pete had invested into Starboy's recovery. "How much is this horse worth?" Dr. Copeland asked. "Oh, about $100.00 on the open market, but it's my wife's first horse," Pete replied. "Oh, I see," replied Dr. Copeland. "Let's see if there's anything else we can do."

After much deliberation, they decided that nothing more could be done. Starboy was euthanized and is buried in the recovery stall at the clinic. Eddy Keirns, a loyal employee, dug the six-foot-deep grave by hand. Jody ordered an aluminum placard reading, *Starboy, July 1956 – March 1970*. But Pete didn't want the placard in the recovery stall. He said he didn't want to answer questions from clients who might see it. Jody understood his reluctance to discuss it further. The placard hangs in the family barn.

When friend, client, and horse trainer Sherry Indestadt heard about Starboy, she brought gelding Mighty Preak to Jody. Mighty Preak had been the 1956 Ohio County Fair Trotting Champion, now retired. Jody later received a trophy for Sportsmanship for riding Mighty Preak in a fifty-mile endurance race. Mighty Preak was eighteen years old at the time.

"Pete wasn't much of a beer drinker," Jody says. "It was a really, really hot day and he rode our big Standardbred Mighty Preak out to work in the woods. I told Pete that Mighty Preak couldn't be trusted to ground tie, and that you had to hang on to him. Pete was checking trees. Mighty Preak trotted off and left him. Mighty Preak came back to the barn. Pete came up the hill to the farmhouse, cussing all the way. He sat in the hammock and drank six beers. Of course, he was overheated, and he got really sick.

"Cricket was Pete's black Morgan mare with a white snip," Jody continues. "In 1964 I mortgaged my jeep to buy the mare for Pete. Cricket was sired by Captain McCutcheon, a good lineage. A memorable endurance race was Pete's ride on Cricket in the relay race with me, Fritz Bookman, and Jerry Hartley. We entered the fifty-mile race for experience and fun. I was riding Mighty Preak. Jerry's horse was a new three-year-old mare. It was the first time he had ridden her. Pete and Jerry took the mare into a nearby plowed field, sedated her, and put shoes on her before the race. Fritz was riding Bad Boy. We waited and waited for Fritz to finish his leg of the race. It was a good thing that the local guys were ahead. For one thing, they had miss-marked the trails to throw people off. Incidentally some other guys, not from the area, had a sudden accident and were dragged off their horses. Now, I tell you that if anyone had dragged Pete, Jerry, or Fritz off their horse, they'd have had a hell of a fight. We were safe because we were so far behind. They were pleasant to us because we were losing. Needless to say, we didn't come in first place, but we had a good day."

Johnny Appleseed, also known as Apple, was the first foal of Cricket and Alrod. His lineage was Standardbred, Saddlebred, and Morgan. Apple became one of Pete's favorite mounts. He had a wonderful ground covering trot and a fast walk. Pete loved Apple and penned a poem in his memory:

Requiem – My Horse
by Pete Smith

How I loved you, Apple!
(and love the memory of you still)
Rush of hare-brained gallop,
Earnest walk, flashing trot

Honest smell of sweat and manure
Of Levi's and leather
Esthetic experience of flow
Of form and function
Raw joy of oneness with nature
Your crafty innocence
Solo time with my therapist
Illusion at its best
Thank you, Apple, for the chance
To glimpse the power
And the glory
And the majesty
Of God himself!

Cricket's second foal was Maverick. He was half Arabian. His sire was Irene Vanscoy's beautiful Arabian stallion Silver Sheik. Maverick was ornery, bucking Jessica off and being a handful. Pete castrated him early and sold him to John Branner, who later rode Maverick while tending the Smith sheep.

Persimmon is on the Milliron Clinic mural. A steady grey-jenny, Persimmon was a fun companion for Jessica and Pat. Jessica suggested Pat drop out of the nearby apple tree while she held Persimmon still. Pat came out of the tree, found his seat on Persimmon's back, only to be bucked back up into the tree.

Silver Dollar was a Shetland pony who is in the mural as you walk into Milliron Clinic. "We purchased Silver Dollar from Sherry Indestadt," Jody says, "and Jessica drove him in a race at the Meigs County Fair. Silver Dollar was eventually sold to Laird Gassin after Jessica outgrew him."

Standardbreds are Jody's favorite horse breed. "One of Pete's clients told me about a Standardbred mare for sale," Jody recalls. "Her name was Jody Custer, but I called her Dee Dee. She was a pretty bay, right off the track. The reason they wanted to sell her was because you couldn't tie her up. She would flip over if you tied her. They didn't tell me. I had the pickup truck with the stock racks. She loaded fine, but when I started to drive, she reared up and put her feet on the top of the cab. I slammed on the brakes and she fell back in the truck. After three times of that, she just stood there. I had wrapped her legs before I loaded her, so I hoped she would be all right, but I was worried that she might have been hurt. When we got back to the clinic, Pete checked her and said she was fine. To stop her from rearing and flipping over, Pete put her in a stall at the clinic and tied her to a rubber inner tube. She fought being tied for three days. She'd throw herself back and flip from side to side. Each day I would ask Pete if I could untie her and lead her around. He said, 'No! Just leave her there.' She had water and a hay net. After three days you could have tied her with a string."

Dee Dee also had a cystic ovary and would back up on the trail and kick at other horses. Pete had to spay her. Eventually Jody sold her because she had her at an endurance race and all the other horses were out trotting her. Quarter horses were trotting by her. Jody expounds, "We wrote on her papers that she was spayed and sold her. A year later, this guy comes into the clinic wondering why his mare can't get pregnant. Pete told the guy that the mare had been spayed. It was Dee Dee. Pete had a good chuckle. The Standardbred trainer who bought Dee Dee from us pulled a prank on his 'friend.' He had gotten a reissue of the papers, saying he'd damaged the original. He'd spilled coffee on them and covered up where Pete had noted the mare was spayed. He then sold her at a 'bargain' price to get back at the man who had one-upped him on a previous horse trading deal."

Sailor was a beautiful Quarter Horse gelding, but spoiled and a biter; he purposely reared and threw himself over backwards. One day, Pete stepped off Sailor and caught his foot in the stirrup as Sailor reared and nearly killed Pete, but Pete escaped without injury. Sailor could be a nightmare in the pasture, attacking the other geldings when Cricket came in heat. He drove Junie across the cattle guard once; fortunately, Junie jumped it without injury. "I once rode Sailor to Strouds Run, around the trails and back," Jody says. "It was the worst ride of my life. I had to watch him all the time. The only reason I rode him was that Jan Worthington was already on her way with her horse when I discovered the horse I planned to ride, Mighty Preak, was a little off. I couldn't reach Jan to cancel the ride. She was driving down from Tipp City to condition her endurance horse on our hilly trails. Pete and I had met Jan at a relay race. She went on to become one of the foremost endurance riders, riding in Dubai and other exciting places. She still has a farm with many endurance prospects. Her son Guy is a prominent farrier."

Finally, Jody convinced Pete to sell Sailor. They had made a bad mistake and sold Cricket instead – definitely sold the wrong horse. Ralph Guthrie was interested in buying Sailor. Jody told Ralph how dangerous Sailor was and to take him straight to the kill pen. She talked to Ralph a month later when he came to swab their oil well. He still had Sailor and was trying different bits to see if Sailor would cooperate. The next time Jody saw Ralph and asked about Sailor, Ralph said, "He's in an Alpo can. That son of a bitch nearly killed me."

One of Jody's most beloved horses was Junco. A beautiful New Forest Pony, Junco was the delight of the Smith family. "We got Junco, or Junie, many years ago from Jerry Hartley, a friend and client," Jody says. "Jerry had bought Junie, a stallion, from a small stable in Rockbridge, Ohio, who had purchased several New Forest Ponies from England. They had the ponies shipped to Rockbridge, and began a small herd. They were the only herd of New Forest Ponies in the United States at the time. They are an iconic mountain and moorland pony from the British Isles, well-known for their connection to kings and queens. Junco was a beautiful steel grey, flowing mane and tail, really sweet."

Jerry remembers loading Junie at the Rockbridge stables and getting a surprise from the owner. "That price we gave you? We've changed it," she said.

"Awe, I wish you had told me that before I loaded the horse!" Jerry told her.

"I want $50 less than what I told you because we are going to give you all the papers and you are going to have to do all the transferring of the papers," the owner said.

Jerry had the stallion for several months when a woman from Canada called and said she wanted to buy Junco. "I sent her pictures," Jerry recalls, "and agreed to sell him to her. The Canadian woman came to see Junco and she really liked him. Junco was stunningly beautiful. The woman told me that Junco's mane was not what she liked, his tail was not perfect, and his hooves were not right. Well, the woman was trying to convince me that Junco was not worth the price I was asking. I was upset; Junco was perfect the way he was and for the woman to degrade the stallion in that manner was unacceptable! The woman went up to my house to get a cup of coffee. I picked up the phone and called Pete: 'Pete, what are you doing tomorrow? Set me up an appointment to castrate Junco!' The woman overheard my conversation to Pete. 'No! I want to buy Junco the way he is!' she exclaimed. 'Ma'am, I have never sold a horse that bad to anybody in my life, and I am not going to sell it tonight!' I said in a loud voice to her. The next day I took the beautiful stallion to Pete for castration. I gave Junco to Jody that day."

Jody continues, "Junco was one of the best horses I ever had. Tom Wagner helped me to break him to pull a cart. Pat would put motorcycle tires on my cart and I would drive him through the woods, over logs; he would stand there while I would lift the cart over the log, and then he would go on. I had so much fun with him. Junco placed third in the Senior Division of the Ohio State Trail horse championship when he was 28 years old. He lived to be 35 years old."

Jody remembers a more temperamental horse, Tall Speed, a hearty Standardbred who kicked Apple in the leg while out in pasture. Apple had to be euthanized. Tall Speed was an aggressive horse, even once chasing Pete's dad, a horseman, over the pasture fence. "Pete wanted to get rid of Tall Speed," Jody says. "We sold him to the Amish. I have always regretted selling Tall Speed.

"Pete was a midnight cowboy. He would ride with his pistol in his pommel bag and wear night vision goggles," Jody says. Riding Raybar, his favorite trotting Quarter Horse gelding, Pete rode at night, in the moonlight through Milliron Farm. Pete first met Raybar when he was brought to the clinic with a terrible colic. He was very thin and nearly dead. The client did not want to pay for Raybar's colic surgery. Pete asked to buy Raybar for $1.00. The clients agreed, and Pete performed the surgery, a difficult surgery and a long recovery, but Raybar never coliced again. After Pete saved Raybar, he rode him many miles. Raybar had a smooth gate and good breeding. His Grandparents were both Thoroughbreds.

Pete and Frank Lamp, a friend, client, and fellow hunter from a town near Marietta, Ohio, took Bud and Raybar to Colorado for an elk hunting adventure. Pete passed on shooting an elk the first day, hoping to get a bigger one. He didn't get another chance at an elk, but did get a mule deer, the antlers of which are mounted on the wall of the clinic's large animal prep room. The high altitude and arid climate was uncomfortable for the horses. During the excursion, Bud passed out and spent the rest of the trip at the camp. Raybar managed to get stuck on a ledge with Pete astride. Raybar was able to leap to safety after Pete dismounted and unsaddled him. It was a memorable event for horse and rider.

"We liked to trailer our horses and go riding. On a summer morning, we trailered Raybar and Barney to the Hocking Hills to trail ride with Gussie Anderson. Raybar could be a rough ride if you don't post, Raybar could be hell on wheels. Gussie and Pete had ridden together through some of the meanest territory in Hocking County."

"It didn't matter to Pete if the trail was too far or too rough," Gussie picks up. "I was riding my spotted mare Fancy that day and she could walk like a trotting horse. She had a little running walk that was super. We rode and rode, stopped and rested and rode some more. I think we went all the way to Airplane Rock and back around. Coming home, Pete rode up beside me and he kept looking down. I said, 'Is there something wrong with her?' He said, 'No, that mare sure can walk.'

"Pete kept looking at Fancy's gait," Gussie explains, "and I thought something was wrong with her. Pete said, 'I never saw a horse walk like that.'"

Jody continues, "Later, when his hip gave out, he got a gaited horse, Unique, a lovely blue roan gaited gelding, a Peruvian Paso stallion, Tennessee Walking mare cross. He bought Unique because his hip was bothering him so much. Pete rode Unique to Middle Mountain, West Virginia, for long weekend trail rides with his dog Smokey, friends Jim Hoon, Eric and Rhonda Curfman. After a successful titanium hip replacement, he went back to riding Raybar. Unique, a slower ride than Raybar was Pete's backup and guest horse. At 28 years old, Raybar was still going strong."

Alrod was a registered non-standard Stallion. He had Saddle-bred as well as Standardbred in his breeding, but he was able to trot to a specific standard. Alrod was extremely well-mannered. He was trained by Sherry Indestadt. Alrod was a gift to Jody from Sherry and Newt and Wade Humphrey.

Barney - Barnabus Bay Buddy - is the bay horse in the family picture. Jody says, "If I didn't watch Barney, he'd hit the water every time. I had to hold him up. Pete and friend Dana McAtee thought that was hilarious when I wasn't quick enough and had to get off and pour the creek water out of my boots. Barney was a Hocking College reject. He would attack the students coming into the stalls. He was standing in the back of a trailer stopped at the clinic when Steve Shingler was taking him to the killers as he had been chasing students out of his stall with teeth bared and ears pinned back. I talked Pete into trading Steve's vet work for the horse. Barney and I came to a quiet understanding with the help of a tap from my handy plastic baseball bat, and he was a loyal trail mount for many years. He knew when I saw deer, I loved to watch them, and so, being a bit lazy, he became an excellent deer spotter. I learned to look in the direction of his nose and ears when he stopped to point out deer. He had a lovely single foot but also could do my favorite gait, a ground covering trot."

Traveler, a gray Arabian, was given to Pete by Bud Strouss, D.V.M. Traveler was four-years-old and had never been weaned. He was difficult to ride without following another horse. He bucked Jody off and ran back to the barn. She had to walk back to the barn to get a different bit and rode him back up over the ridge to where he had bucked her off. He balked and tried to buck again, but she was able to keep his head up. When she returned and saw Barney standing in the paddock, she went back to riding Barney. Jody returned Traveler to Dr. Strouss and he sold Traveler to a three-hundred-pound lady in Pennsylvania.

Big 'Un killed two of Jody's favorite sheep - Sampson and Delilah; they were Jacob sheep. Jody says, "I can understand how a horse eating grain could do that. Some horses are very aggressive when they eat. I always made sure he was tied up when he was eating grain. That son-of-a-gun went after sheep if they came near hay. He was known to strike at dogs, too. Big 'Un was a horse we had for too long. He was a handsome black gelding Pete bought from Charles Shields, Sr. Pete always liked to have two horses in case one was lame. He took Big 'Un to Middle Mountain one time, and Big 'Un got away. Pete finally caught him. I talked Pete into selling Big 'Un. When we sold him, we made it clear to the buyer that he was aggressive towards dogs and sheep."

Apollo was a four-year-old gray Arabian stallion that Jessica rescued. Pete castrated and gave Apollo to Jody. Apollo and Barney did not get along and would fight in the pasture. They were not great riding buddies and had to be watched on the trail. Pete sold Apollo and used the money to repair the farmhouse bathroom. Dana McAtee bought Apollo for endurance riding, and then Dana sold him to Sonny Place. After several years, Jessica bought Apollo back and leased him out, two or three times. Apollo ended up back at Milliron Farm and made it to thirty years of age.

A well-read scholarly horseman, Pete enjoyed this passage from Albert Borgmann's 1992 *Crossing the Postmodern Divide*. A copy is posted in the large animal prep room.

> You cannot remain unmoved by the gentleness and conformation of a well-bred and well-trained horse - more than a thousand pounds of big-boned, well-muscled animal, slick of coat and sweet of smell, obedient and mannerly, and yet forever a menace with its innocent power and ineradicable inclination to seek refuge in flight, and always a burden with its need to be fed, wormed, and shod, with its liability to cuts and infections, to laming and heaves. But when it greets you with a nicker, nuzzles your chest, and regards you with a large and liquid eye, the question of where you want to be and what you want to do has been answered."

"We would go riding," Russ Smith, an employee, client, and friend remembers. "We would stop and chat, grab an apple from the saddlebags. He would always lead as a rule. He walked and trotted, occasionally cantered, but he rarely stopped. If we had sandwiches, we would stop. I always took the sandwiches."

The Cattle Herd

Jody tells of Pete's love for cattle and life with the herd. "We tried to be self-sufficient in regard to sustainable food. Pete liked a thick steak as well as fresh milk and eggs. Pete *really* liked cattle. He was a cowboy at heart, after all. He liked herding, lassoing, healing, and eating them.

"Our cows typically weighed about eight hundred pounds," Jody says. "Working with them can be challenging, even painful. They have their own special diseases, in addition to the general conditions common to all ruminants. We had our private herd of cattle. Pete sold my part Jersey cow and bought a Holstein from a farmer who bragged about how much milk she gave. Pete had repaired some defect or other and traded off the surgery for the cow. She was gentle to milk for about the time she was used to being on the automatic milker, and then she moved, a lot. I couldn't milk fast enough. I told Pete it was his cow; he could milk her. *Goddamn-son-of-a-bitch.* Another volley of curses could be heard from the barn. Pete had milked a bucketful of milk before the cow stepped in the bucket. He threw the stainless-steel bucket in the pond (I retrieved it) and called another farmer to come get the cow. Pete's dad was visiting in the interim before the farmer picked up the cow. Abbott was a fast milker and got along fine with the cow."

Pete kept Angus cattle on the side of the hill, by the farmhouse. He liked Angus cattle, even though they tore through any fence they couldn't crawl under, roamed local roads, and invaded the neighborhood. Jody had rarely been around cattle until they moved to Milliron Farm. Pete needed somebody to help him inoculate the cattle and pressed her into service instead of having to drive them himself, one by one to the head gate. But cattle have "sloppy tails" - wet with manure – and Jody balked when Pete ordered her to twist a particular cow's tail to get her into the head gate.

"Wait a minute, I'm going to put my gloves on," Jody said.

"Oh, *blankety, blankety, blank,*" Pete annoyingly muttered.

"Twist it yourself!" Jody insisted wearily as she walked up the hill to the house. "It was the only time he had ever cursed at me," Jody says. "He cursed around me, but never at me." She could hear Pete banging around down at the cattle chutes. About a half hour later, he strode up the hill.

"Do you have time to *please* help me?" Pete asked.

"I'll be right there," Jody replied, as she put her gloves back on.

Jody went back down the hill to the cattle chute and twisted the tail of the same cow that was still in the chute when she left.

Jody vividly remembers the time she was out trying to help Pete gather the cows and calves. "I was riding Mighty Preak, our big Standardbred, about 16'3 hands," she says. "I didn't see the calf. The horse didn't see the calf. A big Angus mother cow came flying out of nowhere and hit Mighty Preak in the shoulder. She pinned us up against a tree. It was a good thing that the tree was there and my leg was out of the way, or she would've just rolled us. Mighty Preak was so mad, he bit that cow like you wouldn't believe; he just bit her and bit her. It was not the cow's fault; her calf was lying there in the underbrush. After that incident Mighty Preak would snake his neck out with his ears pinned down and it was funny to see a big gangly Standardbred herding cattle like a Quarter Horse."

Bookman's Hill

On occasion, Pete would ask his friends to help at the farm, usually just a routine roundup of the Black Angus cattle herd from the Phillips place to the clinic for inoculations. The cattle were content living in the deep woods, having access to fresh water and some woodland shelter. Pete had a great big trailer that he placed silage on for the cattle.

Late in his cattle career, Pete asked Jerry Hartley and Fritz Bookman to help him herd the cattle to the clinic's feed lot in view of State Route 550. Jerry was always around to help, and Fritz, a local farrier and horseman, spent a lot of time with the Smith family. A friend to Pat, Fritz would drive by Milliron Farm early on his way to farrier calls, pick Pat up from the school bus stop (unbeknownst to Pete and Jody), and the two would travel all day shoeing horses.

This day, Pete, Jerry, and Fritz saddled up and headed for the Phillips' farm, which, at the time, belonged to Pete. Fritz was riding his stout black gelding, Bad Boy. The cattle were moseying along when they decided to take a run for it! Approaching the edge of a very steep hill, Pete said, "Let 'em go, Fritz!"

"Hell, no!" retorted Fritz. He plunged Bad Boy forward. *Whoop!* Fritz took a tumble down over the hill, horse and all. They landed against the fork of a tree, shaken, but unharmed except for a broken spur. Undaunted, Fritz and Bad Boy continued with the roundup.

"Pete always loved having the cattle," Jody says. "Finally, we got to the point, I would help him with the cattle anytime he went along to help, but I was through dealing with the cattle while he was at the clinic. One time Pat, Jessica, and I were all ready for church and here comes a State Highway Patrol car up the hill to the house. Cattle were out on the road on Route 550. The cattle escaped from there through the woods down Route 550. This time it was the State Highway Patrol stopping at the clinic. Pete was in surgery so Jessica, Pat and I drove the cattle back through a God-awful tunnel through poison ivy. It was just littered with cow manure. I announced that that was the last time I would chase cattle without him. If he couldn't help I would take my 30.30 rifle and we'd be out of cattle. I told Pete, I said, 'I'm done. Anytime with you, but not by myself and the kids.' Those Black Angus cattle would crawl under the fence. Pete moved the cattle to his recently purchased Phillips place on Route 690. They got out there, too. One was hit by a car and disappeared into the cornfield. He and Jerry Hartley searched for it, this time with the 30.30 because the poor thing had a broken leg. It surfaced a few months later, fat and sassy, with only a slight limp. The cattle got sold. He just didn't have the time."

Farm Cats

"Pete always said that if he landed in a city like San Francisco, he would have a cat clinic. But, I didn't believe that because he loved his horses so much," Jody says. Their first cat as a couple was Pulicides Felis (Latin for cat fleas), aka Poo, who was a finicky large tiger cat who liked to eat graham cracker pie crust. Pete loved graham cracker crust and shared his pie with Poo, who would eat through the pie just to nibble on the crust. Poo came from Kraxberger's Dairy, where Pete worked during vet school, while the couple was living in Colorado. A tomcat, Poo finally left one evening and never returned. Trefa was Pete's favorite cat. Trefa was named for the meat inspection course that, as a vet student, Pete was required to take; "tref" means unfit to eat. Trefa was acquired as a kitten in Fort Collins and made the move to Ohio. She is in the Milliron Clinic mural. Like Poo, Trefa came from Kraxberger's Dairy. One evening Pete was taking his usual bath and Trefa, the family housecat walked by. Pete gently picked Trefa up and put her in the bathtub. Distressed, she jumped out, shaking her feet. Jody watched the entire incident in disbelief, she recalls.

"You are going to pay for that," she told him.

"Nah, she wouldn't dare."

"Trefa sashayed out of the bathroom," Jody continues, "and we went to bed. About three in the morning, I heard Pete cussing away! Pete jumped up and then started laughing. The cat that never urinated in the house jumped onto Pete's shoulder and peed. Pete thought it was hilarious. He went to take another shower while I changed the bedding. Trefa ruled the house. I tried to introduce two kittens, but Trefa swiftly disemboweled them. Pete was out on large animal calls at the time. I rushed them to the Athens Veterinary Hospital where Dr. Bratton repaired them. I was able to find the kittens a new home. We have had many memorable cats. Poo2 was a Siamese cat who was brain damaged and sprayed in his owner's house. He was brought to the Athens Veterinary Hospital to be euthanized while Pete was working there. With the owner's permission, we adopted him, and kept him as a barn cat. Poo2 is in the tree in the clinic mural."

Farm Dogs

Like Pete's horses, his life can't be understood without a complete historical account of his dogs. Since his childhood, he revered the comradery of dogs. While in Wyoming, Pete kept his family's Standard poodle, Zaza. He used her to herd cattle.

How many dogs can a vet have in a lifetime? On his journey, Pete had raised many dogs, several of which were embedded in his soul. He was empathic when a client brought a beloved pet into the clinic that was ill and incapacitated. He treated the pet as if it were his own, trying every remedy and procedure to ensure a prolonged quality of life.

"I remember walking back from our barn with a visiting farm couple," Jody recalls. "They were talking about the amazing idea that some people would even allow dogs in the house. When we got down to our house, all four of our dogs poured out from the house into our yard. There was an awkward silence."

Pete and Jody's first dog together was Shep, a smart Australian shepherd they bought from a couple in Colorado who were looking for a good home for the dog. The couple decided they wanted $50 for Shep, a beautiful tri-color, so Pete scraped up the money. While in vet school and living on Birky's ranch, when Pete would spar with vet pals in the locker room, Shep would bark at Pete's opponent. But when Roger King, who was a big guy fellow veterinary student, entered the ring, Shep took a different side and barked at Pete, cracking everyone up. Shep was territorial and protective, but apparently he drew the line when he decided it was Pete's fight.

"When I was eight and a half months pregnant with Jessica," Jody remembers, "I was at Birky's, walking through what I thought was an empty corral. Unbeknownst to me, there was a bull staring at me from the corner of the corral. Just as the bull began to charge, Shep grabbed the bull by the nose, shaking back and forth, until I made it safely over the fence. When I was safe, Shep let go and flew under the fence himself." Shep was a biter of people, too, however. He had bitten the original owner's young daughter. He bit Pete, and then Jody. When Jessica was a toddler, Shep was rehomed to an older ranch couple without children.

Pete next bought a couple of coonhound puppies in Lamar, Colorado. The breeder did not have the bitch or the puppies vaccinated for distemper, and they died. "We argued about what breed of dog to add to the family," Jody says. "Pete wanted a coonhound, I wanted a shepherd. We decided we would each get what we wanted; we got two dogs instead of only one. Pete bought Melody from a breeder outside of Lamar. She was a large coonhound, coming from a line of cougar-hunting hounds. There was a policeman in Lamar who had gone out on a call for a neglected female German shepherd who had died. The male was chained off to the side, but was still alive but emaciated. They shot him. The officer took the two puppies. The other puppy died, but Shane survived. The officer was transferred to Denver and was unable to take the puppy. We paid ten dollars for Shane. It was the best ten dollars we ever spent.

"When Pete's beloved hound, Melody, had a stroke, I had Melody on a rug in our living room," Jody remembers. "Of course, I kept putting pads and things underneath her that I could wash. She wasn't in any pain; she was just unconscious. Pete just couldn't put her down. The night before the third day I said to Pete, 'Do you want me to take her down to Dr. Schultheis in the morning?' He said, 'I'd really appreciate that.' We woke up in the morning and she was dead.

"My Belgian sheepdog, Champion The Magic Dragon V Siegester (Gates of Victory) Companion Dog/Tracking Dog, also known as Puff, was so jealous of Pete," Jody continues. "Puff was a herding and a guarding dog. If you didn't have anybody to tell Puff to stop and start, he would've just started and never stop. He was Schutzhund breeding which is a line of German protection dog. Puff looked like a cross between a German shepherd and a collie. He was the most expensive dog I'd ever bought. Jessica and Pat were getting ready for 4-H. Jessica wanted to go to AKC shows. I thought that if I was taking Jessica, I might as well get an AKC dog so I can show with my own dog while she's doing her thing with her little Pomeranian, Pombrook's Songkeena. We were out in California to an AVMA meeting. I figured I wanted a Belgian sheepdog. I never had one. The fellow out in California had the best Belgian sheepdogs in the country. I told Pete I wanted to look at them and that it would be a safe time to look because we're clear out there and I wouldn't be tempted. It sounded safe. I had to fly from the city where the meeting was, just a little commuter flight, to where Kurt Marti had his kennels. Guess what I did? I bought the dog! I went back to the hotel with a new puppy. I couldn't believe I bought it. You look at a puppy and you fall in love with it. It was the last puppy. There we were in the hotel. Of course, the puppy was crying. I spent the night on the floor with my hand in the crate with the puppy. I am sure we really bonded at that point. He didn't want to share me with anybody or anything. The flight back to Ohio was an OVMA chartered flight. Puff flew in the passenger seat next to me. The stewardess told me to put the dog under my seat, back in the crate, because people would complain. I asked the stewardess, 'Why don't you ask if anyone would complain?' The entire flight of vets and their wives loved Puff. Everyone cheered for Puff.

"When Puff was in our bedroom he was in a crate at first because he, well, for all of his life, he did not want Pete around me," Jody continues. We couldn't go to sleep with this puppy loose in the bedroom. We had him trained, somewhat. It was kind of funny, when we'd be making love, Puff would wait until we were all through, then he'd leap on the bed and get between us and growl at Pete. Pete would say, 'Ok! I'm done! You can have her!' Puff was a tough dog. He went on trail rides with us. Pete thought it was funny to tease him. We were down at the clinic one time and Pete would call him Puffy Wuffy, which infuriated the dog. He would growl at Pete. I told Pete he needed to be careful. I told Pete for heaven's sake, don't flank him, which means don't touch them in the flank, which irritates a lot of dogs. Pete said, 'Oh, you mean like this?' Puff bit clear through his wrist - all the way through. Fortunately, Pete had enough sense because he had been bitten enough times, not to pull. That's when you do the damage, when you pull or if the dog pulls. As soon as I saw what happened, I told Puff to let go of him. There was blood everywhere. Pete said, 'Well, you're right! I shouldn't have flanked him!'

"When Puff was two years old, I took him to the Belgian Sheepdog Specialty in Chicago since Kurt Marti was going to be there. Being new to conformation, I entered the American Class, which is kind of a nothing class. I figured I wouldn't need a professional handler. The night before the show, Kurt came in the room, he and his wife. Puff wouldn't let him in the room. Kurt knew not to push it. Puff growled and went toward him. Kurt knew to stand completely still and stay calm. Puff won Best of Winners. It was great. I called Pete and he said he thought that was the most excited he had ever heard me. You can ask Pat - he would call Puff my #1 son. Puff figured in a lot of things. He was a character.

"Our animals were a major part of our lives. Still are. Smokey the Border collie was the main one. I still have Smokey, but she was definitely Pete's dog. Ruffian was the other Border Collie. She locked Pete out of his car once. Tess was the one who tore up Pete's backseat.

"One time, our then shepherd Henry Kuykendall accidentally sold Pete a blind dog. Unknown to Henry, the dog had PRA (progressive retinal atrophy). As a sheep dog, the dog could run straight out, go behind the sheep and lay down on command, get up, herded sheep, all by sound and smell. As with all our dogs, I brought the dog into the house to live with us. She'd probably never been in a house before so no one had seen her walk into the vee of the door. I told Pete he'd better check her eyes. He did and discovered she was nearly blind and would be completely blind soon. Henry took her back to where he had gotten her and brought us Bess. I was too sad to tease Pete about a veterinarian buying a blind dog. Bess became known as Bessie Bitch the Basement Beast because she would dart from under the basement stairs to try to bite Pete or Pat.

Ruffian, Pete's dog, was named for the famous racehorse. She was the daughter of Smith Border collie's Jim and Bessie the Basement Bitch. Pete bought Jim from Henry Kuykendall. He was a beloved dog, imported from Scotland. Like her parents, Ruffian was a black and white Border Collie. Client Nancy Bonnett called Ruffian the Roller Derby Queen because she would run in circles and shred the backseat of Pete's car. Pete didn't seem to mind.

Athens horseman Alex Couladis remembers riding one day with Pete and Ruffian in Pete's black Cadillac, Doris. "He had to get back to the clinic for horse surgery, but said he was hungry and that we were going into town first to get something to eat," Alex remembers. "We stopped at Kentucky Fried Chicken. Pete gets the food, begins eating, and begins throwing chicken bones to the dog in the backseat. He saw my expression. *Never feed your dog chicken bones* and said, 'They pressure cook their chicken, those bones won't hurt the dog.'"

When the Smith kids were little, Pat and Pete shared Melody, the coonhound, and Jessica and Jody shared Shane, the German shepherd. But, then, as they got a little older, they wanted their own dogs.

"Tibby was an Australian Cattle Dog given to us by a local dairy farmer," remembers Jody. "Tibby was bred to another Australian Cattle Dog of the dairy farmer's choice for pick of the litter. I told him he could have second pick because my son wanted a puppy. Tibby had five pups. We whelped them in a kiddie swimming pool in the living room at the bottom of the farmhouse stairs. Pat came down when the puppies were being born at five a.m., he said 'I want that one' and went back to bed. Pat named him Smith's Blue Kangaroo, aka Kanga. Pat later won the Athens County Fair in his 4-H class, sending him to the Ohio State Fair where he was one of the Outstanding of the Day. He also was one of the first Australian Cattle Dogs to get the American Kennel Club Companion Dog title in the area.

"Tibby was very smart," Jody continues. "We had a table in the kitchen where I had cat food for the cats. The cat food started disappearing. I put a mousetrap on the table with a paper towel over it. Tibby didn't bother it. I thought, well, I could just have a paper towel there. The cat food started disappearing again. I went back to the mousetrap. To try out my mousetrap, I asked Pete to let Tibby in the kitchen. While I was looking in the kitchen window, I saw her lift the paper towel with teeth, peer under with one beady eye, saw trap, and get back down, leaving the cat food alone. She was smart. If we left her tied up with a chain collar she could hold a chain collar open with her hind foot and back out of the collar."

Pat recalls, "One of my favorite lines, and I think Dad may have only said this to my pets, he always said, 'That's something it's going to die with, not from.' Kanga and Cody were both really old.

143

They were cattle dogs. They had lumps and he didn't want to take them off, he was afraid the anesthetic would kill them. Dad said, 'That's something that they're going to have to die with, not from.'"

There was Colonel, a black and white Border collie who Pete bought from one client to give to another client, but Pete ended up keeping him. There was Hawkeye, another beautiful German shepherd bought at the Athens County Dog Pound. Pete castrated him and used him occasionally as a blood donor as he did all their dogs. "AJ, our grandson, about six years old at the time, came up from the clinic to tell me Hawkeye had died," Jody remembers. "I told AJ that, no, Hawkeye did not die, that he just had a sedative. But, in fact, Hawkeye had died. Pete had used a quicker method to draw blood to try to save a client's dying poodle. Both dogs died. Pete was too upset for me to say much, but it was a sad night at our house."

Tess was Pete's Rottweiler and Australian cattle dog mix who used Pete's black Cadillac as a doghouse. She was happy to stay in the car all day. One day, Tess attacked and bit client Gussie Anderson. "I was bringing my horse Fancy to the clinic for a vet check," Gussie explains. "I wanted to talk to Pete about the new Ohio Horse Council t-shirts that I had. I wanted to talk to Jody and tried to get Pete's attention, but he went off and walked around the building. When I held up the t-shirts, one was black and one was white, so Jody could see it, Tess jumped out of Pete's car."

"Gussie is a loyal client," Jody says. "Pete kept his car parked in the covered alleyway between the large prep room and the recovery room at the clinic. Tess would stay in the car waiting for Pete. Pete normally kept the dog under control. She was not a vicious dog, but she was a Rottweiler mix. She used to lunge against the car windows in the parking lot and I thought she would break the windows. Gussie walks past the car and the dog jumps out at her, and knocks her down. She fell back on the concrete and hit her head. Luckily, she had her hair tied back in a bun.

"We took Gussie to the hospital. They X-rayed her and sewed up the dog bite. Of course, she was in the hospital for three days with an infection. Of course, our insurance agent was quaking. Pete was quaking. We thought Gussie was going to own the clinic. But, she never sued us! How's that for a loyal client? Our insurance paid her hospital bills, but she could have sued for damages. Tess acquired cancer of the leg, and Pete operated. If there was an unruly dog at the clinic, Pete would let Tess shoulder the dog over so he could put a leash on it. She never bit another dog at the clinic. Tess lived for another year, but the cancer returned and spread. Pete was unable to put her down, so one of his vet assistants had to do it for him.

"Tammy, the Australian Kelpie, was my dog. Purchased from a herding puppy mill for $300, Tammy wanted to fight with Tess in the house. Tess was twice the size of Tammy; and one day Tammy started the fight. Tess walked by and bumped into Tammy. That's all it took. They usually kept their distance. They were a couple of bitches, we never left them alone together. It went silent. 'Your dog is hurting my dog!' Pete shouted! He picked up Tess's hind legs and finally got them apart. They were going to kill each other. Pete took Tammy down to the clinic to patch her up.

"Boo was a Great Pyrenees female we bought to hang out with the sheep. She had not been born with sheep. She would leave the sheep and meet Jessica at the school bus. She was much more interested in Jessica than the sheep. Then we got Yank from a guy in Amesville. Yank was born in a sheep barn and lived with the sheep. Yank guarded our sheep for over 12 years. He was a beautiful Great Pyrenees who grew to 150 pounds in his prime. We got Salty as an understudy to Yank because we didn't think that Yank would live so long. Salty was a Maremma and Great Pyrenees mix, another guarding dog who stayed with the sheep. Pete and I were going out one night to an event at the university. I told Pete we needed to check on Yank. I asked Salty where Yank was and Salty took us right to Yank's body. Pete got out the bulldozer and buried Yank before we went into the university event."

Jody likes to foster dogs and remembers fondly Zeus, a black and silver German shepherd she adopted from the rescue Forgotten Four Paws. Pete always said, "You can't keep keeping those foster dogs." But when she contacted a search and rescue group to donate Zeus, Pete said, "You can't do that, he's one of the best dogs we've ever had." "And he was," Jody says. "Zeus was found nearly starved and guarded the food container. He tried to bite Pete once, did bite Annette, Dick, but became a loyal and trustworthy companion."

Pete's policy on rehoming foster dogs was always flexible. Once when he spayed a dog named Smokey, the owners didn't want her. Jody called the breeder and told them that the dog needed a home - as her breeders, they were responsible for her. They said that they would take her, but all their kennels were full, and that she would be in and out of a crate. Pete grabbed the phone and said, "Can't do that. She sleeps on my bed. I'm just going to keep her!"

Oxen

Into her teen years, Jessica was known for equestrian skills. Riding and training horses of refined lineage, as well as Brown Swiss oxen. Large and in charge, Butch and Bam were Jessica's project oxen, trained to the saddle and yoke. They roamed Milliron Farm for many years – sometimes causing terror in the clinic parking lot, other times out of control in the local parade. Butch and Bam hold dear memories for both the Smith family and Milliron Clinic clients.

Clinic employee Jerry Sullivan remembers camping in the field beside the clinic one night because his dog was being treated and he wanted to be there early to see if his dog was alive or dead. "I woke up in the morning and I sensed something there," he says. "I looked up and the oxen were in my face. They were huge! I reached in my pocket and pulled out my pipe tobacco and picked a pinch and gave each one of them a chew. It broke the ice and they were okay. The oxen were quite the critters. That was Jessica's project. She was a wild child. She was such a little sweetheart growing up."

"One time one of Jessica's oxen ate a Christmas tree off a client's car," Jody laughs. "Another time, in the summertime, an older lady was asleep in her car with the windows down. One of the oxen reached through the window and licked this lady on the cheek. She just about had a heart attack. Fortunately, when she screamed, he didn't have his horns in the car."

Craig Higgins, one of Pete's employees, spent an entire day cleaning out the barn. While in the clinic, taking a break, one of the oxen went into the barn and just splattered manure from one end to the other. Craig stomped out of the barn. He was furious.

"My husband Mike was Pete's UPS delivery man, as well as client and friend," Ann Cunningham says. "I always knew that Mike was at Milliron Clinic about 10:00 a.m., so that if I ever needed to call, I knew he'd be here. This particular day, Mike and Pete were standing outside talking in the clinic parking lot. I stopped and I looked over and I could see the big brown ox thirty feet away looking at me. Pete and Mike were talking and Pete looks at me and said, 'He likes red.' Well, I had a red blouse on. I looked at my blouse and felt weak in the knees. Of course, we all cracked up and we started talking about the animal and where it came from. Pete was rotten that way."

On occasion, Pete would invite groups for lectures and symposiums to the clinic. April 15, 1986, Pete and Jody invited the Appalachian Draft Horse Association to the clinic. They hosted a potluck and Pete gave a lecture on reproduction. At the end of the lecture he and Jessica demonstrated how the oxen could pull and maneuver logs.

"We were down at the clinic the night Pete had to put one of the oxen down," remembers client Charlie Watson. "Pete said the ox had fallen and that he had been working on him all day and couldn't save him."

"Butch and Bam were quite the team," Jessica says, "Bam lived 16 years and died on November 11, 1992, when a caregiver took him off pasture for a day and offered him hay instead. He perished from bloat. Butch galloped exuberantly into the barn onto a concrete floor. His 3,000-pound body splayed out on the floor. He never recovered."

Hawks and Buzzards

Living near a highway is certainly good for business. Situated in a rural country setting, the highway means easy access for clients, as well as the beauty of the surrounding woodland; the area is enveloped with tributaries, creek beds, towering trees, and many forest creatures. If any of the creatures became maimed, bruised, or worse, due to the highway, they usually ended up at Milliron Clinic.

A Red Tail Hawk had been hit on the highway in front of the clinic. Jody remembers, "It had a broken wing. Pete set the hawk's wing and strapped it to its side. I trapped mice with a mousetrap for the bird to eat. Pete kept a close watch on the hawk. Finally, one day, Pete took the strap off. He placed the hawk onto the clinic roof. It hopped around, but it wouldn't fly away. Pete didn't want to leave the hawk on the roof overnight, so he brought it back into the clinic and placed it in a cage overnight. A week or so later, Pete took the bird back to the roof. The hawk lifted its wings and flew away, and then circled around and swooped right over Pete's head and screamed as if to say *thank you* for fixing my wing. Many times we would see red tail hawks flying over the clinic, but we never knew if it was the same one.

Pete liked buzzards, crows, hawks. He liked them all. They fascinated him. There is a hollow tree on Milliron Farm. Pete had noticed a buzzard flying down into the tree. He was curious, so he took his chainsaw and cut a big square hole into the tree. He looked in and there were baby buzzards in the bottom, near the roots. He covered the hole and returned to check the hatchlings. They fledged. The tree is still there with a square cut out of it.

"One time we had a quick freeze; it was cold, then rain, and then really cold," Jody says. "The temperature dropped fast. There were several buzzards up in the hay meadow and their wings had frozen so that they couldn't fly. Pete brought them to the clinic. As soon as they thawed, they upchucked. It was a horrible, rancid smell. The ladies who worked at the clinic said that was enough of that, so they put the buzzards into the barn until they recovered. When the weather became warmer, they opened the barn doors and the buzzards flew away."

GALLERY

Pete's Parents: Abbott Pliny Smith II
and Elizabeth Saunders Smith

1938. Betty and Pete

Pete's Paternal Grandmother
Ruth "Smitty" Smith O'Brion

Pete as a young boy in Maine

1949. Learning to ride at an early age, Pete, age 11,
enjoying the joys of horsemanship

1958. Burr and Lou Betts - Betts Circle Two Arabian Ranch, Parker, Colorado. Pete riding Witezar, son of historic Polish Arabian stallion Witez II, rescued by World War II General George Patton

1959. The Milliron Brand

1959. Big Thompson Canyon, Colorado. Pete, Joyann Haley (Jody), Virginia Haley (Jody's mother). Traffic stopped due to rockslide

1963. Betty, Janet, Abbott, Susie, Jim, Jody, and Pete.
Jones Beach, New York

Veterinarian Joins Staff

A 1962 graduate of Colorado State University, Dr. Abbott P. Smith, has joined the staff of the Athens Veterinary Hospital, Pomeroy Rd.

The hospital has two other veterinarians, Dr. Marvin Phillips and Dr. James Bratton.

Doctor Smith has been in private practice in Lamar, Colo., and while in school worked for four years with the Colorado State Racing Commission.

Doctor Smith, who completed the six-year course at Colorado State, was born in Augusta, Me.

Married and the father of two children, Dr. Smith, 25, lives on Elliottville Rd., near Athens.

DR. ABBOTT SMITH

The Abbott Pliny Smith's - Pete, Pat, and Abbott.
Last Resort, Millbrook, New York

1968 Milliron Clinic - Pete overseeing construction

Milliron Clinic1969. Family photo of Abbott "Pete" Smith III (Cricket), Jody Smith (Starboy), Pete's mother Betty (Pepsi), Pete's father Abbott Smith II (Gigolo), Abbott "Pat" Smith IV (on Tinker Toy), and Jessica riding Silver Dollar, with Shane (German shepherd) looking on

Milliron Farm
Jessica, Silver Dollar; Jody, Starboy; Pete, Cricket; Pat, Tinker Toy
Shane and Melody

1970. Jody, Rex (foal), Calico (mare),
Jessica, Pat, Shane (dog), and Pete at a friend's farm

Pete riding Cricket,
Pat riding Tinker Toy

Jody Smith, Pete Smith, Jerry Hartley, Fritz Bookman.
50 Mile Relay Race

1981. Pete at work. Photos by Chip Gamertsfelder

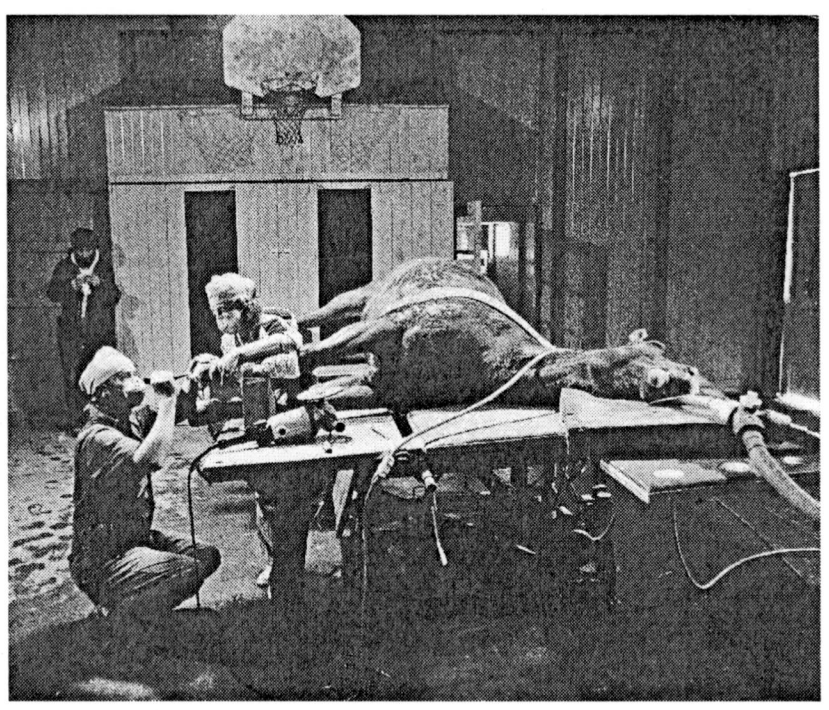

Milliron Clinic.
Equine surgery. Eric Eisenberg, Pete, and Jelea Bookman

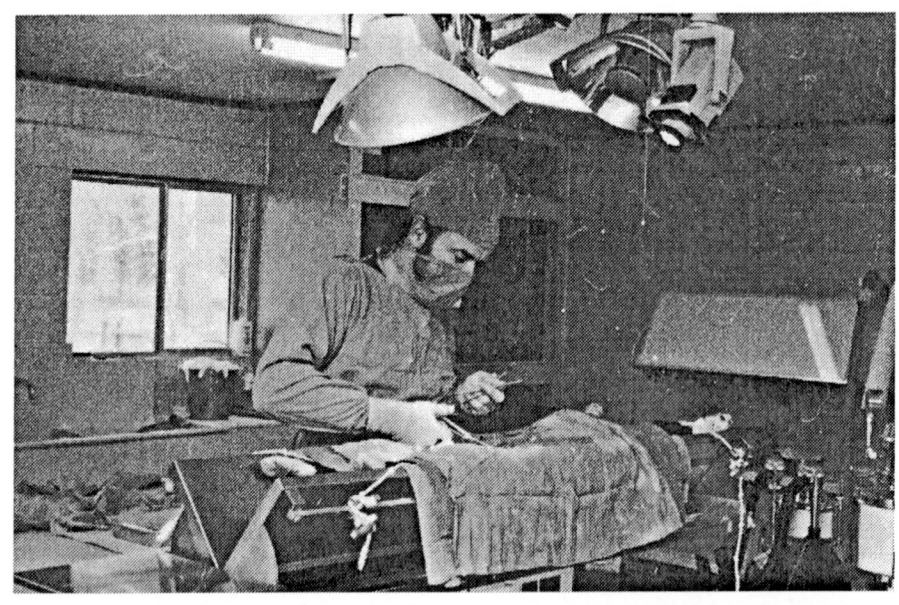

Milliron Clinic 1981. Pete during surgery.
Photo by Chip Gamertsfelder

1981. Pete walking to the farmhouse.
Photo by Chip Gamertsfelder

1981. Pete working at the farmhouse. Photo by Chip Gamertsfelder

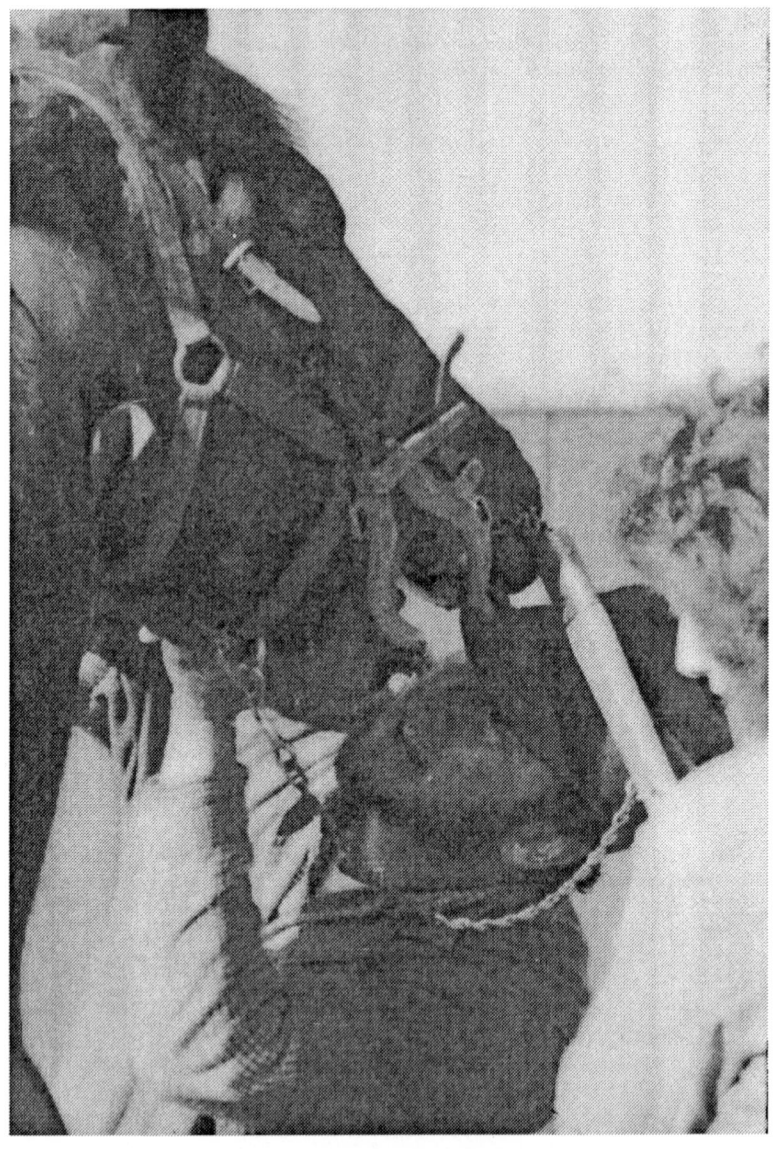

1981. Pete at work. Photo by Chip Gamertsfelder

Pete and a client's dog. Milliron Clinic parking lot

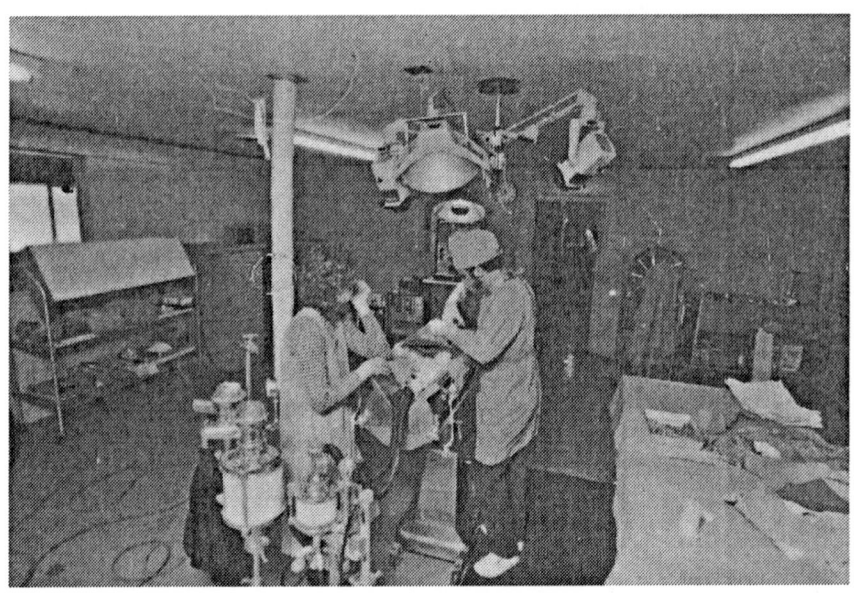

1981. Milliron Clinic surgery room. In background, veterinarian technician, Jelea Bookman; foreground Nanette Rorick and Pete. Photo by Chip Gamertsfelder

1981. Pete and his Cadillac, Doris. The hood ornament was handcrafted by a client as a barter for services. It is part of a larger art piece, made of iron and welded to the car hood; a shepherd with his Border collie. Photo by Chip Gamertsfelder

1981. A veterinarian's pastime. *Top photo:* Pete at the farmhouse, looking through a catalog. Trefa, the cat, is on the kitchen counter (top left). *Bottom photo:* Playing chess with Will Tevis and Carl Lorubbio. Photos by Chip Gamertsfelder

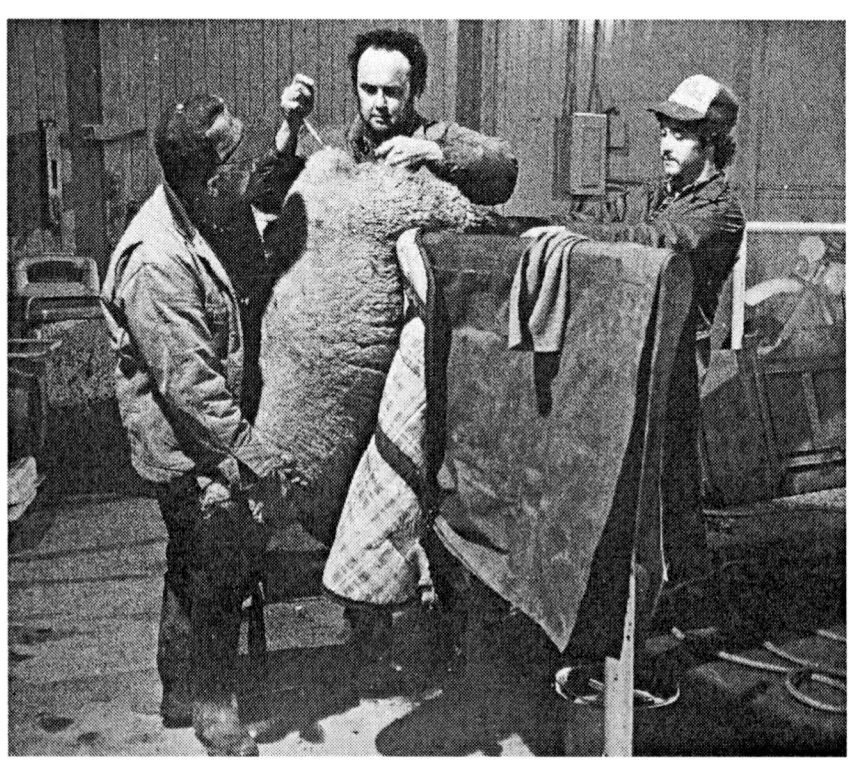

Milliron Clinic. To the left is the washing machine Pete used to agitate the ingredients for sheep dewormer. He made it in large batches due to the ongoing parasite problems. A client and Pat looks on as Pete sews a ewe's prolapsed uterus

Pete and Jody

Panama. Photo courtesy Eric and Rhonda Curfman

Pete and Raybar; Jody and Bud. Riding the trails

October 2006. From left to right... AJ and Barney; Jody and Bud; Rich and Joker; Noah and Winnie; Jessica and Misty; Grant and Apollo; Pete and Raybar; Pat and Luke; Karen and Robie; Smokey. Photo by Downard Photography

October 2006. Pete and Raybar, Jody and Bud, Jessica, Smokey, and Pat. Photo by Downard Photography

2004 Milliron Clinic. Top and bottom photos by Christina Baird

At Milliron Clinic, Dr. Smith laughing at one of his own jokes

2009. Pete, Unique, Smokey, Jody, and Apollo, Middle Mountain, West Virginia. Photo by Eric and Rhonda Curfman

> If you haven't worked a 14-hour day,
> your work probably isn't done.
> *Pete Smith*

---

8 THE PRESERVATION OF BUZZARDS

THE DAY WAS sunny and bright; clouds meandered in a blue sky. Birds sang in the sycamore trees that line the right side of the clinic's driveway. It was a day that Pete would always regret. Always. The semi-trailer was a stock trailer, one that has holes in the trailer walls so that live animals can breathe. It pulled directly into the clinic field under the sycamores.

Pete, Jody, and other spectators watched as 1,200 western Rambouillet cross-breed sheep peered through the holes of the semi-truck. Frightened, the sheep milled in a tight circle. *Baaa... Baaa...* The smell and sound of sheep permeated the bailiwick. This venture promised to be the mother of all financial gains; grand expectations are much greater than unforeseen realizations.

The story is best told by those who lived it.

Poetic Profanity

The first shepherd to the Smith flock was Henry Kuykendall, followed by several lackadaisical shepherds, then finally, John Branner, a local who lived with the sheep for several years, worked for Pete and they became friends, keeping secrets while out on the range; telling life stories, experiences, and future goals. John, a soft-spoken man, remembers, "The concept was good, I think. There was a lot of idle pasture, and, of course, it would be too expensive to

184

fence it in. I think that Pete and his partner in this venture had some encouragement from the Ohio State Extension agents to try a free-range approach. It was kind of unusual around here. It was a time when everybody was pulling out of farming and the fields were still pasture. At that point, everybody had a couple hundred acres. That was the average size farm around here. It was supposed to be a good deal because sheep are good for pasture. They fertilize it and keep it down and move from farm to farm. I think that was the concept.

"The day Pete opened the gate and 1,200 ewes walked out of the truck, Jody was there on her horse," John continues. "It was early February or March and Pete came over. I was renting a house on Route 690. I remember we were sitting by the fire, just like it was yesterday. I had been working for Pete cutting firewood and taking it to Columbus, but that started to play out. People weren't buying firewood. We were just sitting around the fire contemplating our next move. I wasn't married, just out of college. It was the late 70's. There weren't very many jobs, no matter what you had going on. Pete said, 'I'd like you to watch the sheep for a bit.' I said I'd try it. I guess Henry Kuykendall, the first shepherd, had given notice. I remember this as plain as day. The sheep were corralled up there, up where Jan Crall and Dave Barger lived. Twelve hundred ewes, that was a lot. I think there was an extension agent there. And, of course, I had to laugh. I worked on farms here and there, but, I never minded sheep. We were asking the extension agent questions. He said, 'You need to get them out on pasture.' There's always pasture out there, but with Johnson grass…the sheep didn't like that. You just had to walk where you wanted the sheep to go and the dog would follow. So, I did. I took them down pasture at the Nadroski place. Down Route 690 past 550, of course the traffic wasn't as busy as it is now. We had 1,200 ewes; I was walking down the middle of the road. The dog was going back and forth. Then Jody told me how to command the dog: *come-by*, *way-to-me* and all that.

"Henry Kuykendall took his dog Chuck with him when he left," John remembers. "Henry was only there a couple of months maybe. Chuck was the dog he used in trials. I remember Henry had left and Pete had hired another shepherd. I had been contemplating returning to college, but wasn't ready, so I took a job working for Pete. I was repairing the farmhouse roof when the sheepherder and his buddy rode their motorcycles down the road. I wondered who was watching the sheep. Somebody was supposed to be with the sheep 24-7, unless you put them in a fenced area, which Pete didn't have. It works fine out west because those shepherds have nowhere to go. They're out there in the middle of nowhere. You take them supplies; drop them by truck or helicopter, once a week or a month, and it's not a problem.

"When you're a shepherd, you're with them all the time, staying in the camper. I really enjoyed it. It was the right job for the right time. When we saw the missing sheepherder going down the road, sure enough, Pete shows up an hour later! He asked me again to watch the sheep. This time the sheep were up by Joy Creek at Marshall Lowe's place. They had 3,000 acres up there, adjoining farms. By that time, they had lambed already. I went up there. Where they lambed, the pasture was wearing out and the ewes needed to be moved. They were scattered all over the place, so we gathered in as much as we could. We ended up in Morgan County.

"Everything was a routine," John continues. "It got so that I knew where they were going. Some days I'd fall asleep in the saddle. Topography wise," John said, "the sheep had to move, it was their daily routine. These sheep wanted to go up this ridge, and this one lady's garden was there. It was a strip mine. It was a daily occurrence, passing this one lady's garden. But Pete had an idea. He dynamited the strip mine to make a way for the sheep. It was an abandoned strip mine. There was this little path that the sheep could navigate up, then Pete got a couple of guys who used to work in the strip mines; they were experienced. I remember going out there and they dynamited. It didn't go as planned. Nobody got killed, but it didn't block off like it was supposed to. It was a tough business. You had to put money into an operation that you weren't getting money out of. These were commercial ewes. Pete had professional shearers come in. Then the wool market went down. They were using wool to soak up oil spills. I think it actually cost more to get them sheared than what the wool was worth."

"I learned a lot about Pete," John reflects. "He stuck in there. Every problem that he came across he had a good innovative solution to. Round bales of hay were just becoming popular. You see them all the time now. But, back then, everybody was baling them up and leaving them on the field, just like haystacks. Pete had a logging truck and trailer, we hooked up the trailer so that we could get hay round baled up and we could haul, but it was a fight. We had six or seven 2,000 pound bales, stacked on the logging truck. This was before Pete got it all figured out. He had a spear he used. We got five on the bottom, four on the top. He'd take the end-loader and load hay onto the truck. He had a contract with Southern Ohio Coal Company, over in Meigs County. They had a lot of land over there.

"At some point, we're back to Joy Creek now; I was getting to know Pete better. We packed our lunch because we'd be out working all day. He turned me on to those mustard-packed sardine sandwiches. Protein. They're not bad. We were out stringing barb-wire one day. He had a good sense for building fence. We stretched it with the dozer. He got pretty good at it. It got expensive right in the middle of it. It went from $50 to $80 a roll. The prices just doubled. We'd stretch a whole roll at once. We became good friends. We went and saw movies together. Cowboy movies. We got a kick out of going to the movies; *Blazing Saddles*, spaghetti westerns. Pete had his temper, and he could let out a string of words, but be poetic. *Poetic profanity.* He'd throw it out, and we'd be fine. But, he had a sense of humor. We were dipping sheep or wallowing in the mud, in the blood, and after a long day, the humor."

"That's when the foot rot dip spilled into the stream and killed the fish," Jody says. "We got fined by the wildlife department. Formaldehyde. Whoever was downstream reported it, as they should. I do remember the blue cursing."

"I remember we did the sheep dip at the clinic," John adds.

"One day they did it at the Phillips place," Jody says.

"One time we were at Joy Creek," John recalls. "I was down there with Marshall Lowe. Pete decided we were going to bring all the sheep back to farmhouse pasture, fence in the farm, and kind of have them corralled up. At that time, I was building perimeter fence. There weren't as many sheep by then. Some were killed by dogs and worms; the western ewes had no resistance here."

187

"Towards the end of it, Pete said that if they would have shot every one of those ewes as they came off the truck he would have saved so much money," Jody says. "I still remember after they brought them back and they were down at the Phillips place, he was working and going on calls and all that. He forgot something, I don't remember what it was. He went back, and he was going to put the sheep in in the morning. He said there were rows and rows of eyes. It was raccoons. The raccoons were eating all the corn. So, he had to change his program. I think that was when he was doing it all by himself. Maybe you had gone back to school. What horse were you riding?"

"I rode Maverick the Morgan-Arabian," John remembers, "and then there was another horse, too. It was opposite of Maverick. A little calmer. Maverick had one blue eye. The other horse was a Quarter horse. I don't remember his name. Well-broke horse. I got wages, but Pete stuck with it. It was really an inspiration to me. The cards were stacked. I'm just thinking today, I'm a surveyor, these pastures used to be green and clean, but it's all overgrown. The concept, maybe not 1,200 sheep, maybe the wrong breed, if it could've been tweaked a little bit. The thing about Pete, he biggie-sized everything."

"I will say," Jody says, "that when Pete had the rams, something like twenty to thirty rams, they were out in this field, and the rains came, the rams kept going out to a little bit higher ground, but not high enough. They weren't smart enough to go up on the hillside. They got swept down by the little house where his sheep partner lived at the time. And Pete's partner did try to get out there and try to save some rams, but you can't pick up a sheep that's wool is full of water. They drowned. Not all of them, but many of them. So, Pete's partner bailed. Pete lost a lot of money. At least the ram that Pete had bought that was West Virginia State Champion survived. One time, we were moving the sheep in the strip mine. I had a heat stroke. It was so rough. I had taken some water; Jessica, Pat, and Pete and all ran out of water. They drank some water that the other sheeperder had in a canteen. I wouldn't drink out of it. They all got trench mouth and I didn't. We were chasing sheep all day. We lost so many when they ran out of pasture out there by Lowes and we had to move them. Pete was giving away lambs right and left. Even to the County Home. The ewes abandon their lambs when you move them. They wouldn't cross the creek. If it was raining, they just wouldn't go. It was a general disaster."

"When you have fifty ewes they herd really well," John adds. "But when you have fifty ewes and lambs it's like herding cats. They just don't move."

"If it was very high water, they wouldn't go, but, they could swim," Jody said. "They probably never saw anything like that out West. One of our sheep – I had a separate flock, completely different from the other flock, which unfortunately gave Pete the idea, because we always made a little money with that flock, but probably not if you figured out the time we spent with them, but, I remember bringing the dog, Jim, around one time, and this lamb jumped in the pond and swam across, he didn't have much wool. Jim just looked like 'what on earth!' Jim was a wonderful dog."

"We had trouble with dogs," John remembers. "I kept a gun in the camper. Every time I got the gun Jim was nowhere to be seen. It was later when I was talking with Henry, we just happened to be talking; his buddy was a hot head. He said they were herding sheep and his buddy got mad at one of his dogs, shot the dog and Jim was there. He shot the dog right in front of Jim. Jim never forgot that. He was a smart dog."

"I remember one time about the show ram from West Virginia," Jody says. "It wasn't afraid of anything. It would just run Jim into the ground. I remember losing my temper and sic'ing Pat's cattle dog on that ram. There was blood and the minute that ram turned, Jim was right there. Jim saw that that ram was under control. He was a neat dog. He used to be so gentle. I had my crook by the door. If I left the crook where he could see it, he'd stay right there, but if the crook wasn't there, I'd look out the door and all thirty of my sheep would be in the yard. He got cancer when he was about ten. We still had people wanting to breed to him. Pete said he could take the cancer off, but it would always come back unless he castrated him so I had Pete do the surgery and Jim lived several more good years. I was with Jim one time. We had a possum in the trap. I usually let the possum loose. I let that possum out of the trap and

Jim nailed that possum instantly and killed him. I never thought he'd do that. He was a great dog. He was the daddy of Ruffian. Pete had her for years and years. Oh, there were some beautiful moments during the time of the sheep. Sitting there by the creek just watching the sheep graze. Peaceful. But, man."

"It was a pretty sight," John says. "The dogs working and lambing time. It was a unique operation for the area. People came to see the operation. It just needed a little tweak. There were a lot of bugs in it. Every day was drama. It was, oh boy, it seemed like it just happened yesterday. A lot of it blocks out. My relationship with Pete was good. We got along fine. I enjoyed working for Pete and with the sheep. I remember he would be doing surgery to three or four in the morning, the next day would be his farm day, and we would work from sun up to sun down. Quite frankly, I worked hard, but I didn't work that hard. It was great to get up at the crack of dawn outside, work from sun up to sun down, and come back at the end of the day and you felt great. We were out in the woods in the pastures and stuff. Mostly Pete and I, a couple of student veterinarians came down. Pete would kind of siphon them off their vet duties and have them work on the farm. One guy really liked it, but one guy didn't like it."

"You had to castrate all the male lambs, and dock the tails. Some of that is vet work, but not quite," Jody says. "I think he only ended up with 200 to 300 sheep out of the whole bunch that survived. Some guy bought the remnant of them. He took them to an island in the Ohio River, and, of course, they couldn't get off the island and dogs couldn't get on the island. But, I haven't heard from him, of course, that's been years ago. The only time we ever heard back from him, they were doing all right, but that island couldn't support all the sheep."

"Did Pat help with the sheep?" John asks.

"Oh! Pat to this day doesn't want anything to do with sheep," Jody laughs.

"Pete's perseverance was 200%," John says. "Even when things were going sour, he would kind of cheer me up a little. We maintained. It was easier for me because I didn't have the monetary investment that he had. He still maintained his sense of humor the best he could and carried us all. *Positive Perseverance and Poetic Profanity.* I remember when we would run up strays; an experience is what it was. I enjoyed that time in my life. Maybe not everything. Parts of it. There were parts of it. I think Pete was a positive influence. I was in my young twenties. I learned a lot from him in a lot of ways. He was a role model for me. We had our share of jokes. When we would be walking through the woods, you know how you slip on a branch and fall down, or something, he would say, 'There's a slippery spot there.' Some people would say, 'Well, I'll pay you next week, or next week, because things are a little tight.' Even though things were tight, and they were tight, he always, every Friday, he would give me my check. And I bet he had to borrow money to make the payroll."

"Oh, yeah, bunches of money," Jody says.

"I remember one time, too, we were sitting out there. He said, 'You know, John, we have to make $150 a day just to break even on this operation.' Just the farm. Which, back in that day was a lot of money. He started thinking about other ways to move cash flow. He would pay my way into the movies. If there was going to be something really tough, something beyond our normal day, he wouldn't tell me at first, he just took me to Perkins Pancake House and we'd have steak and eggs for breakfast. I sure enjoyed that because I was single. Then he'd start talking about what we were going to do that day. But it was a challenge. Sometimes we'd be out in the woods and we'd have to make or come up with something to get the work done; the right tools for the right job. I never understood his mechanic tricks. He'd take work to a whole different level. Pete was spiritual that way."

Volunteer Shepherds

Pete seemed to have a Pied Piper effect on people; where Pete went, people followed, even to sheep hell. People were interested in what Pete was doing and enjoyed his comradery. It was Pete's convincing laugh, never-ending supply of quality jokes, bigger-than-life presence, and his confidence in living, that mesmerized people. If he needed a volunteer, he made you *feel* like you were his last breath. People perceived that being connected to Milliron Farm was like being in a scene from Camelot; mystical, magical, with lots and lots of sheep.

As a volunteer at the clinic, Jerry Hartley was always available to help Pete and partake in buzzard preservation. The formaldehyde bath was constructed in the area to the right of the clinic. The formaldehyde treated and prevented foot rot. It had a penetrating, offensive odor that remained for days. Sheep were methodically brought to the containing trough, run through, then marked and returned to the flock. Occasionally, the ewes would leave their lambs on the other side of the trough and the workers would have to walk them through the formidable bath.

As volunteers came and went, Jody and Dave Barger were the last two that could stand the intense event. Jody ended up with an allergic reaction to anything with formaldehyde.

When the lambs were of age, they had to be castrated. Flipping the sheep on their backs, Pete would have a helper, usually a volunteer, hold their legs while he made the snip. It was hard work.

Jerry came to loathe the animals' passivity. "The sheep would go and lay down somewhere. If you didn't go pick them up, they would just lay there. I hated them," Jerry says earnestly. "Don't you think that Pete would have been content to work 18 hours as a veterinarian and skip all this other stuff? He sure was an overachiever."

"Sheep's intelligence is survival of the flock, not the individual," Jody quips. "They were a 24-hour nightmare."

Maggots infested the flock, mostly in their manure-caked tails and feet. To avoid maggot contamination, Pete would remove the lamb's tails, as a worker held three of its legs. After a day of working with the sheep, clothes would be smelly and ready for disposal. If the formaldehyde was not enough, the lanolin from the sheep's wool would rub off onto the clothes. The lanolin was so thick that clothing repelled water.

"The lady down at the Salvation Army would keep me in old overalls and stuff to wear around the sheep," Jerry says. "Jan Crall helped with the sheep, too. She was working with a sheep one day and it knocked her over. She wasn't hurt, but to play a trick on Pete, she filled out Workmen's Compensation forms. Jan gave the forms to Pete and it broke his heart. He thought nobody would do that, especially volunteers. He looked at the forms and they were signed *Dr. Deduct.* It was one of those 'getcha-back' jokes that Pete always talked about."

Pete hired a woman to shepherd the sheep. She was living in a trailer alongside the sheep, in the rented pasture. Jerry Hartley was helping Pete at the clinic that day.

"Jerry," Pete said, "will you go get the shepherdess and take her to town? She needs provisions."

Jerry agreed and drove his truck to the woman's trailer out in the sheep pasture. It was a cold winter day, and the drive was not so bad through the snowy terrain. Jerry greeted the woman and told her he would take her to town.

Living with sheep in a trailer for several weeks without the comforts of civilization can have adverse results. She hadn't had a bath for weeks. Jerry was gasping for breath on the drive to the Athens Kroger, which seemed to take forever.

Finally, they arrived in town; the woman went into Kroger's. Jerry decided to stay in the truck while she shopped. He promptly returned her to her trailer amid the sheep.

The day Pete sold the remainder of the partnership flock, everyone cheered. It was the end of the sheep saga; no one would miss their smell, *baaa's*, or wooly touch. Jerry swore he would never wear wool again.

Herbie and Kay

Herbie and Kay Everett are kind, endearing souls. Like John Branner and Jerry Hartley, they were shepherds with integrity. "We were second and third shift workers. We were shepherds. Volunteers," Herbie says, "I worked for the railroad all day, then Kay and I would help Pete in the afternoons and evenings."

"I loved Pete to death," Kay smiles, "but I always said I would never work for him. That was Pete. I didn't work for him; we were volunteers; I could go home whenever I wanted to. He yelled once in a while."

"He would just start yelling," Herbie interjects. "He had a temper, same as me."

"If things didn't go right," Kay continues, "like he said one time when a horse died, 'Get in here and help me get this horse off the table!' I said, 'No! I'm going home!' If I worked for him, I would have to get right back in there!"

"If you don't get paid, you don't have to put up with nothing," Herbie says.

"Sheep and surgeries were much of the same time," Kay says. "When the sheep went away, he didn't need us. Pete finished up most of his surgeries by 9:30 to 10:00 p.m. When somebody needs help, you go help. When the sheep went away, Pete didn't need help at those hours. We always spent time with the sheep during holidays. The only reason it was on holidays is that that was the only time the clinic was closed that you could get that many days in a row. It took that many days, three and a half days, to get to that many sheep. To say that we were going to mess with the sheep on a specific weekend, it couldn't be done. It had to be a holiday weekend. In the spring of the year, Memorial Day weekend is the only long weekend that you've got, and actually it's getting up in the warm weather sometimes, and you want to do that when it's cool because the sheep are hot. One year we helped with the sheep dip. Herbie hung his bib-overalls out on the line with that formaldehyde on them. Every time I'd go outside the door, I'd get sick. I finally told him to get rid of those bib-overalls."

Shearing sheep is dirty work. It's hot, itchy, greasy, sweaty, sometimes full of parasites and almost always smelly. Oil-repelling lanolin coats everything and you smell like a sheep for weeks afterwards. The sheep probably don't like it either, but who's to know? They never really cooperate - bleating, running, dodging, and all that sheepy stuff. A good shearer can shear a sheep in about two minutes or less. It's difficult to find a bona-fide, dedicated sheep shearer. Zipping those clippers through all that wool takes finesse and a steady hand. The Smith's had the good fortune of having several generations of Strode family sheepshearers, pulling in with their shearing palace every spring.

"Jessica! Pat! We need your help with the sheep today!" Pete would say.

"That's all right, Dad, but we have to go to school!" they would reply. Not even a day off from school could entice Jessica and Pat to work with the sheep if they could get out of it.

The contrast of red blood on a white sheep can be exaggerated - sometimes. Sheep can go into shock very easily and die very easily. Dr. Lyle Schultheis, a veterinarian in Marietta told Pete, "Sheep come in to this world looking for a way out." Of course, as the Smith's will tell you, there are exceptions. "One of the ewes had been savaged by free roaming dogs and struggled to live," Jody recalls. "She stayed alive until her lamb was weaned, and then died. Another ewe was injured, but would drink milk from her own udder and survived (with the help of penicillin)."

After a long day of working with the sheep, the Smiths went to the Dairy Queen. "We had evidently become accustomed to the odors leaking from our clothes, but others were accosted by them," Jody says. "We got very quick service and then ate outside."

To say the least, the sheep were a harrowing ordeal. Nonetheless, Jody has fond memories, "Riding the horse with the herd as the sheep filed down the bank, across the stream, up the other bank with our Border collie Jim was ideal," she reflects. "It was picturesque watching as Jim worked the sheep back and forth, and behind them; watching Herbie Everett running back and forth, and behind them, as they moved through the pasture. We had to make imaginary fences, putting sticks and branches into holes in an old decrepit farm fence; usually enough to keep the sheep in as long as grazing was good, reaching down for the perfect stick to plunge into the hole, only to have it slither away."

Jan Thompson, client and the Smith's neighbor said she could see the buzzards flying high, then sweeping low over Milliron Farm. Rambouillet cross-breed sheep were no longer thriving in the Smith pasture. Jan stopped by the clinic one day and Pete told her that the Audubon Society had given him a plaque for the *Preservation of*

Buzzards. When Jan asked to see this amazing award, Pete and the clinic staff just laughed. "There really isn't a plaque," Pete grinned.

November 22, 2008, many years after, Pete wanted to buy more sheep again. First Jody handed him a piece of paper:

> Any decision on breeding present flock of sheep will be delayed until more information is gathered and the decision to breed or postpone breeding will be mutual.

Jody still has it, signed in cursive by her and Pete: *VJ Smith and AP Smith.* It was in writing. No more sheep.

Mikey, let's go get a dozer
and shove that tree down.
Pete Smith

---

9 FEARLESS INGENUITY

PETE WAS VERY good at enticing volunteers to help him around the farm. Hay season was no different. It took a lot of volunteers to put in many bales of hay that the clinic and farm needed to function.

When out on farm calls, Pete would be intrigued by the new and innovative machinery. Upon one occasion, Pete got an idea to build a hay bale gatherer that could collect square bales into one pile for collection later. "It was a sled that attached to the New Holland baler by a rope," Pat explains. "It connected to the baler by long metal rebar. It would collect ten to twelve bales, then you pulled on the rope and all the bales would be in one pile. The rebar held the bales until they were released. Dad had torn down the de-horning chute earlier, and used a lot of the materials from the chute to build the bale gatherer. If volunteers were unavailable, he could hook up the gatherer, bale square bales, and place several bales in the same location for easy retrieval with the hay wagon or pickup truck later. We would alternate between square bales and round bales. One year we would bale square bales, the next year round bales. One year we put up 10,000 square bales of hay. We filled up all the barns to the rafters. We went through a lot of hay."

Farm Work

"Sometimes the house benefited directly from farm employees," Jody says. "One employee completed a good job of putting a

197

brick floor under the barn cistern for the ewes that were lambing. I suggested he construct a brick floor for the carport by the farmhouse. He did a really good job laying the bricks on our garden paths and carport. He used to help Pete on the farm. He was clearing brush up beyond the house. Pete and I were going to a meeting. Pete forgot that he needed to tell the employee something. I sat in the car while Pete went up where he was clearing brush. Pete came back down about fifteen minutes later and said, '*Shit!* That's the end of that.' The employee had constructed himself the cutest little tent up there and was sound asleep. He was getting paid by the hour, not by the job. He already figured Pete was gone for the day and was settled in when Pete caught him unexpectedly. 'It takes a ton of at-a-boys to make up for one ah-shit,' Pete would say, a saying he borrowed form one of his favorite clients, Nancy Bonnett.

"A client of Pete's had a son," Jody remembers. "The client was recently divorced and the son had gone to the city to live with his mother. On occasion, the son came to visit his father in Athens. One summer the son came to spend time with his father, and the father was concerned that his son was becoming a city boy and that he wasn't learning the value of hard work. So, the client sent his son out to help Pete around the farm. The boy came out and did try; lifting hay bales and all that stuff. Pete asked this poor kid what it cost to go to a gym in the city and if he thought the work on the farm was hard work. The boy replied that it was the hardest work he had ever done. Pete said, 'You think I should charge you twice as much as what you pay at the gym?' The kid was suckered in totally. When his dad came to pick him up, he told his dad, 'Dr. Smith said we owe him for letting me work here.' Pete looked at the dad and winked. The kid was relieved when Pete actually paid him for his work that day."

Before Jessica married Rich, he helped in the hayfield. "Rich was a city boy. He isn't anymore," Jody explains. "He pretty much has it down on working on hay now. Rich thought at the time that it couldn't be difficult - after all, Pete was more than twenty years older. Pete worked him into the ground. Poor Rich. The next year Rich planned his family vacation during hay season, in Alaska!"

Pete was always busy. Veterinary work, family life, horseback riding, social events, community involvement, and much more. During this time, he was busy building Milliron Farm and maintaining his acreage. "Pete liked to own the land around him," Jody says. "His mantra 'all I want is to own what borders my property' was always on his mind. In the 70's, he borrowed money from Horace Karr to buy the Phillips' place. He arranged payments with Horace, and finally paid his loan off in full. People asked Pete why he worked so hard. His automatic response, 'If I wasn't under all this pressure to pay off mortgages, I wouldn't work so hard.'"

Owning land requires upkeep. Owning machinery requires upkeep. It was a lot of work. The Hydro-Ax was one of Pete's favorite pieces of heavy machinery. Used by logging companies and the forestry industry to clear dense thickets and brush, the Hydro-Ax was used often on the Smith farm. One day, the Cummins engine could take no more. "He did the typical amount of maintenance on the Hydro-Ax, which was none," Pat said. "It stopped working one day when he was in the process of clearing brush. It was covered in leaves, debris, and brush. The motor got hot, probably had a hydraulic leak, and caught on fire. When it caught on fire, it really caught on fire. The latch to the roll cage was broken, but he was able to get the fire extinguisher, which was out of fuse. By this time, the large ag tires were billowing black smoke. Trying to escape the flames, he took the fire extinguisher and busted the latch off the roll cage so he could get out. He sat on the bank and cried as he watched his beloved Hydro-Ax burn.

"He loved his big excavators, too," Pat continues. "He had yellow-iron disease (infatuation with, addiction to backhoes, trackhoes, dozers, etc.). He bought a Caterpillar 235 trackhoe. It was hauled in on two semi's and came in two parts. They assembled it in the side field because they couldn't get it across the bridge. When they got it assembled, they drove it through the creek to the clinic parking lot. The Cat 235 was his favorite."

According to Pete, farm equipment was not only a necessity, but the more the better. He liked shopping for it, finding good deals, and keeping plenty of it around. He never really discussed the purchase of farm equipment with Jody. He bought what he needed, when he needed it.

"I always thought that if I ever won the lottery, I would buy him something new," Jody said. "Sometimes pragmatic, he saved money buying and restoring used farm equipment. He purchased three used dozers to create one usable dozer."

Client and volunteer farmhand Ron Docie used to help Pete make hay, Pete driving the tractor and Ron on the wagon. Ron admired Pete for his open-hearted spirit, he says, "Pete just had a go-for-broke, all-or-nothing trust in life in general; a true kind of faith that not too many people have. That's the example he set through his deeds of how he would go into things. If you want dogs, get dogs. Some people may be concerned about liability. Some people may have a question about doing this or that. He just went forward and did it. When you consider his position, a lot of people in lesser positions would be more concerned about that than he ever was. He, of course, would never want liability. I don't think that dictated what he did. It was interesting how Pete had an appropriate mix of empathy and acceptance. Think of all the misery that he saw; if you were too compassionate, you weren't going to be able to operate. There's a certain point you have to accept it. I think he did that better than most. I think that he had an important prayer, and that it was an important principal. Obviously, I'm not saying he didn't have any compassion. What I am saying is there's a certain point that to feel too bad about a situation is what you think is best vs. what God thinks is best. So, if you trust in God, you don't worry about it too much. Pete embodied those very core principles. On the other hand, he did make changes where he needed to make changes; positive changes. So, I just always had a lot of respect for him."

Dick Sheets worked for Pete early on and stayed for twelve years. Sitting in the clinic waiting area, Dick and Jody reminisce about maintaining the facilities. Dick laid the clinic floor tiles. Pete had said he wanted the flooring to be urine and blood color. A lot of workers would come and go over the years, but Dick hung in there.

"I've worked on about all of the equipment around here," he says. "The autoclave and everything; mostly maintenance. I've worked on all the houses, the barns, and the sawmill. I didn't have any trouble with Pete."

Jody puts in, "Pete would come up to the house. *Blankety-blank* about an employee. You were the only employee that Pete never, ever complained about. Pete was very complimentary of you and your work."

"That's nice to hear," Dick nods.

"That's the truth," Jody affirms.

"Used to be when they had a horse that they had to put on the table, I'd be the extra help," Dick says, pointing out the window. "I've dragged them up the hill a time or two, too. I didn't mind it. It was part of the job; took them and dropped them in a hole way back on the ridge. I remember building all the fences and wooden gates around. I sawed every board. Sawed them at Pete's sawmill, too. We started with just a real little sawmill and a shed. Pete said the sawmill was always his dream. That's why he was a very successful man. Not very many can have their dreams like that. He worked for it; he earned it. But, Jody would take the checkbook away from him. When he'd go to the auction, boy he'd like to buy things. Actually, I wasn't around him a whole lot. I'd be working on Pete's other houses. I wouldn't even see him. I built Pat and Karen's house. It's about two miles from the clinic by horseback, and four miles if you drive. Russ Smith helped on it. Russ, Jerry Leedy, Craig Higgins, and Jeff Davis. They were all working for Pete at the time. I liked working for Pete. He would tell me what he needed done and I wouldn't see him for a few days. He always had me doing something different.

"I was thinking about that time he broke his ankle," Dick continues. "Pete had assigned me and Russ Smith to build a fence. We were working on the fence when he came down the creekbank to check on our progress. He was drinking a Pepsi, stepped on a rock, and went down! He twisted his ankle and didn't spill a drop of Pepsi! '*Oh, hell!*' He had a few choice words. We had to carry him over to get his truck. Someone took Pete to the emergency room. His bone was sticking out. They sent him up to Columbus. They gave him some kind of pain killer at the emergency room that he was allergic to."

Jody confirms, "I remember that trip very well. He had a plastic bag because he was nauseated all the way up. I took him to Columbus."

"He was tough, because when he got back, it wasn't very long until he hobbled down here on crutches. Remember?" Dick asks.

"Yes! He practiced vetting out of a wheelchair here!" Jody exclaims. "I finally convinced him not to use the wheelchair around horses. He wasn't supposed to work at all. I had satellite TV installed at the house so that he could watch his favorite Westerns, but he was back vetting in two days."

"He was laid up awhile," Dick says. "It was a bad break, but he came down to work every day. They reset his ankle and put a plate in it. Later, they removed the plate."

"He was going to do horse surgery and all kinds of things," Jody remembers. "We talked him out of that. He could only do small animals. He couldn't get out of the way of a horse. Some of the surgeries were elective. Right after he broke his ankle, we went to a vet meeting in Washington, D.C. It was at a luxury hotel, downtown Washington D.C. Pete told me to bring along my old compact vacuum cleaner so he could make a whirlpool bath for his own broken ankle. I was walking through the hotel lobby with the old vacuum while people stared. One of the hotel staff shouted, 'Lady, we do our own cleaning here…'"

"One thing I remember about Pete; he was a hard worker himself," Dick says. "He wouldn't ask me or anybody else to do anything that he wouldn't do. He'd get right down in the mud just the same as us. I worked on all the barns, the house he lived in, and all that. I always found work here. I know I'd still be working if I was able. I've worked all my life. Pete had big dreams and he made them work. Behind the clinic garage, there wasn't anything just some piles of dirt and lumber. When we started I never dreamed it would turn out like that. He knew what he wanted. I remember we were working on an old abandoned highway bridge in New Marshfield. The bridge went over the top of the railroad track. It was wintertime. It was cold. The engineers told Pete he could have the old timbers from the bridge. That's what we used to build the sawmill. We tore down the bridge to get the lumber. I was afraid he was going to get killed when we were tearing down the bridge. He was on the skidder and one of those steel beams came at him. Pete thought the skidder would hold it when we cut the leg off the beam. It didn't. When Russ cut the steel beam, it jerked the skidder back. Pete was wise enough to turn the cable so the beam fell loose. The beam fell into the ravine. I told him that if that had been any of the other guys, they'd been dead. Pete said his instinct kicked in. Didn't seem to shake him up. He just knew. He was banged up several times, wasn't he? Didn't he have his back broken?"

"Yes," Jody confirms. "He broke his back working on that ranch in Wyoming."

"I remember he told me that when he was in college he rented a room in the funeral home where he worked," Dick says. "He came home one night and there was a dead guy right in his bed."

"Oh, yeah," Jody says softly. "Pete never thought he was going to die, he never wanted anything to do with a funeral home. He always said not to take him to a funeral home."

"I know he told me once that he was never afraid of dying. Somehow or another he got caught in the stirrup and a horse was dragging him, too," Dick remembers.

"Yeah, that was when Bud drug him through the woods," Jody adds. "One other time there was a tree that fell on him. Harold Hay found him that time. Harold is the one that was here when the deer had locked together. I found two deer with their horns locked. Harold and Pete tried to separate the deer. They roped the live deer, the other deer was dead. The live deer couldn't go anywhere dragging a 300-pound dead deer by the head. Pete gave the deer an anesthetic and so then they tried to pry the horns apart with a steel fencepost. Then one of us went back and got a hacksaw. They sawed one tine off the live deer, separating the rack. I still have the rack. Pat wanted the rack. AJ, my grandson, wanted the rack. I said, 'No! I am keeping the rack.'"

"Pete was fearless," Dick says. "He wasn't afraid of dying. If he wanted to try something, he just tried it. I used to help in the hay field, then I got bronchitis and emphysema. I helped de-worm the sheep and helped to catch them while Pete gave them a shot. I took some up to the stock sale in Mt. Vernon. Pete was always fair. As long as they treated him right, he'd do anything to help anybody else. Of all the guys that helped me, I think Eric Curfman was the best because he never argued. I really liked him. I had a lot of good guys work with me; some of them wasn't so good and didn't last long. I worked for Pete a long time without anyone helping me. I told Pete that if anyone needed a job, hire them. It was hard what I was doing, working on that sawmill. It wasn't long after that he hired some guys. I even helped clean stables and stuff, too. I never had any trouble with any of the animals. Pete showed me how to lead the horses out. He said not to get behind them. I helped horses on to the surgery table and into the recovery stall. I did just about everything. Plumbing, electrical, and all that. I missed Pete when I left. I always wanted to come back and visit, but the doctor told me to stay away from hay, straw, and the chemical smells."

The Sawmill

Pete loved his sawmill. He was passionate about forestry; the aesthetics and comfort of being in the hills of southeastern Ohio surrounded by timber. Farm employees were presented with a black cap with an artist's rendition of a log and sawblades, representing Pete's favorite pastime. Jody's cap has a white wooly sheep bearing the Milliron Brand. The sawmill was a big production, one that he had waited nearly a lifetime to create.

The sawmill consists of a large wooden building, constructed with timbers logged and milled on site. The ground floor of the sawmill is used for storage, equipment, and, of course, the large industrial log carrier and mega saw. The power to the mill is amped by a three-phase generator. The second story is a beautifully designed area that would satisfy any lumberjack. Approaching the second story steps, the aroma of weathered lumber permeates the air. At the top of the steps and into the first room is Pete's large wood stove. Bookshelves embrace the upper rafters, only reachable by ladder.

Pete knew about timber management. Occasionally, he would consult with the local Ranger for land management advice.

The Smith children learned to operate a chainsaw, learned the importance of trees and their purpose at the sawmill. When you're working outside and working with animals you need to know how to run a chainsaw. When Jessica was a professor at Hocking College, she brought her chainsaw class to Pete's sawmill.

The clinic employees remember Pete's famous wood chopping parties. In the depth of winter, Pete would invite staff, friends and family to chop wood. When appointments were slow at the clinic, Pete would spend time at the sawmill, generating money by cutting wood and selling it.

"There was a really nice tree that had nice low branches hanging down so that we could all sit on a different branch and have our family portrait taken. He cut it down," Jody says. "Even though I had told him 'We were going to have our portraits taken there.' Pete said, 'Oh, that was the tree, wasn't it?' But I told him, 'I picked out another tree.'"

Pete released a lot of stress working out in the woods and cutting timber. He was always looking for ways to earn extra money because he could never say no to a salesman. He loved to cut down trees. He would get frustrated because he felt he had quality logs and not getting quality prices for them. He would load up the timber trucks with logs and the guys would come back with the checks. He would get very angry because he felt he was getting ripped off. That's when he decided to build his own sawmill, selling directly. Pete declared he was going to have the biggest sawmill east of the Mississippi, big enough to saw a 60-foot timber. He felt he was going to generate a lot of income from the sawmill and that was going to be his retirement fund. He had great plans.

Dempsey Sharp worked for Pete for a very long time, especially on the sawmill. "Pete and I just seemed to click. We were very close friends. I became acquainted with Pete when I took one of my animals to the clinic," Dempsey explains. "I was looking for a veterinarian to take care of my dog and my cats. Somebody mentioned the Milliron Clinic. I took the dog over to Pete for shots and that's how we got acquainted. I don't know whether you know it or not, but on my bill he always wrote *No Charge*. Pete worked with all animals, large and small, but I believe he especially favored race horses. Once he expressed an interest in a medication that I was using for a breathing problem. Advair had just come on the market and it had made a marked difference in my life, especially in the control of asthma. He investigated the possibility of using Advair with race horses, but decided it presented too much of a problem to administer an effective dose. He was thinking that if he could keep the airways more open and relaxed, they would have more stamina. He said, 'The difference between a winner and a loser is the small fraction of a second.' I would like to believe that he considered me to be on the right side of that fraction. I know he was.

"I found out that Pete was interested in trees," Dempsey continues. "He was as interested in trees as he was horses. I believe that horses were his real love of life. But he loved trees, too. He said that he had some that I could come over and look at, and I did. He knew I was fascinated with wildflowers. Then this thing came up about the sawmill. That sawmill he had! We had a lot of conversations about how to strengthen certain things, how much stress/weight he could put on certain things, and what kind of timbers he would need to build the sawmill. I did a lot of that figuring for him. I was an engineer in the war. So, we got started. I didn't do the measurements. I did the computations for the strength requirements."

In the spring of the year, on non-clinic days, Pete and Dempsey would go on wildflower tours. They would get an early start and make their rounds through the State Preserves. "We went into the woodland where the wildflowers were," Dempsey says. "Pete was pretty good about recognizing wildflowers. He was interested in botany. Occasionally we'd run onto some unusual flowers and we would talk about them. I gave Pete a few wildflower pictures that I had taken. He hung them on wall of the second floor of the sawmill.

"Pete would take a trip with me back home to visit my kin people," Dempsey smiles. "From the clinic we would take Route 50 through Parkersburg to Clarksburg. Then we would take Route 79 South and cut off when we got to a certain place and take the country roads to my home. Honest to God, I could be driving along at 70 mph and I would see a flower appear on a hillside and I knew exactly what that flower was; most of the time from their color. When Pete and I went, we were out from early morning to late. When you start looking at flowers, and really look at them, you take your time and don't look at anything else. Pete loved all wildflowers. We would never pick them. Well, once in a while we'd pick violets."

Bulletproof Glass

One day, Charlie Watson was at the clinic with one of his mares. Pete was working on the mare and Charlie was intrigued by Pete's sawmill.

"How's the sawmill coming?" Charlie inquired.

"Let's just go out and look!" Pete smiled.

Pete took Charlie on the seemingly endless tour, explaining to Charlie all the creative ideas he had for the sawmill's future. "I'm going to do this; I'm going to do that..." Pete explained, arms pointing and waving.

The windows in the sawmill came from a local jail where Charlie had been working. It was bulletproof glass. The jail was being renovated and the glass was going to be thrown in the dumpster. Charlie confiscated the glass, hoping to incorporate it in his barn. Charlie took the glass home and put it in the top of his barn for later use.

Later, Pete was at Charlie's to see Kate, Charlie's beloved Belgian mare who had foundered and was in bad shape. Pete was going to euthanize her. When Pete was in Charlie's barn, he saw the bulletproof glass.

"What's that glass for?" Pete asked.

"Well, I intend to build out here on the barn. The horses won't hurt it, or anything," says Charlie.

Pete begins looking around at Charlie's barn.

"When I get that sawmill up and running, I'll cut you some lumber for your new addition. You'll have a very unique barn. I'll cut you enough lumber so that the boards go from the top to the bottom – one long board. I'll take care of you. I need that glass for my sawmill control room! Those pieces that come off that sawmill are wicked!" Pete said.

Pete explained to Charlie that if the lumber going through the sawmill kicked back or flew, that the bulletproof glass would take the pounding and protect the operator. Before long, the bulletproof glass was in place around the control panel of Pete's sawmill.

Ten years went by. Charlie was at the clinic on a Monday afternoon. He had a yearling stallion that he had to show and the stallion had a pimple on his chest. Charlie didn't have an appointment, just stopped in to see if Pete was free.

"Hey, Pete. I'm laid off. When the weather straightens up in April or May, I'd like to get some lumber and start residing the barn."

"Okay," Pete replied. "Check the schedule."

Charlie made an appointment for Thursday at 10 o'clock. He talked with Pete a couple of hours before leaving. The next evening, on a Tuesday, Charlie received the phone call that Pete was in the hospital. The barter never came to fruition.

Let's Go Mikey

"1980 and 1990s when I was doing work for Pete, cutting wood; we were logging. I am on Pete's old Allis Chalmers D3 dozer, running it in the backwoods," explains friend, client, UPS man, and farmhand volunteer, Mike Cunningham. Mike stops by the clinic to talk about his adventures with Pete. Jody is nearby, rolling her eyes, shaking her head, intrigued by Mike's commitment to work in the backwoods with Pete.

"We were cutting this big-ass wolf tree, a huge, five-foot diameter monster tree," Mike continues. "Those trees are junk, not good for anything. We had a big 30 or 32-inch bar and a 980 Stihl chainsaw. It was a big saw. It's the biggest saw Steele makes. It was old technology, but it served Pete well. New saws have so much more power, less weight. This saw was all blade. Pete would handle like it was nothing.

"It was hotter than hell outside that day. Most loggers would not attempt a wolf tree. They would leave it out there. It was a soft ash tree. This one was just junk. They're just dangerous trees. We were fully aware of what we were doing. You take your chances. It's not like you're playing with dynamite. People do it every day. But that's what Pete liked to do.

"People don't understand what it's like to cut a tree down like that. Pete was trying to get rid of the weak trees and the ash borer so they wouldn't feed on the strong trees. Just for my own sanity, I saw what he did, saw how he did it," Mike continues. "I just can't explain it. Pete was twenty years older than me. He worked like a dog. That was his reputation. Somethings didn't go the way they should have. We would run into that kind of stuff all the time. Sometimes, we didn't have any rope with us. We had steel cable, and you think to yourself, *how is that steel cable going to get up there? Are you going to climb it?* I don't think so. Pete just took the dozer. There was a tree had set on itself. The tree was hollow, bored out, and it had just set down. Pete said, 'Mikey, let's go get a dozer and shove that tree down.' I said, 'I ain't getting near that thing. Nope. Let's just get a rope or something.' Pete jumped on the dozer and shoved the tree. It pushed off the base right back into the dozer. The tree was so damn big. There is a cage on the dozer, but it would smash the dozer if it hit. All the branches were 70 to 80 feet out; they all hit behind the dozer. There was a wall of branches sticking out over the dozer. I said, 'Ok! I am done working for tonight!' The tree stood there for a week before we could do anything with it.

"I don't mind cutting when it's fifteen degrees or twenty degrees above zero," Mike continues, "but sometimes I just refused to do it. Never once was I in danger when working with Pete. Pete would jump off the truck and he would run up the hill. It was all I could do to get to the hill, and then he would fire the chainsaw and cut down six or eight trees. I was still getting oxygen. Pete was like Paul Bunyan. Before we would go out in the mornings he would walk fifteen times up and down the hill from the farmhouse to the clinic. That was before work. He had a weight attached to a coat hanger and he would take it up and down the hill with him. I was always amazed about shape he was in. He never grunted when he picked up a saw, which were always too big. He didn't need that big of a saw."

209

"I don't know where he got the energy," Jody says, "but he'd go in there and go swimming at the Ohio University Aquatic Center. He opened the clinic at 8:00 a.m. and walked up and down the hill from the farmhouse to the clinic at 7:00 a.m. Where he got the energy to cut timber, I'll never know. Pat would say something to his dad about that's scary or dangerous and Pete would say, 'Yeah, like hunting rhinoceros.' I always tried to get Pete to take somebody with him and he would say, 'No, they'd probably kill me.' I even tried to get him to take a phone with him. I said, 'You don't have to keep it on, just turn it on in case you get into any trouble.' He never thought he'd be in any trouble."

"A tree hugger would say, 'No, you can't go in there and do that.' Pete saw it all different," Mike continues. "Pete called it 'weeding the woods' and he would weed some big stuff! Even to this day I have trouble cutting sizeable trees. He didn't see it that way. Maybe a standing maple or oak needed to go away. Maybe a standing ash and a maple, they had to go away. He didn't care if it was thirty inches in diameter; it was going to go away. I had a hard time with that until now. I've been into lumber all my life. Pete asked me to help him. He would say, 'What are you doing today, Mikey?' We would go out on Saturday and Sunday afternoons."

"I'd look out the kitchen door and there would be this really nice dog running around out there. It was your dog. You were picking up saws," Jody recalls. "You'd come and get the saws, pick them up, bring them back."

"For years we traded our animal care for saw sharpening," Mike says. "We never exchanged money. We are talking big money, and worked it out. That's kind of what started it. He worked far and wide. It's not like he walked behind the house to cut a few trees down. I mean, we walked a long way. Long days. All day. Hard work, when he wasn't vetting, all we did was clean out woods. We'd stack grapevines and brush to burn it or whatever. The sawmill came much later. I helped him to get it running. I helped him as much as I could."

Dozer Tracks

When people get along and like to work together, relationships are built. Lifelong relationships can extend beyond what we know. Pete had such a relationship with Eric Eisenberg. Then, a young man looking for work; now, due to Pete's encouragement and inspiration, Eric is a successful veterinarian. "Pete hired me to work around the farm. The first day on the job, he had me clean the tracks of his bulldozer. I did such a good job, he put me on the schedule to work. I had a background working at a small animal hospital. We got along really well," Eric Eisenberg remembers. "When I was growing up, I never saw a horse, I never saw a cow. Now I know a lot about them, and Pete was a part of that. Pete wanted me to have a horse, so he would wheel and deal with his clients to get me a horse. One wasn't enough, he got me two! I would help Pete in the clinic in the morning, and then in the afternoon we would go out and cut firewood, bale hay, or do another farm work. I remember it would be a bright sunny day and Pete would say, 'At 6 o'clock we are going to bale hay. Sure enough, at 6 o'clock a big black cloud would come and it would start to rain. I would be like 'Oh, thank you God!' and Pete shook his head and said some choice words.

"Everything he did was big. He was a big eater, too. He really liked beans. One day a year he would *let* everyone come up to the farm to cut firewood. I told him I would cook some beans, cowboy beans. I was living in a barn on route 550 at the time. He would be in his doctor's coat and come and check on the beans. 'Did you put the salt in? Did you stir them?' Pete kept asking. When we served the beans, you would have thought Pete had died and went to heaven. He loved to eat.

"One time we were out working in the woods," Eric eagerly says. "Pete had his horse, and I had mine. My horse had the pack on it with the tools. On the way back, my horse spooked and ran off into the woods. We got back to the farmhouse. Pete was really upset. He raised an eyebrow and asked, 'Aren't you worried about your horse out there running around in the woods with the backpack?' I said, 'No, I'm not worried. I know I have you as a friend and if something happens to my horse, I know you will take care of him. Why would I be worried?' Pete said, 'Well, that is true.'"

Gardening

Loving to eat, along with the thought of eating healthy, and the opportunity to use power equipment, Pete liked the idea of a garden. "A lot of people don't know that everything with Pete was always big," former employee Will Tevis says. "I was into gardening. Pete liked the idea of a garden. There was a guy named Eric Eisenberg who worked for Pete, too. He came to us from Belize. Eric was kind of a vegetarian hippie type. We were all kind of friends. We were talking about growing a garden. So, Pete got advice from other people, farmers and gardeners. He had 100 ton of sand hauled in, then dumped 100 tons of sheep manure on it. This was up by the house. Pete had me order $250 worth of seed. Eric took the garden over from there. Everything with Pete was big."

"We grew some wonderful spinach, snap peas," Jody says. "Eric left and Pete was all upset about getting it started again. But we just got too busy. Pete got off on other projects. We didn't keep it weeded, but yes, it was amazing We had the most incredible ragweed."

Surgical nurse, Annette Anderson remembers Pete telling her about his garden one day during a colic surgery. "He brought in tons of top soil, lime, fertilizer, and manure. Then he mixed it up with a backhoe. He didn't have time to weed. Soon the weeds overtook the vegetables. The pig weed was as big as a man's arm when it passed his son's second story bedroom window."

Building Fences

Pete had magical energy, Hemingway persona, and a Tom Sawyer idea that most people revered. He made people feel that whitewashing a fence, or, as it were, baling hay was a lot of fun (baling hay is very hard work). His tanned features, Cheshire smile, and authoritative voice, could talk a monkey out of a tree, or, put a hay-hook in your hand. When Pete wasn't vetting, he was always working on improving the farm: fences, hay, repairs, machinery, you name it. He was notorious for hard work.

"Dad and I were out working in the field by the clinic," Pat remembers. "We were building a perimeter fence where the clinic sign is. Dad put the boards up and one nail in each board, then I would go back and pound in the nails. Dad was two posts away, about sixteen feet away, and the chainsaw kicked, slipped across his throat, taking a big hunk out of his chest. I look at him in disbelief. Blood is squirting out of both sides of his chest. I think, '*He's dead.*' I get in the truck, spin it around and put him in it. I take off toward the clinic."

"Take me to the clinic," Pete tells Pat, while blood is spraying on the windshield, blocking Pat's view. Pat puts his head out the driver's door so he can see. At the clinic, Pete gets out of truck and goes to the surgery room, to the surgery sink. He begins washing his wounds. Blood is squirting everywhere.

"I got him a setup and he starts putting little clamps on everything. He feels around and puts clamps everywhere, trying to stop the bleeding," Pat says. "He has a huge chunk out of his chest and blood is everywhere. He's wiping off the mirror so he can see himself. Finally, he stops the squirting blood and asks me for more sutures. I said, 'Dad, we're going to the hospital.'"

"*Goddamn it*! I can do this by myself," Pete explains, holding the sutures.

"I'm going to the hospital and I'd love to take you with me," Pat said, as Pete continues cussing and being angry.

"We drive to the hospital," Pat says. "We walk in and he's got all these clamps all over his neck and chest hanging down. We walk in; the lady's got her head down. She looks up and falls right over backwards. Then the doctor looks around the corner."

"Congratulations, Pete, you've moved to the front of the line," the emergency room nurse said.

They sewed Pete up and insisted he stay overnight. Pete said, "Nope!" He signed himself out of the emergency room against the doctor's medical advice. Pat drives Pete back to the farmhouse.

"Where you are going?" Pete asks.

"I'm taking you to the house," Pat replies.

"We got to clean all this stuff up."

"Now?"

"Now."

Rush of hare-brained gallop,
Earnest walk, flashing trot
Honest smell of sweat and manure...
from "Requiem - My Horse"
by Pete Smith

---

10 TRAIL RIDE

Welcome to the 1998 Milliron Trail Ride! The main trail is marked with white ribbons. Side trails include..."Bench" trails that move around the side of the ridge instead of across the top; "Fence Rock" is a large cliff faced rock that doubled as a fence when the area was first settled; "Strata Gas Line Road" is a long, straight, grassy road that runs along the valley to the road; "Tryon Meadow" is a large field on the ridge opposite the main trail.

Ride safe!
Enjoy your ride!

THE MILLIRON CLINIC Annual Trail Ride was the talk of the Tristate area equestrian community. The event was Pete's way of thanking his clients and the community for his success. It was a big deal and a lot of work. The staff would begin preparing invitations two months before the trail ride. Originally designed for clients, friends, and family, the event grew so large that there was standing room only in the parking lot.

Always held the last Sunday in October, the ride began at the clinic. Pete scheduled the trail ride for the time change in the Fall because he said, "People who are normally late will be on time because they haven't changed their clocks." Trucks, trailers, and riders arrived at 10 a.m. to saddle up and ride three designated trails through Milliron Farm, neighboring farms, including trails to, in, and from Strouds Run State Park.

Riders were provided a hand-drawn map, indicating trail routes, between Dutch Creek Road and State Route 550, and then finally collecting to the Smith's cabin-in-the-woods where a roasted pig and all the amenities awaited. The first trail was for novice and leisurely riders; the second for a longer, more aggressive rider; and finally, the third trail that was long, mean, and challenging. Trails could be rugged, root barren, steep, rock laden and bramble lined. Other riders were the main obstacle. The challenge was to avoid collisions on the trail. But the main event was the conversation and good eats at the end of the trail.

Many volunteers helped to clear trails, organize riders at the clinic, set up the spread at the cabin, cook food. Everyone would bring their horses and park at the clinic. They would bring covered dishes into the surgery room. The surgery table and wagons would be filled with covered dishes. The covered dishes had to be transported to the cabin. People who didn't want to ride horseback had to be transported, too. Charlie and Betty Watson, among others, were always available to come early and cook. Dr. Robin Byers, musician and friend, frequently helped as well.

It's a hot topic around the Milliron camp. Gussie Anderson always attended Pete's legendary trail ride. "I remember catching a paint horse that had run off from their rider," Gussie says.

"I really didn't understand all of that," says client, rider, and long-time friend Sylvia Snabl. "About half the group decided to make a record time of it."

"You would have thought there was a pot of gold in that cabin," said Tracey Thiele, another rider and client.

"Pete was right there with them," Sylvia says.

"Pete always rode out around and southwest," Jody adds.

The trail ride was a time of preparation and work for Jessica, Pat, and the rest of the clinic staff. "Southeastern Ohio," Pat says. "You never knew what kind of weather you would get. Most of the time it was beautiful. Dad had four guys - four farmhands would work clearing the trails and put markers up for two and a half weeks prior to the event. Dad had a six-mile trail, a thirteen-mile trail and a twenty-six-mile trail. They were all designed to get to the cabin at the same time. The six-mile trail would be a walk, the thirteen-mile a trot, and the twenty-six-mile trail Dad and a couple of other people would race. And the deal was that if you outran him, that horse got free vet work for a year."

"It was a wonderful thing," Dana Gardner remembers. "Pete had the trails marked. He ran cables through the woods to mark the trails. He tried to make it as safe as possible. There was food. Lots and lots of food. There would be a pig in the ground, an ewe in the ground. People would bring food. I mean, there would be a whole table full of food. It was wonderful. What was so awe inspiring was that you when you arrived at the cabin on top of the hillside, you could see hundreds of people weaving through ropes through the woods. But, what would happen is that people would bring friends, which was cool. But then, people would bring friends of friends of friends. There were people who had no respect for anything. People started partying out on the trail. It just got out of hand; it just outgrew itself. The highway patrol would have to get traffic moving around the miles of horse trailers. It was a big deal."

"We parked the riders and horses all in the fields surrounding the clinic," Pat says. "The one year it rained, it was 34 degrees and rained from morning to night. We had log skidders, fortunately, and we pulled out every single vehicle. We pulled the last vehicle out at 4 a.m. We had to pull the trucks and the trailers and all the dumbasses that thought they had a big four-wheel drive trucks, they'd get all wound up and sliding around and got stuck."

"It was well known all over West Virginia, too," Dana says. "We had stickers and banners. Dr. Byers' band would come in after the ride and play. We would be expected to have everything cleaned up and be back to work the next day. Everyone thought it was a Horse Council event, or a public event, and it wasn't. It started out as an appreciation event for clients."

"And then one girl got kicked in the knee and broke her knee," Pat recalls. "Then one guy ran his horse to death up on the ridge. The horse collapsed and died."

216

"It was amazing," Jessica adds. "It was a big deal for a lot of people for a long time."

"They got angry when we stopped it," Jan Crall says. "They got mean."

"A lot of people quit coming to the clinic because Dad quit having the trail ride," Pat says.

"I went on two of these big trail rides," says Rich, Jessica's husband. "I think it was probably the last one. If you ride a horse, you don't have to do all the running."

"Unless you're a son or a daughter, because we got to do both," Pat says. "And I had to lead one of the rides. And I don't even like horses."

"But I remember riding with Pete," Rich adds. "We were obviously on the 26-mile trail. He was crisscrossing and literally avoiding the other riders."

"Avoiding other human beings," Jessica says.

"Five-hundred people," Rich marvels. "I was just, 'How can he do this?' We never saw another rider once we started out. It was a small group; Pete would literally avoid hundreds of people. And we always arrived right on time at the cabin," Rich said. "He would ride those half Arabian, half goofy horses on his trails, in his woods. He would ride places that you couldn't walk...and fast. You couldn't lead because you had no idea where you were going. There were branches, twigs and shit flying all over the place. My horse would usually follow Pete's horse."

"One year there was a girl from Murray City," Jody says, "who was running the horses along the side and pulled somebody else's rein and the horses fell. I told Pete we had to stop it. It was getting way out of hand. When it was just his clients it was okay. People came from Akron and from all over. The thing that ended it for me was a guy who was drinking. We never provided alcohol. He had his trailer down at the clinic. I'm assuming he was drunk and being a jackass. He was trying to get his horse in the trailer, just beating the tar out of it. I got mad because he was beating his horse! I told him to calm down and tie the horse up, that when Jessica got back, she knows all this Parelli stuff, and she would load the horse. He jumped on the horse and took it right up the middle of the highway.

217

He returned late that night for his horse trailer."

Annette Anderson remembers the year she rode the great trail ride. "It was an overcast, mild October morning," Annette says. "Trails of various distances had been marked ahead of time so riders could proceed at their own pace. They started at different points off the open fields. When I reached the summit, there were hundreds of horses and riders milling about expectantly on the rolling hills. Then Dr. Smith arrived on his big gelding. Everyone watched as he calmly sauntered into their midst. He rode to a commanding location and began to give directions, gesturing with his hands the location of the different trail heads. On cue, the masses began to move. Eager riders moved forward, toward the start of their selected trails. Not wanting to be caught behind slower riders, horses moved from trot to canter. In moments, the great throng broke into several groups and galloped over the hills in waves. I was caught up in the excitement. As Dr. Smith sat calmly on his horse taking it all in, I took part in what felt like a huge cavalry charge. It was glorious, and an amazing spectacle I will never forget.

"The people who had come to trail ride that day were a portion of Dr. Smith's large animal clients," Annette continues. "Through the day they told me stories of Dr. Smith's success. 'See this horse I'm riding? This horse should have died. The other vet had written him off, but Pete saved him.' Colics, injuries, and illness, all saved by Dr. Smith. Every year the trail ride grew, as the volume of large animal clients grew. Hundreds of trailers pulled onto the clinic property. I spent the day hauling truckload after truckload of potluck dishes over to the cabin where beef, lamb, and chicken had been prepared to serve the crowds. Dr. Smith was under pressure to turn the trail ride into a commercial operation. But after a mule was injured, and a lady thrown from a green mount, knocking her unconscious, Dr. Smith could see the *lawyers circling*, and in 2000, discontinued the annual ride."

A rider's serious mishap on the trail, and with so many diverse, unknown riders, it was more than the Smith family could handle. Tracey Thiele remembers the final incident. She had let her girlfriend borrow a favorite mare, Babe, that year. "My girlfriend didn't wait for me; she took off with her daughter," Tracey says. "So, I took a different trail. Everyone was racing to the cabin to get something to eat. On the trail, my girlfriend's daughter needed to adjust her saddle or bridle. Instead of getting off of Babe and holding the horse, she was still on Babe trying to hold her daughter's horse. They were all on a hill along the creek bed when Babe lost her balance; she had hopped up trying to gain her footing. Babe fell over on my girlfriend. There was a rock and a log there and Babe and my girlfriend were both injured. Someone called the emergency squad. My girlfriend ended up with a concussion and broken ribs. Later, Pete had to put Babe to sleep. That was the end of the Smith annual trail rides."

"Tracey's girlfriend refused to get on a four-wheeler," Sylvia says. "She gave them a hellish argument and they told her that it was the only way to get her out of the woods."

"I was up to the cabin before I knew of the accident," Tracey recalls. "I kept asking riders if they had seen my mare Babe and my girlfriend. It was when I had made it back to the clinic that someone told me there had been an accident. After they took my girlfriend to the hospital, they put Babe in a stall at the clinic."

"Pete already agreed that things were getting out of hand," Jody says. "He had already seen that there were so many who weren't clients, who weren't invited, and inviting a lot of other people. There were over 1,000 horses at that point. Pete had already made plans, that if 'anybody ever gets hurt, I'll quit.'"

There has never been a more appropriate
time or pressing need for audacious action.
Pete Smith

11 COMMUNITY

THE ATHENS COMMUNITY and surrounding areas embrace all
sorts of diverse people; natives, transits, university students, world-
renowned professionals, and more. It could be said it is the melting
pot of southeastern Ohio. With all the different personalities,
doctrines, dogmas, beliefs, and thought processes, it can sometimes
be difficult to weed out the common sense.

Pete was highly respected throughout the tristate area for his
keen intellect about any given subject, and his common-sense
approach. His early years set the stage for his ability to empathize
just about any human condition. He usually had an opinion on nearly
everything, if asked, and always had the *mot juste*.

As a veterinarian, Pete was closely associated with public
health. He played an important role in the care of livestock and the
prevention of disease outbreaks within herds and communities,
otherwise known as *epizootics*. Often, he would be consulted in
matters involving meat inspection and slaughtering. He emphasized
the importance of livestock inoculations to protect farms and
farmers against disease.

In the mid-1970s, the west side neighborhood of Athens
suffered a long run of animal strychnine poisoning. At first it was
believed that dogs were exposed to poison that was meant for

groundhogs. But too many dogs were getting sick or dying. Some of the dogs that were becoming ill were in kennels or tied. Pete was quickly notified of the conundrum and performed necropsies on the deceased dogs. He determined that the dogs had eaten chicken laced with strychnine.

"I'm aware of about a dozen cases of strychnine poisoning last year and that only about half the animals lived. Strychnine hasn't been used in medicine for 40 years or so. I wouldn't know where to get it," Pete told the local newspaper.

The dogs Pete treated for the poisoning were "really loaded" with strychnine, and taken in large doses a dog can have violent seizures in as little as 15 minutes. If the seizures are not halted, the dog will suffocate and die. To save the dog, the stomach must be pumped, filled with active charcoal, and administered a sedative.

"The only thing dog owners can do is keep their dogs confined and make sure they are not aggravating someone who may be tempted to solve the problem with poison," Pete concluded.

During that same time, Debbie Johnson, a local pet owner, wrote a letter to the local newspaper in praise of Pete:

Dear Editor:

I have a little white terrier. She doesn't bite or hurt anyone. She loves everyone, except Chis, our Siamese cat. She watches out the window when I get on the school bus in the mornings, and when I get home at night she's waiting for me.

I do not let her run loose. She stays in the house or on a chain outside. I let her loose only when we're playing outside and when I take her for walks. Sometimes she's ornery and runs away and I have to go catch her. I've always been afraid to let her go by herself, afraid she might get run over by a car or someone might steal her because she's so friendly. I never dreamed someone would try to kill her.

Recently, we were playing outside and she sneaked up the road. She was gone about a half hour by the time I missed her and found her. She just got back in the house and was awful sick. She jerked all over. We took her to Dr. Abbott P. Smith near Amesville. She almost died while I was holding her before we got her over there. Her tongue was even blue.

Dr. Smith gave her oxygen and worked with her until real late in the night. He's a very good doctor.

I worried and cried and prayed all night. My Mom and Dad and brothers and sisters worried, too.

Well, thanks to the good Dr. Smith and God my Bridgette didn't die. I brought her home. She's still not well yet, but I hope and pray she'll be all right.

I'm writing this because I don't know who poisoned my Bridgette and if they read this they'll know how sick Bridgette was and how sad I was and maybe they won't poison anyone else's dog because it hurts too much.

The treatment for strychnine poisoning needs to be administered quickly, along with charcoal, and counteractive medicine needs to be administered in intervals. Pete frequently called Jody on the clinic intercom to the house to tell her that he would be bringing a dog home that would need monitoring through the night. Jody would get out the large tarp to cover her mother's Oriental rug by their bed, put the special large wire dog crate that opened on the top and the front, line it with newspapers, towels and blankets, and be ready for their overnight guest. Pete would give the dog treatment through the night.

One evening when Jody returned home from helping teach dog obedience classes at the Athens Armory, Pete was quite proud of himself that he had gotten everything for the strychnine poison treatment set up; the cage, newspapers, blankets, etc., everything that is except the tarp to protect the expensive Oriental rug. That night, the dog had vomited fluids from the medications, including the charcoal. This required an expensive trip to Columbus to Menendian Oriental Rugs. They were able to successfully clean the expensive rug. It was all worth it; the dog lived.

Living near Ohio University, Pete was the subject of many dissertations, video documentaries, photo journalist assignments, newspaper articles, and more. Hocking County resident and fellow equestrian, Joy Miller-Upton, was working on her master's degree at Ohio University, enrolled in a video class and produced a video of Pete at work. She showed him in surgery, conducting office visits, and working around the clinic, as part of her class project. "Pete allowed complete access to himself and his facility," Joy says. "I named a dog after Pete. It was a little black and white, Cocker-looking, mutt. It wandered onto the farm about the same time Pete and Jody came out and had dinner with me."

Meetings, Speeches, and License

Staying on top of federal, state, and local laws governing the use of medicine and disease control was paramount for Pete. He was required to obtain the mandated continuing education units (CEU) for renewal of his veterinary license, as enforced by the Ohio State Licensing Board of Veterinary Medicine. The professional standards and education requirements could be earned through public speaking engagements, attendance at Ohio Veterinary Medical Association (OVMA) and AVMA meetings, as well as other recognized CEU events.

"Veterinarians have to have a certain number of hours every two years," Jody says. "Pete almost always had twice as much because he liked to go, of course, to the Equine Practitioners Meetings. He always was interested in what was new. I went with him twice to Western States Veterinary Conference held in Las Vegas."

Breakthroughs in veterinary science constantly occur; new techniques, procedures, and medicines. Pete was more than motivated to attend conventions and symposiums around the world to enhance his skills. He enjoyed the comradery of old colleagues, the trending topics, and the variety of available food. Pete and Jody attended OVMA annual meetings, along with their good friends, including Ohio State University veterinary graduates Hank Akers, Lyle Schultheis, and Bud Strouss.

Through the years Dr. Strouss and Sylvia Snabl enjoyed hosting Pete and Jody at their New Albany, Ohio, farm. When they attended OVMA and AVMA meetings together, Pete was often a guest speaker, giving informative discussions on innovative procedures and state-of-the-art pet care. Once, Pete addressed fellow practitioners during an OVMA Sunday morning general session, giving a presentation on "Tooth Care and Molar Leveling."

Dr. Strouss, Jody, Sylvia, and Pete traveled to meetings around the country. "When I first met Jody," Sylvia remembers, "it was when we came up for the OVMA meeting in 1983. Pete and Bud met at an internal medicine meeting in Chicago. We always stayed at the same hotel. One time, we were in Boston at an Equine Practitioners meeting, Bud's son Jay lived in the Boston area. Jay took us to a wonderful restaurant right on the wharf. The restaurant seated 19 people. There were nine of us in our party. We all ordered, and Pete was the last to order. They had a wonderful menu - seafood, pasta with squid ink sauce, that type of thing. Pete said, 'I'll have the shore dinner for six.' The server said, 'But sir, your entire party has already ordered.' And Pete said, 'It's for me.' The server said, 'But it serves six, sir.' Pete ate the whole thing. The moaning was horrible."

> Press Release
> Athens Veterinarian Convention Speaker
> Thursday, February 26, 1970
> Columbus – Veterinarians from all parts of Ohio met here this week to learn of the latest developments and treatment techniques in their profession. Among more than 1,100 veterinarians and their wives at the 86th annual meeting of the Ohio Veterinary Medical Association were Dr. and Mrs. Abbott Smith, Athens Route 3. Dr. Smith addressed the practitioners during a general session Sunday morning.

Community Events

There were many invitations to speak at community meetings and events. In March of 1967, Pete was asked to speak at the

Monday night Athens Kiwanis Club meeting. The topic was agriculture and pollution. Pete warned the attendees of the perilous world in which they lived.

"A coming food shortage may make survival a common problem for all men." Pete said. "The world will have to increase food production 150% by 1980. The world's population is increasing 2.2% annually, but food production increases 1.5%. In our own time economic and physical hardships will be suffered, and we can't sit by and watch this during our own lives, let alone those of our children."

Pete continued by criticizing government farm polices and government intervention. "It is hard to see the need for continued government suppression of agriculture, mostly an outgrowth of the 30s, which has removed domestic goods from the world market," Pete wrote in his prepared remarks.

In June of 1978, Pete was one of the guest speakers at the Athens County Animal Health Care and First Aid Workshop, held at Ohio University's Morton Hall. The topic was "What to do With Your Pet in an Emergency Situation and How to Maintain Preventive Health Care." The workshop was arranged by the Athens County Humane Society and the Athens Kennel Club. The event was covered by the *Athens Messenger's* student reporter Carol Jordan. Jordan's article included a picture of Pete with his signature mutton chop sideburns, a plaid flannel long-sleeve shirt, bending over a pet while securing a white bandage. The picture caption read, "FIRST AID – Dr. Abbott Smith, veterinarian from the Milliron Clinic, demonstrates how to bandage an injured pet, assisted by Joe Ann Croxford of the Athens County Kennel Club."

In June 1979, as president of the Athens County Taxpayers Association Inc. (ACT), Pete went on record saying, "We have to make our elected officials accountable. The only way we can have any control of this burgeoning bureaucracy is to control the purse strings. What we want is to let those who pay the bill pay what we want when we want them to." Pete continued his role in the taxpayers group for several years, even signing a political letter in 1981 along with fellow ACT to the *Athens Messenger* stating the ACT disagrees with the Ohio Department of Tax Equalization regarding property value rates and that a survey should be conducted by the County Auditor before hiking property taxes. As a land owner, Pete was resilient in promoting equitable tax laws and regulations.

The Unitarian Fellowship of Athens invited Pete to speak. Sunday, February 12, 1984, Pete delighted his audience. The synopsis of the symposium was as follows:

> Everyone's favorite vet, Dr. Pete Smith, will be with us to speak on "Animal Humor." Surely he will know whereof he speaks, since he has been delivering, doctoring, patching, and whatevering our animals in these parts for, lo, these 21 years. Having earned his D.V.M. degree at Colorado State University, Pete practiced in Lamar, Colorado, for a short time; he and Jody were attracted to Athens by the lure of cheap farm land. In 1963 he associated with Drs. Phillips and Bratton; a year later he established his Milliron Clinic near Amesville, where his practices have been about half and half in respect to large and small animals. He is the only vet in the area that has a horse operation table, which rotates to a vertical plane until the patient is led alongside it and strapped thereto, then rotates to any angle needed, including horizontal after the horse has been anesthetized. The wisdom of anesthetization is apparent.

Safety Town, a course for children sponsored by local civic organizations and businesses in cooperation with the Athens City School District, city administration and area police, fire and natural resource organizations, requested Pete to present several times. The summer course promotes safety awareness and is offered to local elementary students. Pete explained to students the perils of encountering dangerous and sick animals.

Pete was nominated and elected to serve as a supervisor to the Athens Soil Water and Conservation District (SCWD) Board. His introduction to the Board read:

Dr. Smith is a veterinarian. He, his wife, Jody, and their children, Jessica, 10, and Patrick, 8, enjoy horses and trail riding on their farm in Ames Township. Dr. Smith is also interested in racing Standardbreds. He says that his interest in the conservation program is based on a desire to "increase the wealth of his clients and to improve our environment for our children."

In January 1992 there was a concern about wild goats roaming the hillsides near Athens. The black-coated goats, which could be seen from time to time, favored the vegetation on a cliff overlooking the University Mall, on State Street. Pete informed the community via an article in the *Athens Messenger* written by Roy Cross that the goats are remnants of abandoned farms in the Dow Lake and Stroud's Run State Park region. Pete said that in the 1960s the goats were known for their destructive grazing, especially throughout orchards. The state rangers were brought in to get rid of the goats, but to no avail. "They probably missed some," Smith said.

Pete kept up-to-date about ongoing issues within the community regarding missing pets, informing pet owners of methods identifying their pets, such as branding and tattoos. An article published by the *Athens Messenger* headlines incidences of valuable, stolen dogs in the Athens area. Inset is a picture of Pete with gloved hands, gently holding Dave Sturbois' sedated family dog's hind leg. Pete gently engraves a tattoo on the dog's inner hind leg for identification. The second photo coinciding with the article is a picture of Mathew Sturbois, son of Mr. and Mrs. Dave Sturbois of Long Run Road. The caption continues, "Mathew is shown comforting his dog, Luke, before the animal is tattooed. David Sturbois urges owners have identification numbers tattooed on their pets to thwart what could be a dog stealing ring operating in the county."

Trying to Stop Dognappers
Dave Sturbois had his valuable cattle dogs tattooed. He's hoping that he won't have another dog stolen or if one is, it will be returned.

Sturbois had a cattle dog turn up missing last December – and he thinks it was stolen.

While looking for the missing dog, valued at more than $500, Sturbois said he found evidence of a possible dog theft ring in Athens County. He said many valuable dogs, both mixed breeds and purebreds, have been reported missing on Saturdays.

Just in the area of his Long Run Road home, Sturbois said he discovered that four other dogs had turned up missing the same day as his – all within a mile and a half of his home.

One of the dogs was a trained German Shepherd. Another was an Irish Setter.

"There's no reasonable explanation for that many dogs missing on one day. They were all good dogs without any history of running away or not coming home," he said.

Sturbois said that during his search for his cattle dog, he learned from a half dozen other people that their dogs had also turned up missing on Saturdays.

Sturbois placed an ad in the lost and found column for three weeks hoping to locate his dog, but had no luck. In addition, he has been calling all numbers of ads where dogs are reported missing, trying to put together a pattern in case there is a theft ring working in the area.

If there is a ring, there are only so many places the dogs can be sold, Sturbois said. One is to laboratories which conduct medical tests on adult dogs. Other sources are kennels or pet stores which attempt to sell the dogs.

"It is unrealistic to assume that someone is selling these dogs to individuals," Sturbois said.

Having dogs tattooed will make the dogs worthless to pet shops or most individuals and will increase the chances of having the dog returned to the owner.

Laboratories which operate on the animals will report the tattooed dog to the National Dog Registry for a $25 fee per number. Once the fee is paid for a number an unlimited number of dogs can be registered without additional cost.

Although there is no solid evidence of a dog theft ring working in the area, just tattooing a dog's inner leg can be relieving to the dog owner, knowing that the chances of a missing dog's return is improved.

Also Sturbois and Jody Smith, Amesville, have agreed to conduct a survey of missing dogs to supplement the information Sturbois has already collected, in an effort to get more information about a possible dog theft ring.

Pound Rescue

In 1999 and again in 2000, Pete was Rosanne Krager's guest on the local TV program *Rescue Matters Live*. Rosanne, a volunteer with Pound Rescue of Athens invited Pete to talk about pet adoption, pet care, and anything else that came to mind:

Rescue Matters Live with Dr. Pete Smith Transcript
DVD November 16, 1999 DVD #1002

Pete is sitting in the TV studio in khaki slacks, white t-shirt, plaid long sleeved cotton shirt, and a tan corduroy blazer/jacket. His small beard is white with splashes of dark grey. He gently twirls the small glass of water on the table beside him.

RK   My name is Rosanne Krager and I am a volunteer with Pound Rescue of Athens. This evening we have Dr. Pete Smith from the Milliron Clinic with us. Welcome

PS   Thank you.

RK   To start off tonight, we want to begin talking about greyhounds. I know you have worked at a greyhound track.

PS   Yes. I spent four or five years at the Mile High Kennel Club during their race seasons and as I was going through school as an assistant veterinarian. I

229

have a very high regard for them. They are so exquisite anatomically. Graceful in many respects, the most beautiful dog there is. Certainly the most graceful and the most aerodynamic [chuckles and smiles]. And good natured by and large.

RK There probably wasn't anything at that time such as rescuing greyhounds off the track?

PS Yes, there was a little bit, but not much.

RK Really.

PS Basically it was that type of thing, like with racehorses, if you don't run fast enough you die. So, since they are runners, there's very little hip dysplasia in greyhounds.

RK What's the age for a greyhound?

PS Well, they live about any dog that size; 12 to 14 years. Very nice dogs and incredibly socially competent in spite of not being socialized as young animals, which we all know is critical if you want a good pet, you need to socialize them for 6-12 weeks. It is a critical time.

RK What age do they take them?

PS I don't remember for sure, but I assume it's about a year, a year and a half.

RK So, they just keep them isolated then, until they race?

PS Pretty much. Yes.

RK And they race them at one year to two years of age?

PS Yes, I think so. Some of them are very durable. They race for many years. But, of course, if they aren't fast then they either find an adoptive home or they put them down. My class in vet school, all Colorado State University anatomy classes were done on greyhounds. It was a tremendous advantage because of the great muscle definition – no fat. They are incredibly fine anatomical specimens. We benefited greatly from that. They are good pets. I had close association with a lot of them, and

I have a greyhound skeleton at the clinic that's very dear to me. I call the skeleton Sidney.

RK Awe.

PS I really liked greyhounds.

RK So, you are saying they would make a good pet.

PS They are like people and other animals. Some of them are good and some of them aren't. But, on the average good.

RK But, you wouldn't want to let them lose to just run.

PS If they run, they're gone, typically. It's very difficult to have them come when you call them.

RK Can you ever really teach them that there's a place to go back to? Because they've never known that.

PS It's not their nature. They are a coursing hound and they love to run, and they do it so well. That's when they're happy, so that's what they do when they get the chance, and they just keep going. You don't always get them back.

RK I know we were also talking about some concerns that pet owners might be aware of. I know we are speaking of the parvo virus.

PS Yes. It's a really difficult situation in Athens County, which is a very poor, and probably the poorest county in the state. So you have a huge resident population of unvaccinated dogs which allows these very infectious virus' to build up steam and the same thing with distemper and cat leukemia.

RK Would the parvo virus stool be contagious?

PS Any body fluid really. Any stool.

RK It can be spread from cats and dogs the same way?

PS No. When parvo first hit, the only thing we had to use was cat the distemper virus, which was antigenically similar enough that it saved millions of dogs before there was a good parvo vaccine.

RK So, if a dog comes in, even as it's being diagnosed, is there a timeline you look at?

231

PS   Yes, but it's so important to prevent the virus. To kill a virus you can't typically use antibiotics because you can't kill a virus as such because the DNA in the virus is so much like the DNA in the cell nuclei. If you kill the virus, you kill the host. So, you can give them antibodies by way of blood. You can vaccinate, which gives them an interferon response, antibodies and so forth in a couple of weeks, but it's going to cost. Just the IV fluids and blood transfusion can run a couple of hundred dollars quickly. If it happens to be a Rottweiler or a Husky, one of those breeds that are incredibly vulnerable to it, then it might die anyway. So, you need to vaccinate them in advance. But parvo virus is not very antigenic. So, in a hot area like this, we've only been successful in preventing it with a twice a year vaccination. It's a challenge and the dog show people typically do it at least four times a year. It's just not a great vaccine. It's sort of like the Chlamydia organisms in the cat cough and lemoniids thing and it's just not very antigenic.

RK   You mean to give frequently?

PS   Yes.

RK   Well, that's interesting.

PS   So, that's one of the ones that's given to the puppy, but as a dog owner you should have that done say at least twice a year. You have to give them a series to start with, to bump them up where they can coast for a year. Then after that, you can give in six month intervals. About all the other vaccines will last about a year, but parvo, it's one of the tougher ones to get a good immunity to.

RK   The other one, I know we had spoken about is heartworms, too. We were talking on the last show. You would think you would see it more in the summer.

PS Yes, but we've had such mild winters, like the last ten, really, every winter since the late seventies has been mild enough that there were mosquitoes every month of the year.

RK If you are buying heartworm medication, you think it's okay if you don't give it over the winter? Do a lot of people have that feeling?

PS Yes. Most of the ones we use nowadays do a good job of worming them, too. It's not a bad idea, I think, especially if you are in an endemic area like Sunday or Monday Creeks locally, to just do it all the time. Athens itself is not a particularly high-risk area, but the outlying areas to the north definitely are. Starting at The Plains right on north, all of that is pretty rough.

RK So, what's the timeline for heart worms? Are there signs?

PS It's probably going to be at least six months before he even shows, before you can test it. As far as the microfilaria in the blood, then it's going to be another six months to a year before you'd see any cough or weakness or whatever.

RK At that point, is it beyond...?

PS Well, we had a couple of boxers that came through the Panama Canal on the deck of a freighter; you can imagine what the mosquitoes were like there. They had more microfilaria than they had red blood cells and they made it, but it was hard on them. The treatment is very successful and very simple nowadays.

RK It's just hard to keep them still for six weeks, or keep them calm for six weeks.

PS Well, you have about ten weeks actually, of course, the fate of the adult heartworms on the right side of the heart is to act as emboli and they die. Once they die they carry into the lungs where they are broken up and broken down and sort of re-assimilated, you

know, then gotten rid of, but that is a lot of clots in
your lungs. You have to be relatively careful,
especially if it's a bad case, to keep them kind of
quiet through that time.

RK So, let me ask you, as you get them and they've
successfully gone through the treatment, you
presume that they could not miss heartworm
medication?

PS Well, that would be stupid, wouldn't it?

RK You think, but you never know. Does it make them
more susceptible to getting it again?

PS Just do the same thing over and over again. Parvo,
heartworms, whatever.

RK I mean, do they get it easier?

PS Well, not really. But you can't go through
something like that without a little damage.

RK Right, and if it was really far along...

PS Your lungs are going to be a little less functional if
you had a hundred worms, maybe a foot long,
break up and carried out as emboli, blocking off
and plugging all these areas. You can't be as good
as you were. It's rough. In fact, interestingly, in
Dade County, Florida, where, of course, Florida is
the heartworm capital of the universe. In Dade
County, Florida, they crack about a chest a month
on people where the heartworms have made it as
far as causing a lump in the lungs that is taken for
cancer and they are opened to get it early and it
turns out to be a heartworm larva, so you just kind
of wonder how long it will be before they figure
out how to do the same thing to us and we will be
on the heartworm pills.

RK Wow.

PS Terrible disease really.

RK It is because I don't think you see anything right
away to let you know what it is.

PS   It's like hookworms, you might be dead by the time you know you have them.

RK   That's awful. Something else we thought might be real important to bring up is this time of year people are bringing their plants in the house. Any specific plants you can think of that people might need to be aware of?

PS   Of course, everybody knows about poinsettias, but they aren't really as poisonous as we once thought. I don't know of a house plant that isn't kind of poisonous. They can eat a lot of spider plant, for instance, and not get hurt much, but if you want to do something for your dog, in that light, you might give it sprouts or something. You see, in their natural state, a dog, or a cat, would get its salad from the partially digested gut content of the rabbits and the chipmunks, so forth, that they eat. That's important to them because the food that they eat out of the dog food bag is petrified, it's extremely over processed. So it has no vitamins, no life to it, no way of keeping up their gut flora, no vitamins, and so they try to duplicate that by eating houseplants and grass which they can't digest because their guts are not designed for that. A cat, which is a strict carnivore, has a gut about as long as it is. Where a horse, which can make meat out of hay, has a gut eighteen times as long its length, it's specifically designed to process forage. The best way to compensate for that is to give them vitamins. They have a definite need for them because there is really none in the food, and there is no significant bacterial content or the stuff wouldn't keep on the shelf. It's dead. Dead. Dead. So, the two things you need to make up for that petrified stuff that you feed them, which is what I feed my dog, too, is yogurt, Dannon Yogurt. It is by far the best culture. Keep them full of good bugs so the bad guys can't set up.

RK   How often do you give them that?

PS   Every day, all their lives. Every dog and cat.

RK   How much?

PS   Say about a teaspoon per ten pounds of body weight. Teaspoon for a cat or a small dog; a heaping tablespoon for a bigger dog. So, that keeps them full of good bugs, keeps everything perking right, keeps them satisfied, and then the vitamins, because there are really none in the food.

RK   May I ask you this, have you ever heard of giving them vitamin C?

PS   Yes. It's a great antioxidant, but there is no proof of any kind that vitamin C is beneficial to dogs or cats. I certainly don't know any harm, other than over doing it and they have an acid problem, or something, but, uh, it's not a biggie.

RK   What about dogs that they say eats grass if they want to regurgitate something?

PS   If you wanted to duplicate that, it would have to be a very fragile, delicate, easily digested thing like sprouts. That would be the only thing they could possibly digest with their limited gut length. They have very little time to digest it as it goes through quickly. In 45 minutes the vegetable matter or whatever they ate in a normal healthy dog or cat gut is through the stomach, through the small intestine, through the large intestine, just waiting to be expelled.

RK   No kidding, that fast.

PS   It doesn't take long. We know that from doing barium series. I mean, if the guts working right, it doesn't take long to process.

RK   Ok, so what about dogs that eat dirt.

PS   They're trying to find vitamins and minerals. Minerals in that case.

RK   You would think it would be awful, but I've seen them eat a clod of dirt.

PS   Awe, they eat worse than that. [hearty laugh]

RK   And the dogs that tend to eat their excrement. And what about that?

PS   Well, you can see they're missing something there. They're looking for something.

RK   Unfortunately, we don't know what it is. And cats, too?

PS   Cats are much more discrete than dogs. Much more discerning.

RK   Do they eat grass?

PS   They eat good stuff. Dogs are scavengers.

RK   So, I guess I am thinking, more so that I've heard cat owners say that they have used the plants, the potting plants, they are the ones that get more into the plants, more than dogs.

PS   Sure. Cats are into decorating [splays his arms] and entertainment.

RK   But, I heard that if you keep catnip that they...

PS   They'd be swinging from the chandeliers if it was catnip. Everything is a playground to a cat. You know, he's going to make the best of it.

RK   That might not be to your benefit [laughing] So, maybe you shouldn't have catnip.

PS   Oh, catnip's great, I'm not knocking catnip, I am just saying that it doesn't have any nutritional benefits, it's just for fun. It's a recreational drug. [laughing]

RK   Any closing comments?

PS   It's been great fun, I've enjoyed it very much. I just want to encourage everybody: if you want to have an animal, make sure you really want it. And, if you get it, commit to it; spay it, neuter it, vaccinate it and hold the number at an affordable, happy level for you so that you can enjoy it.

RK   Now when do our tags go on sale?

PS   Oh, I think they are going door to door as we speak. Arresting people [laughing] that don't have them. It's so much better than raising the rates on those of us who do buy them. I am really heartened to see that. I think it's wonderful. I think they should be commended for that. And, they could do things like charge less for licenses on neutered dogs, on intact dogs, rather than gouge the people who are doing the responsible thing and paying their fees. And, they are making a step in the right direction right now.

RK   People don't realize the importance of their identification. If they find your dog, they can contact you. The dogs that I find, I always look to see if they have a tag.

PS   They are making a step in the right direction. If you have a 'lavatory retriever' this way you get it back. [laughing…]

My home and life were filled with wonderful books,
reference materials and suitable mythological heroes
(as perfect heroes must be) …
Pete Smith

———————

12 A VETERINARIAN'S PASTTIME

BESIDES PETE'S INVOLVEMENT in keeping the community
abreast about pet care, breeding, and overall wellness, he was
interested in the community's history and antiquity. The area in
which he practiced and lived is rich with historical relics, bygone
stories, and forefather residue. Amesville, rich in historic sediment,
houses the Coonskin Library. The library was built in 1804 funded
entirely by the sale of coonskins. It was built almost a century before
Dale Carnegie's widespread library beneficence. Pete's mother,
Betty, had a nasty fall while perusing the library shelves. She
suddenly fell and broke her wrist. Pete took her to the local hospital.
He asked how long it would be, then discussed it with his mother,
left her there to be treated, and went to a movie. A practical
arrangement, rather typical of their relationship.

Pete was in the highlight of his career at this point, well-known
throughout the tri-state area for his healing hands, precision surgical
techniques, and cutting-edge ideas. He retired from farm calls,
mostly, and worked out of the clinic. He had gained respect and
confidence from the locals, his colleagues, and animals. With age
and work, his body sometimes worked against him, aches and pains
set in, a typical sign of aging – exacerbated in his case by the wear
and tear from decades of wrestling animals, farming, and logging.
Jody reflects, "He had the look of an Amish man there for a while
with his mutton chops. He had long sideburns. I didn't care much

for those. He had a mustache and a beard for a while, too, which I liked."

Pete and Jody were fervent advocates of the local arts. Movies were a favorite pastime. Pete would sit through the very end of a movie to view the credits. He appreciated and enjoyed everything about a movie: casting, direction, music, sets, etc. He was an avid reader, and enjoyed returning to work by Pliny the Elder (AD 23-79), a Roman Statesman, naturalist and philosopher. The Smith home remains saturated with magazines, obscure farming and veterinary periodicals, popular and reference books - words and writing too valuable to throw away – a treasure trove of reading material, mostly books which any librarian would be proud of. In his second-story sawmill office, Pete built high bookshelves lining hand-hewed walls showcasing his lifetime collection of literary finds. An avid reader and connoisseur of the arts, Pete read everything. "He had several magazines he read," says Jody. "He really didn't read for fun. He did like Westerns. That was his main diversion. But we read; the two of us."

Whenever time allowed, Pete and Jody attended lectures at Ohio University, theater productions at Memorial Auditorium, and other local artistic events. They were members of The Dairy Barn Cultural Center. When Pete first arrived in Athens, he treated the therapeutic dairy herd in the same barn.

Joy Miller-Upton, a former public relations employee of a local hospital, remembers a fancy benefit for the hospital at the Dairy Barn. It was to introduce new doctors to the hospital's staff and the community, as well as being a fundraiser with all the upper crust of Athens society there. Everyone was dressed up, milling around an exhibit of paintings and sculpture. "Halfway through the event, in the midst of all this Pete and Jody walk in," Joy recalls. "Obviously they were in between farm calls and didn't have the opportunity to change clothes. Their boots were covered with what you are covered with when you come out of the barn. They just kind of wandered in. They were members of the Dairy Barn. Pete said, 'We just wanted to see this show. Aren't we allowed to be in here now?' I said, 'Of course!' They wandered around, not only looking at the art in the show, but talking to the people. Pete fit into any situation. He knew everybody, they knew him. Pete and Jody were as comfortable as those who had on their go-to-Sunday-meeting-clothes. Next thing you know, they had a plate of food in their hand. It was that whole thing - Pete fit wherever he walked into."

Jody remembers driving with Pete home from a classical concert at Ohio University's Memorial Auditorium. It wasn't terribly late at night, about 9:30 or 10:00, but there was a crowd on either side of the road by a bar called Sweet Water Station, later dubbed the Silver Saddle. Wisely, Pete slowed way down. There was a guy crawling up the center line on State Route 550, too drunk to stand. Pete had to drive off to the side a little bit as the crowd moved away from the highway. Jody noted when they passed the 50A Inn that Pat used to play pool there during his high school years.

As well-thought-of, culturally-minded residents, Pete and Jody would often be invited to uptown social galas, art exhibitions, fireside chats, neighborhood picnics, and dances. "Pete was a fair dancer, but his aches and pains from injuries bothered him too much," Jody says.

Once they received an invitation to a local birthday party. They decided to attend, unsure of the party aesthetics, but felt the need to venture from the farm. Driving along the host's driveway, they spied a little hut donning a sign that said, "Nobody Under 16." Jody couldn't get Pete out of the car. It was a cornucopia of social awkwardness.

"This place is going to get raided!" Pete claimed with complete certainty.

The distinct fragrance of marijuana could be whiffed while still in the driveway. The perils of living in a university town includes invitations to all types of venues, but this one was not for Pete and Jody. Without any further ado, they returned home.

Being in the public eye and talking about vetting could also have its adverse consequences. Veterinary work is not for the squeamish, nor for those listening in on tales of that day's surgeries. Once the Smiths were at the annual Equine Practitioners meeting in

San Francisco, and they and some friends all went to a fancy restaurant afterwards. Jody remembers, "And they started talking about taking a dead foal out of a mare in pieces. And the waiter just about went under the table. He couldn't handle it. We had to get a different waiter!"

Jerry Hartley invited Pete over to his home for dinner many times. Afterward, Pete liked to relax and watch a movie. Pete enjoyed watching movies and would catch a movie whenever he had free time. They enjoyed watching Katharine Hepburn and Peter O'Toole starring in the classic film A Lion in Winter. "Pete would watch it time and time again, just to relax and unwind," Jerry says. "He liked Henry the Eighth. Pete watched it so many times, I just couldn't watch it anymore."

In1984, Virginia Haley, Jody's mother, penned Pete a letter in response to his empathy for Jody's father, Bart, who was experiencing terminal cancer. The letter documents Pete's compassion towards his father-in-law as well as his prevalent thoughts of the afterlife. We shall never know what Pete wrote to Bart, but we can surmise the contents of Pete's letter from Virginia's response.

> Dearest Pete:
> Your masterpiece of such a wonderful letter to Bart – so well expressed your feelings to and about Bart's present and future life gave us both the relief of our grief that we needed. I had to have Betty, the aid that was taking care of Bart, read your letter to him. At his request, have read it to him, Pete, every day since. You will never know how much you helped us both. Just beautiful, and so promising for the next life.

As children, Jessica and Pat were required to attend Sunday school and Christmas Eve services. "On Christmas Eve Jessica would be wide awake at the church service and Pat would fall asleep in the pew," Jody remembers. "Pete always said, 'If you are eating at my house and sleeping here, then you are going to go to church on Sunday!' As youngsters, Jessica and Pat would alternate between the Athens Episcopal Church and the nearby, rural church.

Jessica was in the church program once, Jody remembers, but Pat was too young, about five, and he sat in the pew with Jody. "All of a sudden he walked up through the pews to the front of the church. As soon as the church was silent he sang solo *Jesus Loves Me*. It was adorable."

One Sunday, coming home from the local church, Jody noticed that Jessica and Pat were whispering away in the back seat. They were eight and six at the time. Jody could see that they were very concerned. "What are you worried about?" Jody asked. Jessica replied, "Oh, that preacher said that if we don't get all of our little friends to come to church, they are all going to go to hell." Jody said, "Fortunately he is not in charge of that." That was the end of attending that Sunday school. The family did, however, return to church for homecomings and social events.

"Jessica never cared for liturgical church," Jody says. "She is now a Quaker. When Pete had a broken ankle, we had to drive him right to the door of the Episcopal Church to let him out of the car. All of the Bishops were standing outside in their robes. Jessica said, 'It looks like a gathering of the Klu Klux Clan!' I said, 'Take a really good look daughter!' Our Bishop was very African American."

The Christmas season was a bit leaner as clients were on holiday and appointments slowed down. One Christmas Eve, Jessica brought a friend home for the holidays, an Ohio University student whom Jessica invited to spend the holiday at the farmhouse. Pete, Jody, Jessica, and Pat had a gift exchange, re-giving something they already owned. Jessica's friend watched with raised brows as the Smith family opened their presents. Each present contained a gun. They all were marksmen and each one appreciated the gift. "Later that week," Jody smiled, "Jessica's friend saw me on Court Street in Athens. We were walking down the same side of the street, until he saw me and he crossed to the other side. I suppose he remembered that we exchanged guns for Christmas."

Traveling to McDougal Cemetery once with Willie LaFollette, Pete and Jody looked around at the headstones. Willie talked them into buying four burial plots. There were quite a few for sale at the time, now it's all sold out. "We were walking through the cemetery," Jody remembers, "and Willie said, "Oh, you'll really like this one. Come up and see this one. The view is great from here." I said, 'Willie, I hope we'll be looking down. I don't think we'll be looking out.'"

Pete did not believe in astrology or horoscopes. He would read his Gemini horoscope in the daily newspaper as a joke. However, he was aware of the astrological chart on castrating animals within moon signs. It was a common event that clients would request castration of their livestock according to the astrological charts. Pete thought there was something to it; animals castrated within astrological alignment statistically had less bleeding than those who were not. He had witnessed the effect first hand with good results. "In his early days, he would de-skunk skunks once a year on the 4th of July," Annette Anderson said. "That's all he did that day. People would bring in skunks all day. It had something to do with the time of year. He finally stopped doing it due to concerns about rabies." Nancy Bonnett provided Pete with an astrological calendar every year. Pete used the calendar frequently to schedule castrations and to pinpoint the setting of the full moons.

A little superstitious - just a little - when in doubt about yes or no questions, Pete would flip a coin. Pete knew the Scriptures well. He knew Acts 1:26 referenced how the disciples prayed and cast lots when indecisive. Pete was known to flip a coin when in doubt, usually going for two out of three, tossing the coin high in the air and watching it fall. He had used this method of discerning many times, even back in high school.

As a fan of American mystic, Edgar Cayce, Pete and Jody would attend A.R.E. (Association for Research and Enlightenment) meetings throughout the area. At one particular meeting, they had the opportunity to meet Hugh Lynn Cayce, Edgar Cayce's son. Country neighbors Connie and Jimmy Lowe would host A.R.E. meetings at their lovely old farmhouse.

"We would get up early in the morning before Pete had appointments and read the Bible. We read completely through it several times," Jody reflects. "We were rarely interrupted in the early morning; hopeless to read in the evening. We read through *The Urantia Book*, which is a huge book. Pete really liked that book. He got a lot more out of it than I did. It's got the most beautiful description of Jesus that I've ever read. The Urantia Fellowship is based out of Chicago. If you read down the list of writers, one of them is the Archangel Michael. Pete read it two or three times. When we read the Bible, either I would read it while he was eating his breakfast, or we'd read a chapter back and forth. We each had our own bookmark within the same book. Pete liked to read *Comparative Religion* and *The Christian Agnostic* by Leslie D. Weatherhead, it was one of his favorite books. He always tried to seek greater heights of love and understanding."

There is one book that you will not find in his sawmill library. It is Napoleon Hill's *Think and Grow Rich*. Along with a few other treasured books, Pete valued it too much to be kept with just any book collection. It is labeled as one of the world's most powerful books, claiming both personal and financial power. Hill studied the methods of philanthropist Dale Carnegie's secret to wealth and influence. The premise of the book is that you subconsciously determine your own success and financial status; that each individual is responsible for opening the door to untold riches, literally think and grow rich. Pete's copy is slightly worn and smells a little musty.

As a believer in the theory that God helps those who help themselves, Pete was continually willing to grow and persevere in all areas of his life. He liked the company of well-read, scholarly individuals, those who could challenge his way of thinking and bring new ideas and thoughts to the table. Pete's idle time was filled with classic entertainment; movies, theater, concerts, a good book, a game of chess, and much more. He was conscious of current events and watched the evening news whenever time allowed.

"One time we took a meditation course at Ohio University with instructor Cecilia Renaldi," Jody remembers. "I really wanted him to go. We fell asleep during the first session. It was winter, Pete had just come in from the woods, and I came in from barn chores. The university building was overheated. The first two classes, Cecilia would kindly say it was all right, that we would absorb some of the material subconsciously. Finally, she'd had enough, 'Can't you two ever stay awake?'

"To relieve stress and tension," Jody continues, "Pete would go swimming at the Ohio University indoor pool. He loved to swim, a trait he passed on to Noah, our grandson."

Jessica remembers how Pete loved jogging in the community. "He jogged the ten-mile trek around State Routes 690 and 550, Dutch Creek Road," Jessica says. "He loved southeast Ohio."

Pete relied on God, all of the time, to handle his finances - and God did, on occasion. Long-time client and friend Marie Phillips willed her family farm to Pete. It was at a time when Pete was almost bankrupt; too much yellow-iron disease (three bulldozers), too many bad (sheep) investments, too many land mortgages to service, too many clients off-the-hook with their vet work, and too many big dreams. But at the end of the day, God intervened in the form of Marie and her gift. Marie had several animals and the Smiths took their stock trailer to pick them up. There were chickens, two dogs, Bullet and Sissy, and a lot of cats. The will stated that the Smiths were to take perpetual care of the animals. After contemplating his good fortune, Pete decided to sell Marie's property. The chickens were given free-range in the Smith barnyard. Bullet and Sissy lived with Pete and Jody.

Another great fortune was the natural gas wells on Milliron Farm. Pete signed a lease with L & B Oil Company for $60,000, a large sum for mineral/gas rights at the time. It helped to keep the family and clinic staying afloat and solvent. Later, L&B's representative came to the clinic. "Pete was busy and signed the addition to the lease without really reading it," Jody says. "The oilman said we would get another $10,000. I was excited about that because I had fallen in love with Bob Evans' Spanish Mustang stallion, The Gambler, who was for sale. I told the rep that I wouldn't sign it unless our attorney looked at it first. The oilman grabbed the papers, left the office and we never saw or heard from him again. They never drilled and the lease ran out. I've always wondered what those papers contained."

Bill Hines' Thursday Night

Social time included a weekly rendezvous with the local men, usually at the home of Bill Hines, known for his brown Swiss cattle, homemade peach brandy, fresh milk, homemade butter, and buttermilk. Pete was Bill's vet. "Pete rarely over-drank, except for those Thursday nights. They evidentially drank something besides beer, maybe moonshine." Jody says. "I would always say, 'Take your keys out of your truck.' But he would not. After he came back from there, for some reason or other, he would always take his keys out of his truck. I don't know if he was paranoid, or what."

Brad Maxwell, a local cattleman, one of Pete's clients, was one of the regulars to Bill Hines' place on Thursday night. Brad says, "I was at Bill's place and one of his cows was in trouble. Bill needed a vet right away. I went in Bill's house and called Milliron Clinic. It wasn't the regular receptionist who answered the phone and she said that Pete no longer made farm calls. I told her to tell Pete that Bill Hines needed him. She said, 'Well, that really doesn't make a difference.' I said, 'Just tell Pete, Bill needs him. Just do it.' She said, 'Well...' I said, 'Just do it.' Finally, she said, 'Well, here's Pete, hold on.' I heard Pete in the background to tell me that he would be at Bill's farm in fifteen minutes. I heard the girl say, 'Well, you don't make farm calls.' Pete said, 'For Bill Hines I do. I'll be there in fifteen minutes.' Pete came and we worked on the cow.

"Pete wasn't a very good drinker at the Thursday night gatherings," Brad laughs. "We used to sit around, shoot the shit and drink Lord Calverts and 7Up. Most people are smart enough to put two fingers in the bottom of a glass and fill it with 7Up. Well, Pete would fill the glass half full of whiskey and then add 7Up. It just didn't work well for him.

"There was me, Pete, Bill, Gene Hines occasionally, Bill Gasgella was another one. Just various people throughout Ames Township. Usually about 9 p.m. everybody would show up at Bill's house. We solved world problems. It was a getaway place for people to go. We would talk about everything. Local news and bullshit. It was a place where Pete could get away from being Pete Smith, the vet. Pete was a good guy. He always dealt fair with everybody and I always liked bullshitting with him on Thursday night. Pete was my vet for years. I had cattle and dogs. There was one night that he got too much moonshine and we had to take him home. In the early 80s Pete was on his way to Bill's, not on a Thursday night. Pete used to buy milk off of Bill. The one night he stopped over in Glouster and bought a pizza. He sat in the front seat of his car. Pete never locked his Cadillac. He stopped at Bill's to pick up his milk. When he got back to the car, his dog had bumped the locks and locked the car from the inside. The dog flipped the pizza box and ate all the toppings off, everything but the crust. He finally got a clothes hanger and unlocked the car. When he got to his pizza and found that it was half gone, he said, 'Now there's man's best friend. At least he left me the crust.' Bill Hines passed away in 1998. That was the end of Thursday nights at Bill's."

President Obama

On February 1, 2009, Pete felt it his patriotic duty to write President Obama a letter in regard to legalizing marijuana. Yes, you read it correctly, legalizing marijuana. A prolific thinker and people advocate, Pete penned his thoughts and ideas before marijuana was legalized in Colorado, the first state to do so in the USA.

Dear President Obama,

Congratulations! Along with the vast majority of the world's population, I'm delighted that you are now the man!

There has never been a more appropriate time or pressing need for audacious action.

First, we should legalize, tax, and regulate marijuana, cocaine, and heroin, which would generate untold reve-nue and eliminate most crime, since most drug related crime is caused by the money. The better the interdiction the more expensive the drugs and thus more crime. Cheap legal drugs mean lots of money for the U.S. Gov-ernment, but none for organized crime and obviously a

$6.00/a day habit has no social consequence compared to a $600.00/a day habit. Our shameful prison population would be quickly reduced by about 50%. Cheap, clean drugs from a government health source would reduce Hepatitis C, Aids, etc. and each time a drug purchase was made the addict would be exposed to help, education, and counter-addiction strategies in a legal, safe, confidential non-threatening environment. Our current system is a dismal and expensive failure so why not talk to the folks in Holland and see how the idea has been working for them. A trillion or so a year at almost no cost would come in handy right now.

P.S. Your reaction (and mine) to this idea is probably to blow it off as perhaps an interesting concept, but totally impractical and unacceptable due to political unpalatability and moral, ethical, religious and emotional issues, but stop a minute and think. Alcohol can be a terrible taskmaster and we all personally or peripherally know of the tragedies that can accompany its use. Always was and always will. However, before prohibition ended, remember Al Capone types and Valentine's Day massacre were events which are now almost unheard of because alcohol is now legitimate, available, and cheap. Not to mention the billions in revenue produced. Look at your daily newspaper or police blotter or TV news and there is almost no mention of crime related to legal personal addictions to alcohol, nicotine, or caffeine. A veritable artesian well of trillions of dollars badly needed by the government goes untapped in drug money other than graft. Marijuana is well known to be the largest dollar agricultural commodity in most states, but being criminalized and unregulated causes only trouble rather than producing billions in state, local, and federal revenue.

There would be little point in criminals recruiting addicts for money if drugs were cheap and legal. Addiction has been and will be with us always, but ending drug prohibition can stop the associated social consequences of crime, graft and corruption.

A vibrant economy and functional social programs produce meaningful work and negate many of the gateway factors to drug use. We know that prison time graduates hundreds of thousands of hardened criminals with connections each year besides impoverishing and breaking up those families. No other society imprisons the percentage of the population that we do. You can balance the budget in just a year or two and eliminate most crime with the old bold stroke of ending this era of drug prohibition.

Ecuador

"Pete!" sister Janet said on the other end of the line. She had been in a riding accident and was laid up with a bad back. "I have a ride scheduled to Ecuador. I won't be able to go. Will you go in my place?"

Without hesitation, Pete replied "Yes!"

Janet had been "legging up" - getting herself in shape for the Ecuador ride - when she injured her back. She was an expert rider, but had taken a bad spill. The trip to Ecuador was a trip of a lifetime. It was a custom ride "for competent and experienced riders" the Andean Rodeo Ride, November 24 – December 3, 2000. Limited to eight riders, the ride "journeyed back in time along ancient Inca and Spanish colonial routes, between prestigious Haciendas in two stunningly beautiful, yet very distinct areas of the Andean highlands."

Janet faxed the itinerary to Pete. He was excited and ready to go, but there was a problem. His passport was about to expire. "Someone told him he had to go to Chicago to get a passport extension," Jody remembers. "We left after clinic office hours ended and arrived in downtown Chicago about 2:00 a.m. and everything was fine except, according to our map, all the one-way streets were the other way. So, we finally find the cotton-pickin' place. We found a nearby parking garage, but needed to find a hotel. It cost $400 a night to stay in a hotel! I told Pete there was no way we were going to pay that price to stay in a hotel. We ended up sleeping in the car in the parking garage. The next morning, we were first in line at the passport office. The lady tells us that they can't fulfill Pete's request. Pete, upset, began hollering. A very large armed guard came forward. I told Pete to please go sit down. I asked the clerk if I could please talk to the person in charge. I explained the whole thing; a last minute situation. She gave him an extension. This lady was reasonable enough."

On November 24, 2000, Pete flew into the Quito airport and was met by a bilingual guide. After a night at Quito's Hostal Mi Casa, Pete and his fellow riders were driven by bus north of Quito, to the Otavalo area where they visited the colorful local market. By nightfall, they were assigned rooms at the picturesque Hacienda Pinsaqui. The next morning, the group saddled-up and rode for five days to Mojanda Mountain, San Pablo Lake, and the Zuleta Valley, finally returning to Quito by way of Cayambe and the Equator Line.

Provided horses were warm/hot blood lines (English, Arabians, Pasos) crossed with Criollo (descendants of the Spanish Conquistadors), ideally suited for the rugged terrain and high altitudes – as much as 12,600 ft. Horses were matched expertly with riders. Each rider was provided South American western tack, mostly US Cavalry saddles.

November 30, 2000, the group departed Quito and drove south to the "avenue of volcanoes" to a working Sierra cattle ranch, the Hacienda Yanahurco. The next day, along with the Andean cowhands, Pete helped to round up 2000 head of cattle, including chogras, the Spanish fighting bulls. Along the way, Pete had connected with interesting people who shared his enthusiasm for the outdoors and horsemanship. It was a great adventure for Pete, and a grand vacation, reminiscent of his days in Colorado; the smell of the herd, mountain views, and the thrill of the ride. He embraced every moment. There were strong bulls kept in a separate pen only to be challenged in the bullfight arena that night. The giant herds of cattle, exotic people, patchwork of fields, and the spectacular scenery would be the topic of conversation once back in Ohio. After several days in the lush Andean highlands, the tour was over and Pete was taken back to the Quito airport to catch his flight back home.

Panama

The Panama ride was organized by Bill Sprayberry and Bob McIntosh. Bob is Australian, but has lived in Panama for the last 50 years or so. Both are intriguing, charismatic horsemen who connected with Pete at their first meeting. Bob considers it his good fortune to have met Pete on the Ecuador ride in November 2000. Bob reminisces, "We interchanged jokes continually during the ten day ride; what a character."

Pete enticed fellow equestrians Eric and Rhonda Curfman to travel to Panama with him. The threesome flew into Florida in early February, meeting up with Bill and Bob, then finally Hal, who would journey by horseback across the Continental Divide through the Panamanian jungles. "When we slept," Eric remembers, "we didn't have electric, we just had candlelight and torches, or whatever. We took along a few snacks, and ate local nuts and fruit. All along this road, there would be cut out places, and there would be bamboo like huts and a little garden with corn where people lived. The next morning when we got up we would meet little kids walking to school. No matter how old they were - five or fifteen - they all carried machetes. They were all real friendly.

"I have a panoramic picture of Pete with his arms up in the air once we arrived at the Gulf of Mexico. It had stormed that night and it was rough. It looked like Jurassic Park. One of the first times we stopped to take a break, Pete had this habit, no matter where he was at; he would just fall down on the ground and lay there. He'd actually go to sleep if we had time. He was lying there one time and the air turned blue. He was up out of there. Fire ants! He moved and screamed with a few choice words! Seconds later, everything was back to normal."

Near the gulf, Eric and Rhonda stayed in a woman's hut, sleeping in a homemade bamboo bed, while Pete didn't get a bed and slept on the ground. Eric was struck that, unlike everyone else, Pete didn't take any pictures - he didn't believe in picture taking.

"So, we get back to the little village," Eric continues, "and we tie our horses to the road bank. That was where they were when we got them; threw the saddle off mine. We had ridden up there in the

252

car, but we walked back to the hotel. We go in and the lady asked us if we were hungry and she fixed us a chicken dinner and, boy, it was really good. We're sitting there and our chicken dinner comes out and Pete walks in. So, what's Pete do? He grabs a fork - there goes my piece of chicken, and he grabbed the biggest piece!"

Pete wrote an account of his Panama trip. He was going to send the letter to his guides, but decided to tuck it away for posterity:

> One can only imagine why Bob decided to undertake an outward bound eclectic, psycho challenge ride of such unique proportions. At least in retrospect I think we are grateful. He and I had both fondly recalled the basic joys of humans needs met. To be really tired and find rest - thirsty and drink - cold then heat - sexual abstinence - and well, you get the idea. This ride with its small compatible group definitely accomplished most of those objectives. I immediately lost my wallet in Panamanian security while rushing to avoid being bumped from the Miami to Panama flight due to extremely slow hours of processing i.e. forty-five minutes in line without moving then running through to catch the plane strewing pocket contents, shoes, etc. Bet they get a lot of loot that way. Airport lost and founds are large rooms stuffed with such stuff but of course not my wallet since it had some money in it.
>
> Bob picked us up at the airport in his beautiful new Mercedes station wagon and installed us in The Executive Hotel in downtown Panama for the night. Very nice and reasonable too at $175 a night. We had a sampling of Panamanian liquor and a vision of night life. Definitely a five-star experience.
>
> The next morning, we left our excess luggage at Bob's house which is a wonderful four story home with a swimming pool and gardens on the third floor. Very nicely kept by his lovely Panamanian wife and her maids. A large ebullient Weimaraner, two chicks, and

two bunnies rounded out the entertainment section for his boy and girl – nice kids.

The morning dawned on a pretty tropical day and we left the city on a five-hour drive to Santa Fe from which we would ride through the jungle to the Atlantic coast and back.

The trip took us up the Pacific coast, through West Texas type scrub, and sugarcane holdings and then inland toward the mountains and Santa Fe. We arrived at a motel in the foothills which was to be command post for our venture. It was entirely adequate at $15 a night and meals were tasty and cheap.

With typical manana urgency the wrangler/guide finally assembled a scruffy assortment of tack, horses, and mules. Three hours late we started off into the jungle. As Bob put it "IT doesn't get any better than this." Certainly prophetic, as things were to get progressively worse before our return "home" to that motel. We had seen many good horses with reasonable flesh but the gringo's horses were cachectic and plodding with tattered flapping tack and nonadjustable short stirrup saddles. We were quite a sight. The jungle road quickly deteriorated into a muddy rut traveled only by monster 4X4's, equines, and people. From horizon to horizon the jungle was evenly settled by indigenous natives using slash and burn plantations of a few acres each and a few livestock and chickens. The chickens hold a special place due to their food and entertainment potential. We had watched a very ritualized series of cockfights the night before in Santa Fe. A special arena very prettily constructed with auricular tiers of seating and a special cage for the referee, indicates great esteem for these events. Careful weighing and matching of opponents preceded a fight to the death with razor spurs strapped on with masking tape. Feathers had been plucked from underside and throat to facilitate scoring marks. These sad heroic deaths together with all those rum-soaked

Indians gave us our fill quickly and we left while we still could.

Due to our three-hour delay in departure, darkness overtook us before our intended destination so we took shelter for the night in our wranglers old home town's community center. The only thing not rusted through was a bronze plaque indicating that the building had been constructed as a cooperative project with the USA. We slept fitfully on rough concrete a little concerned about snakes so that when one of the local dogs licked Hal's face a great hullabaloo arose from him and his leaping and cussing scared the dogs away.

Fortunately, the vampire bats in that area prey almost exclusively on cattle so there was no significant blood loss during the night and at least at this writing no one of us has developed rabies.

The natives are sturdy, good natured mostly and industrious. Everyone no matter what age carried a machete as an extension of their arm. Probably very little mugging among them I suspect. Most were barefoot or wore rubber boots or shoes which were often abandoned on the road. Most natives are handsome people at least as compared to other Indians of South America. Dental integrity ran high except in the old women who, probably depleted by constant child-bearing, usually showed no teeth. I saw only one deformed (hunch backed) local and that was just outside a medical clinic in Santa Fe.

Almost no sign of logging was visible as the terrain was extremely steep and without access for extraction. The really huge trees often remained as their canopies; they were so high as not to interfere with farming. Apparently bananas, cassava, yucca, and corn were popular. We were told that (as at home) marijuana and moonshine were big cash crops probably due to transport logistics.

The horses were excruciatingly slow but sure footed and in constant forward motion. The mountains rose and fell with extremely steep, slippery grades that would continue for miles without any benches or plateau. In spite of obviously minimal tissue and blood resources they did not breathe hard or want to stop. Figuring they knew more, were pretty much left to their own discretion. My mare was blind in her left eye and had a big hock but though pessimistic seemed resigned to her duties.

Apparently all monkeys and other wild mammals and edible birds having found their way to the dinner fires, only songbirds and vultures were now reduced to one juvenile river otter – never a track in the soft mud of the "road" other than people and livestock.

Most spectacular were the black and white swallow tailed kites, one of which was trailing a leather jess, which I assumed represented a failed falconry experiment.

Hummingbirds, kera kera, parrots, and songbirds in the up lands and frigate birds, pelicans and egrets flew along the Pacific coast.

We reached Rio Luis too late to ride to the Atlantic and so determined to hire a canoe to take us down the river. The "Town" was typical with a small bar, nice school and a little police station with two bored rag-tag policemen in their shack next to the school.

The dugouts were single piece affairs carved out of a single log. Ours carried nine people counting the navigator and his helper/first mate. Due to low water, we negotiated about thirty portages which were exceedingly taxing due to the slippery round rocks covering everything in the river bottom. The water was very clear and beautiful with an intact riparian zone. Brahma cattle grazed all the hillside fincas (farms), a very pretty sight altogether. Our captain told us he had taken a group of New Zealanders down two weeks earlier with no portages necessary. Seating in the canoe was quite painful so at least the portages were a diversion from that. When the outboard motor lost its propeller the captain got out his snorkel gear and searched until he found it. We arrived at the Atlantic coast at dark. The community was small but we were able to locate a fish/rice/bean dinner and a place to sleep for a dollar. Bob and I felt it compared favorably with a Vietnamese bamboo torture cage.

Morning came with a coconut falling off a tree uphill and rolling through the building to hit poor Hal in the head, a tropical version of breakfast in bed.

We negotiated meals of casaua gruel and coffee and took a swim in the river while waiting to head back up river. The Atlantic was fierce with huge crashing surf which was met by rip tides causing great plumes of water spraying twenty feet in the air. The water was warm but way too dangerous for swimming so the Atlantic experience was limited to beach combing. A wild, romantic setting was fortified by a parrot saying, "I love you" in Spanish. Two large ocean canoes with outboards tried to get through the surf with a load of lobsters bound for a town one hundred miles or so up the coast. The biggest canoe capsized in the surf – lucky lobsters! Repairing the motor and reorganizing for another assault took all morning but they finally made it out.

The return upriver was particularly long and painful but finally accomplished and we bathed in the river with neo blue and yellow frogs which we assumed to be poisonous.

On our return we discovered the horses all tied where we had left them without food or water for thirty-six hours. They didn't seem much affected by it – probably used to deprivation. They drank a bit at the river and we turned them out all night in the school lot to graze.

Rain started early evening and continued all night and all the next day making the home journey very cold and wet especially for me because my plastic poncho tore apart early and I was really miserable. In order to raise my core temperature enough to function I walked a lot with a painful ankle in sticky red clay. We had filled our canteens with water collected off the roof using pans and lids so fortunately had resupplied with amoeba-free water.

Our pack mule and horses were loaded more lightly now since we were headed home and left supplies we wouldn't need with the teachers at the school; candies, canned meats, cheese, and toilet paper were appreciated.

We went back the same and only road but the scenery while wet was good. The houses are well constructed for tropical living. They are uniformly built on stilts with bamboo roofs thatched with palm fronds. The rivers were roaring and waterfalls and suspension bridges from before the time of the road added interest.

Since the horses knew they were headed home the pace picked up a bit almost to a normal walk, which was merciful in my hypothermic distress. The extremely steep and slippery grades and corduroy roads were all negotiated successfully and finally the motel at Santa Fe came into view.

Having forgone the luxury supplement there was only cold water to shower in but I was so cold from the all-day rain that it was pleasant.

Rhonda and Eric had to abandon their room due to swarming termite similar to the fire ants that had stung me badly on the trail. Shortly we were all well fed and well rested for the ride to Panama City and the luxury of the Executive Hotel. One of the two motel dogs had cancer on his penis – fortunately easily treated with chemo therapy which a lady doctor working at the Santa Fe clinic said she would pursue.

On the way to Panama City we visited one of Bob's agricultural warehouse/offices and dined at a magnificent resort overlooking the Pacific with its incredible peaceful vastness and shorebirds. The food was great with lobster thermadore and other dishes.

The Panama Canal was a real treat as we watched a Maersh container freighter and Norwegian cruise ship lock through using eight locomotive "mules" cabled to them each as there was only a twenty-four-foot clearance.

An amazing accomplishment costing about $108,000 per ship. We drank excellent tequila and beer at a canal bar and played a couple games of pool and went back to the hotel. Charles Mewa from the Ecuador ride met us for dinner of American beef at a great Argentine restaurant.

The Panama trip will forever be remembered by those who attended. After their return and several years later, Pete invited their guides Bill Sprayberry and Bob McIntosh to Milliron Farm. "I went on a hunting trip on Pete's place in Ohio with Bob McIntosh," remembers Bill. "We hunted deer in the mornings and rode horses with Pete later in the day. Pete introduced me to Tennessee Walking horses. It was great."

Take kindly the counsel of the years,
gracefully surrendering the things of youth.
Desiderata by Max Ehrmann

---

13 EVENTIDE

ARTHRITIS DID NOT stop Pete from doing the things he loved. Now, retired from farm calls, Pete's schedule at the clinic continued to be busy. He continued occasional farm calls to West Virginia to stay in contact with long-time clients and friends, but, even though clients knew that Pete had pulled out all the indoor cattle stalls and chutes at the clinic, they continued to bring in cattle by the truckload.

At one point a client showed up with rowdy cattle without an appointment. The guy was obnoxious; a real complainer. Pete told the cattleman without hesitation, "No." Through the years, this particular cattleman had disrespected Pete and it was without regret that the cattle left the parking lot.

Now in his senior years, Pete was in great shape. The morning's started slower now and he would sit on the side of the bed before rising to avoid dizziness. He was a breakfast eater and required a big breakfast every day. Up early, Jody prepared Pete's favorite breakfasts including steak and eggs or milk toast. Vitamins were an important addition to Pete's morning regime. On Monday, Wednesday, and Friday, Pete attempted to fast to maintain his weight and health by drinking only grape juice and taking blue-green algae Spirulina tablets, which Jody purchased at the Farmacy on Stimson Avenue in Athens.

"Pete had a lot of pain," Jody adds. "He had so much arthritis. He took a horse medicine for his arthritis. He had been through a few things – broken bones, hip replacement, sprained ankle, and cancer. In 2006, he was diagnosed with prostate cancer. He had no warning signs; his doctor found the cancer during a regular doctor's visit. Pete had surgery at Riverside Hospital, Columbus. The surgeon removed the gland without complications. No chemotherapy or radiation was required, and Pete was back to work sooner than later. He was in really good shape; best shape he'd been in for years."

Getting Older

Through it all and growing older now, Pete and Jody's relationship seemed to be standing the test of time. "I am actually three months older than Pete," Jody says. "I was born in April; Pete was born in June. Pete's mother was three months older than Pete's father. Both Abbott and Pete would say that they had married older women. It was a family joke."

As Pete got older, he shaved his signature mutton chops and Jody cut her signature braid. "I used to have a long braid," Jody reflects. "I was leading a horse at the clinic and the snap on the lead rope was not closed completely. My braid got caught in the snap. This horse is practically lifting me up off the ground. Gordon Bolon was there. He helped Pete a lot around the clinic and farm. I said, 'Gordon, will you please help me.' He was hesitant to help me, but he finally came over and helped me. After that, I decided to cut my braid."

It was Jody's quietness, submissiveness, simplicity, humor, and loyalty that are intriguing. It was her love of Pete, family, horses, and nature that connect the sands in the hourglass. "We had our ups and downs," she reflects. "Pete and I had been to a divorce lawyer. I said I didn't have a divorce to give him. At that time, you had to live separately for two years before he could get a contested divorce. Tom Eslocker, my lawyer, said that if I could get along with all the hurt and pain, that Pete really didn't want a divorce, that he was just being pressured. There were other lawyers who said, 'Go get that son of a bitch.' We went to a marriage counselor briefly. The marriage counselor assumed we were going to get a divorce. Several years later, I called him and left a message after we celebrated our 50th Wedding Anniversary."

Pete wrote this letter to Jody on her birthday, April 2, 1996:

Dear Dear Jody,

How do I love thee? Let me count (some of) the ways! It's easy to love someone who loves you and it's mighty obvious that you <u>do</u> love me. Thanks for that!! I <u>do</u> love you, too. Thanks for a wonderful sex life, comfortable homey home; good food (wonderful, in fact) and a <u>happy</u> life. You basically raised our son and daughter with minimal help from a struggling young vet searching for success and an identity, un-mindful that he already had it all!

We share a love of horses, dogs, farm, classical music, sheep, cats, family, and each other. I really can't imagine how we could be more compatible. We have clung to and comforted each other through every kind of economic, physical, moral, mental and emotional crisis and great strength of fiber has been thereby derived. That we would travel this life together to our ends was and has and is never a serious question although it may have been darned uncomfortable at times.

We have tried on a daily basis to grow spiritually and both are happy in the Episcopal Church and I think it is wonderful that we read the Bible and Urantia Book, Daily Word, etc., daily and pray together at home and at Good Shepherd. Although not always on the same wave length, we always honor each other's views and opinions. Pretty amazing and unusual I think!

Although occasionally on both sides some have tried to break up this union, it's obvious that it ain't gonna ever happen – it's too strong.

Happy Birthday and I look forward to sharing the rest of them with *you*.

Love, Pete

Grandchildren: AJ, Grant, and Noah

AJ was born to Pat and Karen, the first grandchild whom Pete doted over. Grant followed soon after; both boys winning Pete's heart and devotion. Pride in the lineage and the posterity of being Pete's grandchildren are evident when they talk about the times they spent at the farmhouse and Milliron Clinic. AJ remembers, "When my family lived in Westerville and we were little, during the summers we would come up and stay with Grandma and Grandpa. I remember Grandpa at the clinic in his uniform with his big mask on his face, his cap, and gloves. I remember thinking *this is kind of disgusting*. While I was there, he did a procedural check to see if a horse was going to be able to have its baby. I remember Grandma telling this story that I went around telling everyone at Kroger's or Wal-Mart or somewhere what my Grandpa does with horses and his entire arm. I think I was just wee little. We spent lots of years running around the farm and just fooling around. I never helped with surgery. I was traumatized a couple of times.

"I remember when he was clipping the tails off Rottweiler puppies, like fifteen of them," AJ continues. "He kept clipping their tails off. I was crying. I was a little three or four-year-old. That was kind of traumatizing. He didn't really say anything about it. He wasn't really affectionate or anything."

"But you know he cared," Grant adds. "He came to our sporting events at times when he had more important things he should have been doing. I don't know how much he always enjoyed it, but he enjoyed the concession stand. He would eat a lot."

"Grandpa would do surgeries until seven or eight at night sometimes," Grant says. "We were swamped as kids. We played three sports a year apiece. We both played baseball, basketball, and football. And we played summer league baseball."

"He read the Bible every morning with Grandma," interjects AJ. "That's an important fact about him. Every single morning they'd get up and go to the table and read their daily book, and then the verses out of the Bible. They'd both read aloud to each other every morning, which I thought was pretty neat. Always working. Sunup to sundown. Extremely busy, always doing something. I've probably had a hundred people come up to me and say, 'Your Grandpa is the greatest guy in the world. He saved my cat, or he saved my dog. He's so nice.' I've heard that many times. And everybody always says how nice he was. He really was a nice guy. Really funny. Definitely busy and you could tell he was always thinking about what he was going to do next. He was amazing. People have always said that dad and I resemble Grandpa.

"He taught us how to ride," AJ continues. "I've ridden three or four times this past summer. I rode Unique, Grandpa's gelding, the last couple of times, which is his newest horse. We rode on the annual clinic trail ride. He told us to have fun. I will definitely have lots of animals when I get older. I will have it fenced in; horses and different kinds of animals. I love horses."

"I was young," Grant says. "I think I rode on a double saddle with my Grandma the first couple of years. Grandpa always had a good time. He loved that cabin up there. He loved to ride. They both do."

"He had a llama," Grant goes on. "I remember he smacked the llama in the face for spitting on him. It was one of his personal animals. We always helped Grandma with chores at the barn, like throwing hay down to the horses and feeding the sheep. It was fun."

"When we stayed at Grandpa's he would come in everyday and make Grant and me untie his boots," AJ says. "He had big logging boots. They come up to the knee and they lace up. All the way up. And they have these huge spikes. They weigh about twenty pounds apiece. They are really heavy. One of us would go over to where he was sitting in his chair, undo his boot and yank it off his foot. Then he'd sit there in front of the fireplace in his whitey tightys and kick back. I think that's kind of cool that when every time he came into the house when Grant or I were there he'd yank them off and he'd sit there doing whatever, eat dinner. He would sit at the head of the table in his captain's chair with a big sheep skin laid all the way across it. It was real comfy for him; right in front of the fireplace. He would sit there on that chair and stock the woodstove and that's where he'd read the Bible every morning. That's where he inspected Grant after he fell on the playground and hurt himself in his man parts. Grant had to stand up on the table and drop trousers. He was nine or ten at the time."

"Well, I didn't want to go to the doctor," Grant interjects. "I was embarrassed. I was all swollen up."

"He gave me four or five stitches once," AJ said. "One time I was driving down the road - you can see the scar on my arm right there - an electric company truck was driving by me and knocked my side mirror off. My window was down and it came in and sliced a big chunk out of my arm right there. It was on State Route 690. I just turned around and drove over to the clinic. Grandpa came out; he was seeing a client and her dog. I walked in and showed Grandpa my hand. I was bleeding everywhere. He took me right back, stitched me right up. One time I fell off the back of a pickup truck when I was cleaning out the barn with my buddy. I was standing on an old board. When I snapped it, I flipped backward and hit my head on the tailgate of my truck. I was knocked out. My buddy drove me over to the clinic. Grandpa shaved my head and stitched my head. I was a teenager at the time. There were probably four or five times he stitched me up. He would give me X-rays, too."

"I remember my sophomore year of high school," Grant says. "I was in shop class and I was using a bandsaw. I wasn't paying attention. I was 16 years old. I cut my thumb deep, almost completely off. It was in the middle of basketball season, so, I was like…I don't want stitches because I won't be able to play. So, we get the bright idea to go to Grandpa Pete and see what he had to say. He decided to put in metal stitches that he puts in animals. He puts those in and that was probably the most painful. Grandpa said, 'Toughen up, this will only hurt for a minute.' He had no sympathy for anybody's pain. If he was hurt it didn't matter. It didn't slow him down. He said, 'I'll give you metal stitches so you can go play your basketball game.' He put them in and then a couple of days later he took them out. He was always my doctor."

"Our first doctor anyway," AJ says.

"Grandpa always led by example," Grant explains. "I mean, you know my Dad. They're not the most talkative people. But, they always lead by example. He and Grandma never got anything they ever wanted, I don't think. But, they always got us something that would help us, or something that they thought we needed, something practical."

"Grandpa was very, very humble," AJ adds. "At Christmas, as soon as everybody would quiet down, he'd tell a joke, one of those jokes that took like five minutes to tell. They were really crude and dirty most of the time. I don't know if you ever heard the joke about the midget and the horse. The midget gets shoved up the horse's rear end, but it's a five-minute joke. He'd always tell jokes at the dinner table. Quiet, but funny.

"I joined the Marine Corps, and, obviously, he thought that was cool," AJ says. "Once I was able to do the max amount of pull-ups, which is part of a physical fitness test, when I was able to do 13 to 20 pull-ups, he was real proud of me for that. He always worked out. He really did. As much work as he did, he'd walk 10 times up and down the big hill, the driveway to the house, then back to the clinic. He worked all day, do surgeries, then go to the woods or whatever. He'd walk up and down that hill 10 times. He had to wear himself out to sleep. He really worked hard. He would go to a movie, though, every week or so for entertainment."

"Grandpa and Grandma took us to the movies," Grant confirms. "We were about nine years old, and it would be all in subtitles; a really cultured movie," Grant said. "AJ and I would go and we would have no idea what was going on."

"We'd make our own words up to what they were saying," AJ laughs.

"They'd be sitting back behind us just shaking their heads," Grant laughs, too. "Yeah, they were very into things like that. We always had fun with them. Whenever we'd go into the clinic, the receptionist and vet techs would give us some mints and some candy and stuff. Everybody went there. Everybody went to Pete. He was like a friend. I think that growing up we were more aware than most kids our age and he understood that. He treated us like friends. He'd call us Cletus, and all kind of crazy names."

"He always had a name for us," AJ adds. "We would show up at the clinic. He'd say, 'Hey, Cletus!' He was very funny."

"Grandpa took three days off a week from eating and only drank grape juice," Grant says. "It was his routine for a long time.

He and Grandma took vitamins daily, too. But when he ate, he ate a bunch. Every day he'd come home for lunch, well, not every day, obviously, but when he did come home, Grandma would have something waiting on him there. He'd eat and eat and eat, then back to work. He always had a joke for you. Every time he saw us he was happy to see us. He was always happy, but when he wasn't happy, he wasn't fun to be around either."

"One time when I was pretty small Grandpa told me something about a tractor or a lawnmower," AJ remembers. "It made my Dad so mad. I got in the car and told my dad what my Grandpa had said. My Dad said, 'Oh, that's not Grandpa's mower, that's my mower.' My Dad started cussing. Dad and Grandpa didn't always see eye-to-eye. Dad had a rough childhood as far as affectionate wise. Dad always tried to give us everything that we could ever need or want. Like the year before Grandpa died, Dad and I were sitting out in the garage drinking beer, he came to tears and said, 'I really didn't get to know your Grandpa Pete. I really didn't get to know how good of a guy he is. I didn't as much as I should have."

Nearby, Jody is listening to AJ and Grant tell their stories. Jody spent time with AJ and Grant, too. "I used to make Grant and AJ walk the snare lines," Jody laughs. "Oh, they hated that. It was really cool to begin with, but then it wore off. One time we walked the snare lines and I was in a hurry for some reason. It was a muddy day and Grant was behind me. I hollered at him, 'Would you hurry up and catch up with me?' He mumbled something that I couldn't understand. Turns out, his boots were stuck in the mud. He ended up walking out of his boots to catch up with me. He must've been five or six at the time.

"On one part of the snare line there was this little spring that flowed through a little hollow," Jody smiles. "Grant and AJ were complaining and fussing about how cold they were. So, we get around that and they wanted to slide on the ice. The whole way they had been whining about the cold and the mud. They get up there and would slide on the ice, they weren't too cold then. Then they went through the ice. They were really wet then and they wanted to keep sliding on the ice. I said, 'No, we're going to the house.' They were so cute."

Noah, Jessica and Rich's son, is tall, athletic, and sensible. He shares Pete and Jody's love of horses. He is the youngest of the three grandchildren. He has his own memories of his Grandpa Pete. "I was seven when Grandpa fell down by the creek and broke his ankle. He wasn't supposed to walk," Noah shares. "He was riding around on his four-wheeler. I rode on the back with him in case anything happened to him. If he got into trouble, I was supposed to run back to the house and tell Grandma. Grandpa and I would ride back into the woods. It was scary sometimes. Grandpa used to hang out in his underwear. One time I was taking a nap at their house and I woke up. Grandpa and Grandma were standing over me when I woke up. They were adoring me. It's hard for kids to be adored."

Lenten Address

Pete was baptized and confirmed in Falmouth Foreside, Maine. He was devoted to church. Most of the year, on Sunday mornings, he would dismiss vet calls and all appointments to attend the Episcopal Church of the Good Shepherd in Athens. He attended the half-hour eight o'clock service where communion was served. During the summer months when Ohio University was on break, Pete would attend the 9:30 am one-hour service with Jody. He enjoyed the music and connecting with the community. One of his favorite songs was *"American the Beautiful"* and the line *"O beautiful for spacious skies."* Living in Colorado, he certainly had seen a lot of spacious skies and long sunsets.

On March 21, 2001, Pete gave an address to the congregation of his beloved Episcopal church during Lent.

> Dear Lord, we thank you especially for interesting lives on this beautiful planet and ask for the wisdom and will necessary for its repair and maintenance.
>
> Hi! I've been invited to share with you my spiritual journey from the mellow perspective of my 63 years, with the caveat that it can't take over 10 minutes. I commend Mike on his good judgment in scheduling the

mildly irreverent Dr. Smith for Spring Break, so as to minimize what Swartzkoff termed collateral damage.

I'm a cradle Episcopalian baptized and confirmed at the Church of St. Mary the Virgin in Falmouth Foreside, Maine. My father was a lay leader who delivered over 300 sermons. As a student at Harvard he kept a string of polo ponies, which served as a 30s version of a babe magnet. Due to an apparent lack of prey he moved them to Bates, where he attracted my very beautiful mother, who happened to be putting in her four years there. They then returned to Harvard to graduate work.

Mom and Dad raised three girls and two boys in Maine on a dairy farm, which is now a State Park on Casco Bay. As farmers often do they went broke and moved to the city...so at fourteen years of age I embarked on my own adventures rather than live in Denver or New York. Things happened to work out and I graduated at twenty-three with my doctorate in veterinary medicine in an all-male class where the average age was thirty-two. The school of hard knocks had served me well and in spite of my total lack of any economic help from loans, scholarships, or parents, I graduated debt free with a wife and two kids and $3,500 in the bank – probably my last fond memory of solvency.

Sadly that educational opportunity is no longer possible due to an endless series of 6% tuition hikes which have put education out of the reach of students who work long hours and therefore have average grades.

Like most of you I explored many religions before deciding that Anglican Christianity is as usable as any even though it is more a religion about Christ than the religion of Christ, Christianity by committee you might say.

Of course we're not altogether to blame, though, since Christ himself left us nothing in writing. His choice was to teach with often-difficult parables and sayings that force us to think for ourselves and come up with what seems right for the present hour.

Anyway – we more or less accept the total package by (as the great jurist Oliver Wendell Holmes put it) generally agreeing on at least the first two words of the Lord's Prayer. We do this in order to 'gather together' as instructed by the Bible even though we're in disagreement as to the details: (of creeds involving mystical cannibalism, mythic cult tradeoffs of a winter solstice, Christmas, Virgin birth, and so forth.) That's all probably irrelevant since as those of us who tried Ben Franklin's daily chart to emulate Jesus and Socrates found out that it's unlikely that one turn on the planet was enough time to pull it off anyway.

It becomes obvious that we can only hope to become partially wise and relatively true in our lives.

We struggle to develop, choreograph, and coordinate body, mind and spirit in order to live full, happy, and meaningful lives. There can be no doubt that God does not need me to carry out healing of his animals, but he delegates almost everything so that we can find meaning and fulfillment.

We are given the Ten Commandments not as a formula to please God, but as a technique for a simpler and more peaceful and satisfying life.

We are given great teachers like the late humanist Ken Keyes who crystallized most of the causes of our unhappiness into the addictions to security, sensation, and power. What do we have to offer God in return? In a word, experience. The I AM who is himself incapable of imperfection is amazingly interested in our imperfect personal life tapestries into which are woven – our personal life designs. We all acquire each strand of warp and woof in unique and wonderful ways according to our experiences. As Albert Einstein put it "the most beautiful thing we can experience is the mysterious" and again "imagination is more important than knowledge." Our lives properly and excitingly lived are mysterious! Who would guess for instance that hydrogen and oxygen – two extremely flammable gasses could form H2O, which puts out fire?

Every tiny fragment of life is mysterious and faith inducing. This week for instance, it's the tiny unsterilized protein prions which cause Mad Cow disease.

Statisticians may announce laws governing large number of either atoms or people – but not for us or the atoms individually.

So, how do we develop a working spiritual conception of God - a being who can create an entire universe with a thought? A God who loves me personally like a favorite child and shows intense personal interest in everything I do? Even if I didn't believe in Him, I'd follow out of curiosity!

Unlike our late beloved Calvinist Lew Kemmerle, I do not believe that there is a great gulf fixed between God and me. I do feel that although I cannot find God by searching that if I submit to the leading of my personal God-fragment of Indwelling Spirit that I will be as the Urantia Book says, unerringly guided step by step, life by life, through universe upon universe and age upon age until I stand in His presence, at which point I'd probably choose to do it all over again because it was so interesting.

When I submit to God's leading, my experience suggests that the immediate next step is usually obvious so I take that step and observe the resulting fresh landscape and then seeing the next obvious best step take it and soon, this makes for a wonderful adventure since that new next step is often 180 degrees from what was anticipated.

Submission to God's guidance involves admitting His higher perspective of my life much like viewing the entire course of a river and knowing intimately and lovingly each molecule in it is compared to my personal perspective of the river from standing at one point on its bank. To experience this surrender of self will and the subsequent guidance is sort of like having a totally benevolent father teaching me the 120 dimensional chess game of life in order to show me new and wonderful experiences.

Surely this Father wants me, His son, to evolve as best I can to my personal limits rather than sit and wait for my inheritance of salvation. Of course I can't lose that way! My choice though is to improve so that my understanding of yesterday is nothing compared to my understanding of today. My truth is probably not your truth or even what will be true for me tomorrow.

When we accept this guidance we accept apparent contradictions as necessary for a full experience of life. We must experience hardships to learn courage, betrayal to learn loyalty; falsehood to learn truth and we must do all this with an immature mind – a mind which knows always less than it can believe so we can learn faith. We must be fallible and free to make dynamic choices if we are to evolve.

Episcopalians don't typically have vanity plates – but if I did, it would read EVOLVE.

He was a self-made man.
The greatest man I never knew.
Abbott Pliny Smith IV

---

14 THE TREE

TUESDAY, FEBRUARY 2, 2010 was a cold day. Groundhog Day. The thirty-third day of the year in the Gregorian calendar. It was an afternoon to saw the ash tree in the far pasture about a mile from the house. Pete had contemplated its demise the day before. It was a weak ash tree, having all the attributes of a tree that could be threatened by a deadly insect. The tree could eventually fall victim to the destructive emerald ash borer, an ugly invasive green bug. Its larvae serpentines and girdles a tree, disrupting the flow of nutrients and water through the xylem and the phloem.

Pete was passionate about trees; the touch of bark, the woody aroma, and the sound of leaves melding with the summer wind. He knew every tree on his 1,500-acre farm. He knew which trees were earning their keep, which trees were getting by, and which trees were destined for the sawmill. Being destined for the sawmill was not a bad thing for one of his trees; it would be repurposed with the utmost respect and decorum. But this tree was different.

The day had begun like any other. Morning devotions with Jody at the breakfast table, thoughts of how the day would unfold, and the ever-present need to succeed. Time at the clinic, then regular rounds. It was late afternoon when Pete drove the dozer up to the high meadow to weed the woods. The surrounding area was deserted. He made his way to the weak ash tree and parked the dozer. The sound of the chainsaw ripping through bark and wood rang through the woods.

273

Nobody was there when the massive limb fell and racked his body. It was a logger's nightmare; a rogue "widow-maker" branch hit Pete directly on the left side, breaking bones in his left leg, snapping ribs and shoulder. It all happened so fast. When Pete realized the extent of his injuries, he knew he had to get help. But, the chainsaw… he was too weak to lift the chainsaw onto the dozer. *Someone might come by and steal it*, he thought. Barely moving, Pete gathered the energy to hide the chainsaw under the leaves of a nearby oak tree.

Truly, God only knows how long it took Pete to climb back onto the dozer, start the engine, and head for the farmhouse. Only God knows how Pete felt, with his high tolerance for pain and a will unsurpassed. But he was mortally hurt, and surely he knew it.

Jody was coming down from the barn. She and Pete were looking forward to going to Ohio University to hear a lecture that evening. She heard the bulldozer coming up the hill to the farmhouse. *Wow! We are going to be on time for the lecture!* Jody thought.

Then Jody realized that Pete normally didn't drive the bulldozer up to the farmhouse. She continued walking down the hill to meet him.

"I'm hurt bad. I need to go to the hospital," Pete gasped.

"You stay right there; I'll call the squad."

"No, no. Just take me."

"Wait a minute."

Pete started off the bulldozer as Jody put a five-gallon bucket to help him step off. He was light headed and woozy. Jody was thinking that if he passed out, she could call the squad. But Pete made it down to the car and Jody drove him to the local emergency room.

Upon arrival at the emergency room entrance, the security guard took one glance at Pete and told him to wait there. "I'll get a wheelchair," the security guard said.

While the security guard was wheeling Pete into the emergency room, Jody parked the car. By the time Jody entered the emergency room, in a matter of minutes, the hospital had summoned Life Flight to transport Pete by helicopter to Grant Hospital, in Columbus.

Jody watched as the helicopter took Pete away. Pete's injuries were worse than she feared. She called Pat, Rich, and Jessica, and told them what had happened.

Rich drove Jody to Grant Hospital, an hour and a half from Athens. The weather was terrible; the roads were icy - there was ice every day while Pete was in the hospital. But no one realized at that point that Pete might not make it.

Pete was taken into Grant Hospital's intensive critical care unit. He was immediately medicated. His leg continued to swell. Most of his ribs were broken and his heart was unstable. He was in serious condition.

When Rich and Jody arrived at the hospital, they headed for the intensive care unit. The first night, Rich stayed overnight and drove to work the next morning. Once stabilized, Pete had surgery to repair the open wound where swelling had split the skin of his leg. He was on a respirator and dialysis. Vince Yates, CEO of Grant Hospital, and friends with Pat, knew Pete was in ICU and visited frequently. Many people came to see Pete while in the hospital. Jessica had to turn many of the well-wishers away due to Pete's inability to visit for long periods of time. Pat, a successful accountant, was in the middle of tax season and was not able to visit as often as he would have liked, but he kept in contact with Vince and learned of his Dad's day-to-day treatment. AJ, in the United States Marine Corps, was stationed in Japan. Grant came to see Pete between classes. Either Jody or Jessica stayed with Pete night and day. They relied on family and friends to pick one up, and leave the other. Pete and the family were showered with cards of concern and prayers.

Dear friend Pete Smith,

I was very sorry to hear about your accident, and hope you're recovering well by this time. We bought hay off of Glenden Bonnett and he told me about it. I've had ribs broke several times, but just 1 or 2 at a time. It normally stings and hurts for four to five weeks. As we get older we should be more careful as we don't heal as fast anymore.

Now with the break in our winter weather we want
to tap some maple trees. It normally serves for an income
for us throughout the spring.

We are now through with lambing except for eight
young ewes for later. I have been standing up once in the
night for around a month checking the sheep and still do
to feed the orphans. I think we have 67 lambs from 43
ewes. We gave them their tetanus and overeating shots
yesterday and now want to dock tails in the next days.
We normally put bands on for 12 to 24 hours, then take
a pruning shears and pinch off the tails next to the bands,
then remove the bands.

We are still shipping milk and feeding heifers as we
used too, but will have to in the future make different
arrangements as the family grows up and leaves the nest
my help gets less.

In closing, I want to wish you a speedy recovery in
health, and will be anxious to hear how you are. Glen
Bennett also asked.

Your friend,
Levi H. Miller

"Rich said he saw that tree and it definitely snapped where it
wasn't supposed to," Karen, Pat's wife says. "It kicked out instead
of falling over. I only went up one time when he was still good
enough to take his mask off to say, 'Hi.' I told him not to talk, that
he looked good. I came back that day and I picked up Jody and said,
'He's going to make it.' I only went up one time when he was still
in good shape; the two other times I went up he had deteriorated,
and then the time that we said we needed to be done with this. That
was awful. We talked about it some; Pat couldn't bring himself to
talk about it. Jessica would call me and tell me what was going on,
if Pete had a really bad day or, one day she said, 'Dad doesn't want
to live like this anymore.' I said, 'I can't tell Pat that, you have to
tell him.'"

"We knew Pete was going to have a rough time, thinking about a rehabilitation center early on," Jody says. "As he started to go downhill, and get worse, Jessica didn't let anyone in to see him."

Pete never really wanted to talk about the accident. He was always thinking ahead. That's what he did his whole life; think ahead.

Jody was at the hospital sleeping in a recliner in one of the hospital's conference rooms, on another floor, when she heard *code blue*. The nurse met Jody as she entered the elevator to Pete's floor. Pete had had a heart attack. His heart stopped beating for nineteen minutes. The hospital chaplain took Jody aside and stayed with her until Pete was stabilized.

Friday, the family gathered at Pete's bedside. He was on life support. Pat knew that it was Pete's wish, that if he was ever in that state, to disconnect the power.

After a conference with the doctor and nurse, Pat suggested they go home, regroup over the weekend, and return to the hospital on Monday morning. As they drove home that Friday afternoon, everyone was thinking of Pete's recovery and his arrival back to Milliron Farm. Wearily, Pat was hopeful, but knew in his heart that his Dad would not recover.

Monday morning, Pat, Jody, Jessica, Karen, and Rich traveled to Grant Hospital for the last time. It was a somber morning. All was still and reverent. Pete, with tubes and pumps keeping him breathing, did not arouse or make signs of revival.

Beatrice Hagari, a member of the Threshold Choir, came into the room. She remembered Pete from his hip surgery, she had been one of Pete's nurses at the time. She stood by Pete's bedside now, along with the family, and softly sang a hymn. Pete's attending nurse gently disconnected the power from Pete's life support. He soon took his last breath. Peaceful now, the room was filled with an imperturbable silence.

The journey back to Athens was solemn. Pat and the rest were tired, hungry, and depleted. Driving southeast on Route 33 from

Columbus, everyone felt pain and loss. It was surreal. The Millstone Barbeque marquee was in sight and they stopped for a meal before driving the remainder of the way home. Sitting in the restaurant, reflecting on the weeks Pete had been in the hospital, now his death, thoughts were collected and the need to move forward pressed.

"By the way, Mom, Dad purchased a herd of Black Angus cattle," Pat quietly announced. "I was able to stop the delivery."

Jody, lost in her own thoughts, felt no need to respond, knowing that Pete always wanted another herd of cattle and that she had reluctantly always said "no."

Pete had seen the advertisement for the Black Angus at the Beverly feed store over a year ago. He couldn't resist. He really liked having cattle around. Pete bought the cattle, paid the man, and said he didn't want the cattle delivered until a certain date, after he had talked with Jody.

Jody wasn't surprised that Pete never told her about the cattle. He knew she would be upset. Fences needed mending, bills needed paid, and Pete needed to slow down. But now it really didn't matter. Jody didn't really care about the cattle. She had just lost her soulmate, her life companion, and her love.

Jody felt the heaviness of her steps as she walked into the house without Pete. There are no words that express the sadness and dismay she felt. Memories swelled through the house and comingled, creating a sense of deep surrender; a sense of unity. Ancestral paintings, reverenced books, fleece-lined captain's chair and posterities throughout the house now have new meaning, all to be given as creative tokens to generations to come. Now the house sighs with contempt at the unfairness of being human. The animals convene to find out where their master has gone. Pete's Border collie, Smokey, waits in the farmhouse yard, looking down toward the clinic.

Several days after Pete's passing, Pat made the arduous journey to the culprit tree. It was a massive, murderous tree. A plethora of rampant emotions overflowed as Pat scourged the tree with Pete's chainsaw, chopping it at the base. It would only be a memory now as Pat ran every twig through the wood shredder.

When Jody heard that Pat had shredded the tree, she told Pat, "If I die on a horse, for heaven's sake, just let Jessica have it!"

"Mom, I wouldn't kill a horse," Pat said in his deep, accurate, Pete Smith voice.

The Memorial

On May 22, 2010, 4:00 PM, there is standing room only in the Episcopal church. Tears, sorrow, grief, disbelief, pain, disappointment, angst; a gamut of emotions filled the Church that day. Reverend R. William Carroll, Rector of the Episcopal Church of the Good Shepherd, Athens, Ohio, gave this sermon to his congregation:

> Pete Smith was a tower of strength. He was certainly that for his family. He was also that for this community. Pete lived in Athens County for nearly fifty years, but his influence, especially when it came to his veterinary practice, extended well beyond and indeed worldwide. The massive outpouring of support for Pete and his family shows the magnitude of his impact on so many lives - and the depth of loss we feel. What can we do when a solid rock like Pete dies? It didn't seem possible, did it? Pete was like a mountain range or a force of nature. I think most assumed he'd always be there.
>
> He died the way he lived - without a safety net. The story of Pete climbing up the hill after that tree fell on him and driving home will become part of his legend. Fifty years from now, as the tales are told, he'll be bigger and stronger than Paul Bunyan. But in Pete's case, at least half the stories will be true.
>
> Pete was so very, very tough; it's hard to remember that he was seventy-one years old. A lesser man would have stayed there in the woods and died. But Pete managed to get himself home. In fact, if some Good Samaritan had stopped to help him, Pete might well have refused. He was fiercely independent – even ornery. He was also wickedly funny and smart. At times he had to be to survive. He left home very young.

There must be something in the water up in Maine – or maybe it's the weather. Pete reminded me of lots of folks from Maine, who are some of the strongest, most independent, most determined people on earth. But Pete also called to mind the West, where he worked on ranches, met Jody, studied veterinary medicine, and rode rodeo. And he was very much identified with Athens County, where he chose to make his home.

There was a tender side to Pete. Those of us who did not know him in his personal life probably saw it best in his care for animals. I have an eleven-year daughter who is still grateful for the miracle he worked for her guinea pig. I can only imagine what miracles he worked for some of you. Here too, his legend will only grow. Pete's care for animals went beyond his consummate professionalism as a vet. With Pete, this came from a place of deep empathy. There was part of him that identified with suffering creatures in ways few of us manage for our fellow human beings. His passion for horse rescue through the Last Chance Corral speaks volumes about his priorities in life.

How deeply he will be missed-this strong and compassionate giant of a man. Again I ask us, what can we do now that Pete no longer lives among us? How do we go on now that Pete's days of cheating death are over?

In the first place, we turn to God. Pete himself often did that. The way he lived his life, he needed to rely on his faith more than most. In God, he found the One he could count on when his own strength failed. In God, he found the Almighty who created the people, the land, and the animals he loved. In God, he found the Savior, whose love is stronger than death.

Even now this Savior – the Lord Jesus – is leading Pete by the hand into paradise. For he is the Good Shepherd, and Pete is a member of His flock. His sheep – even the ornery ones – know his voice and follow him safely home. Even in the tomb, they hear his voice and live. Through death's dark vale, they follow him into larger life.

The Lord's presence with us cannot remove our sense of loss, this "cry of absence" we feel so sharply now. But it does provide hope and strength for the days and weeks ahead.

For, in this Easter season, we remember the victory of Jesus over sin, death, and the grave. And we remember his promise – that nothing can ever, ever, ever separate us from His love.

Death is not the end – not for Pete, not for us – but is instead the gateway of eternal life.

"Pat had a very difficult time at the church service," Jody quietly says. "Before it began he left the pew where the rest of the family were sitting, including family from Mansfield and other relatives. He went up in the balcony, thinking he'd be alone with his grief. As the balcony filled up, Pat went outside and neighbor Art Gish, a very wise and compassionate man, said words of comfort to Pat."

After the memorial service, the family gathered together for dinner. Then, later, Jessica hosted a dinner and a hike. A portion of Pete's ashes were divided and scattered on Milliron Farm meadow, and his beloved sawmill. Later, a portion was scattered in the Milliron Farm pine grove where many of the family pets are buried. The pines were planted as three-year-old seedlings on Pat's third birthday. Susie took a portion of the ashes to bury in the family plot in Reedville, Maine.

"My father was very excited about this physical world," reflects Jessica, in a letter to the community, "where everyone's needs matter and people can have skills to be peaceful, heart connected members of a civilized society, contributing to well-being in a meaningful loving manner! I mourn Dad's physical absence and know that each of us can forge ahead by contributing to well-being in every thought we choose to focus on and every action that we take each moment of our precious lives on this planet."

Pete's obituary, written by Jessica, reflects on how this man, one of America's best veterinarians, long settled in the remote hills of southeastern Ohio, simply loved life, loved living on the edge and living the width of his life, manifesting his big ideas. Pete Smith knew that God's will for him involved dedicating his life to making this world a better place for animals, his best idea about how to serve his God.

Epilogue

When I was growing up, my Dad and I were literally mortal enemies. I absolutely hated him. The mantra of my childhood was how little I was doing with so much, and how much he had done with so little. I never felt I could live up to his expectations, let alone all of them. It just doesn't make for a real loving, friendly relationship. I spent my entire childhood trying to earn his respect and never felt like I came anywhere close. I was hit by a car when I was sixteen years old. He had the opportunity to prove to me that he cared whether I was alive or dead.

Now that I am older and an adult with children I have a tremendous understanding and respect for what he was trying to accomplish. I don't know if it would have done any good for him to sit down and try to explain it to me, but, certainly he never did, and he never tried to.

He was always one step away from losing everything all the time. He lived his financial life the same way he lived the rest of his life. All the great stories you hear about how tough he was, how he never missed an appointment, and all those things, certainly it was tough, but, that was because if he lost a day's work, he would lose everything. He was that close to the edge. He lived his life in such a way that he had to make every penny he could make just to make the next month's payment. He almost lost it all on several occasions.

He was extremely passionate about everything, but he didn't share his passion. You had to follow along pretty close and figure out about the passion he had. He really cared about animals. He was the greatest man I never knew. He cared for me, which I never knew. He certainly cared about his land. He was an incredible human being. One thing that I tell people, which I tell most sincerely, is that if you look up self-made man in the dictionary, it has his picture.

With all that said, there is no one for whom I have greater respect. We were never buddies. We were never to a ball game together. We never played catch or went camping. We never did Scouts together. He never coached my little league team. He never did any of that. I don't know if that is important, but it is amazing to me how much appreciation he had for how much time I spent doing all those things with my sons.

He seemed to really have regrets. He always said that he wanted to write his own story. He was extremely literate. He had a great sense of humor. I don't think anyone really knew him. Everybody knew a little bit about him, but I don't think he wanted everyone to know everything about him. I say this with great admiration, Dad just didn't give a shit what other people thought. He was extremely confident. The only thing that was important to him was his opinion of himself and God's opinion of him. He was absolutely confident that all the people's opinions would take care of themselves.

There were very few people who my Dad admired. Sam Jones was one of them. It wasn't because he thought Sam could whoop his ass. It was because he truly believed Sam Jones was a great man. I don't know of anybody else that Dad looked up to. I know that Les Rivers, the cowboy from Dad's days in Colorado, was important to Dad, but Les used to visit us and he had become an alcoholic. Dad was disappointed in what Les had become.

My Mom might disagree with this, but he never did anything that he thought was the right thing to do at that time. I am constantly doing things because I think that's what somebody else expects or in their best interest. Dad lived his life finding the best things for him to live his life. He didn't need anybody else's opinion. He did, however, listen to people and their opinions. He would listen as intently to the opinions of a professor emeritus just as intently as he would listen to the welder who came to work on his equipment. He would ask questions and respond with the same amount of interest and enthusiasm. He did listen to people, but I don't think he let someone else's opinion influence him in any way. I don't think he let anyone else except God influence him.

God was extremely important to him, but also extremely personal, and extremely private. He was definitely going to church for himself and not for someone else's opinion. If someone told him he was going to die if he stood up and said he was a Christian, he would be the first to stand up. He would never tell anybody he was Christian, but if they would have asked, he would have told them, and told them why he was a Christian.

There's just nobody I have greater respect for. Every time I talk to anybody, every time I do anything, I learn something new about him. I really believe that he was the greatest man I never knew. I have really struggled with his passing because of all the things I should or should not have done. I think saving his legacy was important to him, and it is important to me. A lot of things I have done since he passed, I would certainly like to do over.

I was convinced that dad would outlive me, or perhaps never die. Even when he was in critical care, until he went into the coma the final time, it never crossed my mind that he would die. Even though everyone said he was going to die, my whole-hearted response was, *He'll pull through, you'll see.* As a result of that, I never asked about anything. Every time we had a conversation he would just say, "I'm leaving everything in your hands because I know you will do the right thing." I never once asked him what that was.

After his accident, I thought he was thinking he would go home in a couple of days, then a couple more days, then I think he realized he was hurt worse than he first thought he was. I think Dad made a conscious decision to give up; he had that much power. He was afraid they were going to save him and he would go home in a wheelchair and never walk again. He had all the 'do not resuscitate' and all those orders in place. I was in charge of that because I didn't want my mom to make that decision. My Mom was there with him when he had the heart attack, and all the medical team came and they asked what to do. Mom naturally told them to do whatever they could do, and they did; they saved him. He went into a coma. His regular medical team was gone for the weekend. They called me up and apologized for not doing what they were supposed to do. It was on a Friday. We decided to wait until Monday to see if there was a miracle. Monday came and there was no miracle.

I came home and tried figure out what we have and what we don't have. I have been doing books and accounting since I was 16 years old. I had a pretty good understanding where he was financially. I tapped his 401K money to try to save the farm. He had a pile of metal crap around the clinic. I cleaned that up. Neighbors said they appreciated me cleaning it up. It gave me enough time to come up with a plan.

Abbott Pliny "Pat" Smith IV

.

Appendix

Abbott Pliny (Pete) Smith III, D.V.M.

ATHENS – Abbott Pliny (Pete) Smith III, D.V.M. passed away February 22, 2010, with family at his Grant Hospital bedside after a logging accident in his beloved Milliron Farm woods. Pete was born June 16, 1938 in Augusta, Maine, graduated from Colorado State University with a degree in veterinary medicine in 1962 and moved to Athens, Ohio in 1963 with family, including equines, dogs and a cat.

Pete was an honor roll member of the American Veterinary Medical Association, Ohio Veterinary Medical Association, and Athens County Chapter of the Ohio Horseman's Council. Pete was preceded in death by his parents Elizabeth Saunders and Abbott Pliny Smith II. Pete is sadly missed by his wife of 50+ years, Virginia Joyann (Jody) Haley Smith, son Abbott Pliny (Pat) Smith IV, daughter Jessica Smith Fox; daughter-in-law Karen Carsey Smith; son-in-law Richard Fox; grandsons AJ and Grant Smith, Noah Fox, all of Athens; sister Carol Robinson (Colorado) and family; sister Susan Davis (Maine) and family; sister Janet Riben (Sweden) and family; brother James Smith (Colorado) and family.

Pete Smith is also missed by his dogs Zeus and Smokey, horses Raybar and Unique, cats, and other critters far and wide. As a vibrant member of the community, he is also missed by many friends and other family members. A memorial service will be held on May 22, 2010, 4:00 PM, at the Episcopal Church of the Good Shepherd in Athens, In lieu of flowers, please feel free to make a donation to Last Chance Corral Horse Rescue, Good Shepherd Church or the American Humane Association.

In many ways, Pete Smith was larger than life. He knew practically as soon as he could talk he was going to be a vet. He spent his childhood growing up on farms in Yarmouth (48 West Elm) and Freeport (now the sales office for beef at Wolfe's Neck Farm), Maine. Pete worked on a ranch in Laramie, Wyoming, as a teenager. His school sport was bronc busting. When he met Jody Haley, he was living in a station wagon on the rodeo grounds.

For years, Pete Smith was the western hemisphere vet for descendants of Austria's famous white Lipizzaner's. Pete was one of America's best vets. Horses, even today, are often simply put down unless they are multi-million-dollar breeding stock or were blessed to have Pete Smith as their vet! Pete was also passionate about forestry and horseback riding. He simply loved life, living on the edge and living the width of his life, manifesting his big ideas. Pete Smith knew that God's will for him involved dedicating his life to making this world a better place for animals, his best idea about how to serve his God.

Professor Emeritus Recital, April 17, 2010, 8:00 p.m.
A Professor Emeritus Recital was held at Ohio University's School of Music Recital Hall on Saturday, April 17, 2010, 8:00 PM. Richard Syracuse played a classic concert dedicated to the memory of Pete. The selected works of Chopin were enjoyed as follows...

Scherzo, Op. 39 in C-Sharp minor
Nocturne Op. 9, No. 2 in E-flat major
Fantasy-Impromptu, Op. 66
Intermission
Waltz, Op. 64, No. 2 in C-Sharp minor
Prelude, Op. 28, No. 15 in D-flat major
Prelude, Op. 28, No. 24 in D minor
Fantasy, Op. 39 in F minor

Grant Medical Center May 16, 2010
A Service of Remembrance was held at Grant Medical Center. Jody and Jessica attended in memory of Pete. They lit a candle in Pete's memory and received a rose and coin of remembrance. The invocation reads: *You will not be forgotten. God created you to shine in my life, to guide me and teach me wrong from right, even though you are no longer here, every time I look at this coin, I will remember how special you were.*

Milliron Clinic Memorial Service May 22, 2010 11:00 a.m.

A Memorial Service was hosted by the staff, family and friends of Milliron Clinic. The service was held early morning at the clinic, May 22. A Memory Booklet was given to all who attended. The booklet contains pictures and memories written by Pete's siblings and immediate family. The cover is a picture of Pete standing tall in the clinic parking lot. He is wearing a hearty grin, navy coveralls, a tan hunting coat and gumboots, all while holding a dead possum in his left hand and a rifle in the other. He was younger, light brown hair, groomed mustache and beard.

> Memorial Book Dedication: This document is a gift of Pete Smith's cousin Joe Saunders and his wife Ava, who always made Maine a delightful place for family and friends to visit. Their food, fellowship, generosity and hospitality have been such a gift for the Smith family over the years. Thank you! The picture following is of A.P. Smith II and family in 1972.

A potluck dinner was served as hundreds of people lined up to pay their respects and reminisce. Vocalist and client Mimi Hart sang a lovely song. Jody brought Pete's horses Unique and Raybar to the clinic barn as part of the service. Brother Jim videotaped the event and can be seen on YouTube. Upon Susie's suggestion, each family member recited a two-minute memory.

Carol Smith Robinson, Sister

I'm Carol Robinson. I am the eldest of the five Smith kids, but Pete was close behind – just a year and nine months behind. Whether it was a year and nine months or two years depended on the subject because typically he resented being told he was two years younger.

My memories of life with Pete began at Little River Farm in Freeport, Maine. It was a wonderful place on an inlet of Casco Bay – a point, as it was called, and accessible over a single-lane wooden bridge. Diving from it – when the tide was in, of course, really was great fun. Pete, of course, probably would have had me do it at low tide. I recall that his challenge was to do this race barefoot – on this gravel road. I have noticed that he and I have very wide, big feet. Wonder if that's why…

Actually, I do recall a funny story about living in Yarmouth, before Freeport, also near the water. I know that we were very young then, because Smith kid Number 3, Suze, hadn't been born. The story goes that Mom wanted Pete to go up to the garden – in my child's recollection it seemed like a long way - but might have been just the equivalent of two or three blocks – to get her some green onions. There was a thunderstorm threatening and a reluctant and scared Pete got up there in record time - Mom and Dad often talked about how fast he must have run.

But back to Freeport, Little River Farm held great memories. One questionable memory for me was Pete teasing me with garter snakes – he'd toss them at me and make me scream for help. He also liked to snap a damp tea towel at me when we did dishes. Dishwashers always were the two-legged variety in the Smith house.

It was there that he helped an injured crow and in the process taught that crow to talk – probably more fiction that fact. That was a subject of family delight for a long time. The crow was named Pliny, the family middle name. Pete also knew that the only way to kill a porcupine was to hit it in its tiny head with a 22, and I believe he must have dispatched a porky or two on that farm.

One of the most interesting things about my brother was that drawl. Where did that come from? I can't recall that he ever had a Maine accent, but then none of us really did. That, I believe we have to attribute to Mom, that Montana girl. That drawl was a characteristic of Pete's that I think most of us enjoyed.

When our parents left Colorado to go back to the East Coast, I was in college and Pete had just started at what was then Colorado A&M, so we didn't go back with them, but those three little kids did.

At school in Colorado, Pete met the love of his life Jody Haley. I think Jessica was born after Jody finished college and Pat when Pete graduated, or thereabouts.

One of Pete's greater lines was regarding our kids – his and mine – when anyone was heard to say that Abbott and Betty had produced a great bunch of kids, he liked to say, "Wa'al them good genes shore skipped a generation." – because the kids he and I brought into this world have been not only great, but bright and loving kids.

Lastly, I just have to tell you, Pete, you left too soon. I am the eldest – yes, two years or a year and nine months – and I should have gone first. I know that Mom and Dad have welcomed you with open arms. They probably wondered if they were ever going to see any of us, and were surprised it was so soon. I love you, Pete. Yes, you won another race – the biggest one.

Susie Smith Davis, Sister

My big brother – that's what Pete was to me, the third sibling among us five. He was always bigger than life, whether to his little two-year-old sister or to me now. And the adventures in his life were always just as big. He'd survived so many near-mythic accidents, I didn't take this last one as seriously as everyone near him knew it to be. I missed him – and I miss him.

Pete and Jody called me up last Fall to thank me for some Maine newspaper horse stores I'd sent them. We talked for almost an hour, really rare, and in retrospect so special. That time, I found out he'd totaled his truck just months before and was pretty badly hurt himself – a first, he assured me. But he was fine, back to work, no problems.

That call was especially nice because getting his attention as a child or adult sibling always seemed hard for me. The only time I really impressed him, I thought, was when I showed up driving my ¾-ton Dodge diesel truck. The 1910 Stanley Steamer in the trailer didn't impress him, just the truck pulling it. Or so I thought!

Living with Pete was always exciting. When I was about two, I was saving a base for him at a baseball game in our yard at 48 West Elm in Yarmouth. He came racing in, landed on my outstretched leg – and broke it! He was great at knife throwing and he demonstrated it once by making me stand next to a beam on the second floor of the barn while he threw his knife into the beam from the ground floor. I got to pull it out of the beam and drop it down to him, I guess – that part I don't remember.

In fact, it had to be at 48 West Elm that Pete decided to be a veterinarian. We had cows, chickens, pigs, and at least seven horses. Dad, a gentlemen farmer as they used to call them, commuted 10 miles into Portland to work, so Pete probably helped Mom out with a lot of farm chores. By the time we moved to our Little River Farm on Casco Bay in Freeport, there were four of us, so Mom needed a lot of help.

At Little River, Pete was probably just a typical big brother. I remember very clearly his making me put his fishing worms in my pocket. One time he chased me up an apple tree in the front yard. In the excitement, I jumped from one limb to another and missed. That time, I had a broken arm. Our first year in Denver, 1952, all by myself I broke my wrist. With three broken bones before I was ten, I figured out I'd better be more careful, so I stopped breaking bones.

Once we moved to Denver, Pete was gone to me. He was so much older; we were never in school together. I remember proudly how he got a summer job at a ranch in the mythical Laramie, Wyoming – those were the days of great TV and movie "Westerns." Visiting and riding around that huge ranch was always exciting. Then we came back East, and he went to vet school, rode broncs for sport, met and married the other passion of his life, Jody, had kids, and the rest is the history we celebrate today.

Janet Smith Riben, Sister

Pete is perhaps no longer with us physically but there is something about Pete that makes that not applicable in his case – he was bigger than life and is therefore always going to be with us! I was reminded recently about how that actually works – a neighbor has a dog that has been getting sudden cramps which then disappear – he has trouble walking – wobbles along. They have spared nothing in vet costs to find out what it is. I immediately thought, "Let me call Pete!" Knowing Pete, maybe he'll figure out a way to answer us from where he is! Let's hope! We need his animal smarts.

My friend Christine Chauvin who organizes horseback rides around the world had the pleasure of having Pete on one of her rides in Ecuador. I had broken my back and couldn't go myself and knew Pete would love the experience so he went in my place. Christine thought Pete was a wonderful addition to the ride – a rather unusual group as there were several men on that particular ride. That is not usually the case.

Pete was always a source of laughs, great stories and whenever there were animal problems, he had the solution. On a ride she had in Africa, one of the favorite horses of the organizer had been having serious stomach problems which no vet had been able to help. Christine knew one vet that she could count on – she called Pete. He asked questions, and without hesitation came up with a suggestion. Yogurt with charcoal as I recall (don't pin me down on that one!), with instructions on how to actually get it down the horse's throat. Within a short time the horse was fine again. How little sister Janet (he always called me Nanny. From him that was quite ok!) is proud when she hears stories like that. And there are *many* such stories.

When the opportunity came up for our daughter Anna to come and spend a summer working with Pete, Jody and Jessica doing various chores, I thought "great!" At least Anna will get a chance to spend a summer with this amazing family. Chores with Pat were *not* included – probably lucky for both Anna and Pat! She's not a *numbers* person! It was quite a different experience for her to be working on a farm with all that involves and in a clinic seeing operations and understanding that side of a vet's work, and without the big city life she is so used to. I was actually envious of her. I have always loved visiting Milliron Farm and having all the animals around me – being a part of Pete's world.

Pete visited our world when we were living and working in Venezuela. That was a great time for us all. I had long talks with Pete on just about every subject. Pete was well read – he had an amazing frame of reference because of that. He had no trouble finding lots to talk about with people who had never left the city environment!

He seemed to enjoy it all and was always up to learning more! I remember we had a lot of coffee table books in our house. There were some really interesting ones – which most of us just leaf through – checking out the beautiful pictures. Well, with Pete it was a completely different story! He *read* most of them! I can't remember how long he was with us – too short as time flew by – but he managed to read many of those books and came with floods of questions about Venezuela's this or that.

Pete *lived* his life – some of us just let it flow on. That's ok but oh how much more Pete must have experienced in his all too short time with us. He wanted to get the most out of his life and he made sure he did just that. He always had the loving support of Jody which was incredibly important to him. She went into overdrive to make sure he got a passport in time for the ride in Ecuador. I am sure that was standard procedure for her and Pete understood and loved this about Jody. That they had their love of animals in common was an important strength in every aspect of their lives.

We will miss Pete but he's always going to be here with us! After all he was/*is* bigger than life!

Jim Smith, Brother

Age and circumstance kept me from having much of a sibling relationship with Pete. I was only eight years old when our family moved from Denver back to New England. Pete stayed behind, working his way, without parental assistance, through Colorado State University. There he met Jody as an undergraduate and then stayed as a young married man working his way through vet school shoeing horses and working at a dog track.

Before he was married, Pete worked summers at the Bosler ranch north of Laramie. He got paid in Black Angus cattle which multiplied and formed the beginning of his Milliron Land & Cattle Company. The clinic was named after it. A true self-made man. I admired that about Pete.

When I was 13, I was given the opportunity to work on the same ranch. I was a real screw-up compared to Pete. Mr. Bosler made that pretty clear to me!

Later, when Pete moved to Athens, I had the privilege in my early 20s of spending vacation time now and then with the family. I accompanied Pete on his large animal house calls in his veterinary truck with its hot water heated by the exhaust system. I watched Pete do everything from Caesarian section on a cow in some pasture to castrating a horse – I nearly fainted at the horse incident.

I admired Pete tremendously for his independence, his success, his risk-taking, his everything. Despite my limited exposure to him, I can say he was a role model, although I hardly turned out anything like him.

I rarely saw Pete in recent decades, but I always made a point to call him on his birthday, June 16th. The last time we spoke was on Pete and Jody's 50th wedding anniversary last September. Ironically, my only pet is a parrot, and Pete wasn't trained in that part of the animal kingdom. But many may not know that Pete's first pet was a crow that he named "Pliny." That was Pete's middle name, and he hated it, I'm told, so he gave it to the crow. "Pete" was a nickname, not his middle name. My parrot is named Flower, which tells you how different we are. I'll miss him.

Karen Smith, Daughter-in-law

Pete Smith, my father-in-law, my friend. Being a member of the Smith family it is always good to have a story that you can share. They are all known for the stories they tell, exaggerations and all.

I will never forget helping out one afternoon in the woods with Pete and the rest of the family. Not sure if we were cutting wood or moving gas lines, but in typical Smith fashion there were too many pieces of equipment to drive home; dozers, tractors, trucks, probably even a horse.

Pete says to me, "Karen you drive my truck back to the clinic," oh, yeah with his favorite dog inside. Now I grew up with dogs you hunted, fed and petted once in a while, but never a dog that was a companion 24-7, and loved you with all your heart. So I get into his truck with his dog and proceed to drive. Every time I looked to my right, whether to turn or just to check on Ruff, she would raise her lip and growl. Those five miles felt like fifty.

But a Smith story I could share: Pete and I also had a routine. He, always busy working, would take time out to attend A.J.'s and Grant's sporting events when he could. When the game was over he would come up, hold out his hand and I would punch it like a ticket. When I would attend family functions, whether a dinner in Athens or a trip to Mansfield, he would punch my card.

Always laughing and knowing there was something else we could be doing, but this was what was important at the time. I know that when I take my final trip, he will be there waiting for me to hold my hand out so he can punch my ticket one more time.

Pete Smith, my father-in-law, my friend.

Abbott (A.J.) Pliny Smith V, Grandson

Grandpa Pete was a man of few words, but when he spoke I couldn't be happier to listen, his stories were amazing, and his jokes were hilarious. I'm very proud to be able to say he was my grandfather. The dedication he had in everything he did was unmatched. The strength and toughness that Pete Smith had inside of him was unreal.

My brother and I spent many of our younger years during the summer on the farm with Grandpa and Grandma. I loved to sit in on his surgeries, and watch him do his daily work at the clinic. Grandpa was truly a genius at his profession. But, he also had a passion for the woods. He usually wouldn't get in the house until well after dark, but Grandma always had the food warm and ready. I remember many times untying and taking off his logging boots as he sat in front of the woodstove in his underwear.

As I got older, I didn't see Grandpa quite as much, but getting that "good game" when he came to a sporting event meant a lot; or a walk at Old Man's Cave just chatting; or the countless times I went into the clinic for stitches and X-rays; or trying to keep up with him in the fields, bailing hay; or sitting around the dinner table with the whole family and listening to jokes and laughing and laughing...

Pete Smith was one of the toughest men to ever walk this green earth. I hope that in my lifetime I will be able to endure and overcome half the things that he did. I am very thankful for the memories that I have. The time I did spend with Grandpa Pete taught me a lot about the man I want to be. Pete Smith will be dearly missed by everyone who had the opportunity to meet him, but he will live on in the likes of us.

Grant Smith, Grandson

Pete Smith was a hero to many, but only a grandfather to a few. I was one of those lucky few. I spent the most time around Grandpa when I was younger, and it was always interesting. Whether it was watching him work on horses, throw needles into the dart board with pinpoint accuracy, or building a basketball hoop out of a five-gallon bucket in the horse barn for me so he could get some work done, I was always intrigued by Grandpa Pete.

My favorite times, however, were the simpler ones. On the days Grandpa would come up from the clinic to eat lunch, it was always entertaining. He would strip down to his "whitey tightys" and his cowboy boots, and just take a minute to relax. These were good times. He would always tell us great stories of pinning a mouse to a wall with a butter knife, or just pass the time with some of his family. I believe he loved A.J., my brother, and me very, very deeply. Grandpa would always call us funny names like Cletus, and more time than not had a smile on his face.

As I got older I was not at the farm as much, and as a result, not around Grandpa Pete as much. He was very busy and a hard worker, and I understood that, but he always made the effort to come to my sporting events whenever he could. Grandpa Pete is the toughest man I know, and I thought he was invincible. I never thought we would lose him, but I am glad I was privileged enough to call Pete Smith my Grandpa.

Jessica Smith Fox

"Mourning" by Robert Gonzales
I stand before the presence of your absence
And something deep in me responds,
Shuddering in awe,
Moved beyond experience.
Yes, there is a place.
You are not here.
But you are alive
Reminding me that I will never rest
Again in the place of staying.
Showing me that I am riding

The Current of the Living
Ever-becoming, always dying
In wonderful delight and sorrow.
I am moved
Beyond the thing-ness of my flesh,
Never knowing what will erupt
In the next moment – laughter or tears.

Of the many experiences my father gifted me with during the fifty-year long journey together, in physical form, was his absolute unconditional love for life in general and his family and his friends specifically. What a gift it is to feel unconditional love radiating from my hair to my toenails!

Whenever I am not living that compassionate energy of unconditional love, in any moment, I know that I have inner territory to explore with the same exuberance that my father lived his life, all of it. No one, nothing, needs to change outside of me in order for me to be in alignment with life, source energy, *God*! When I am offering my compassionate presence to all of life, I am in the "zone", tuned in, tapped in and turned on to all of *life*. What a gift! Thank you, Dad! Lots of deep and abiding love, Jessica.

Rich Fox, Son-in-law

After meeting Jessica in 1996 and ready for new directions in my life, I remember saying to her that all my personal experiences in life had so perfectly prepared me for her. After meeting the Smith family, I can only imagine that I thought, "not, even, close."

On our first Easter together, I was sent through the clinic to find Pete so we wouldn't be late for church. I rounded a corner just in time to see a horse put down and thought that was pretty dramatic. During our first summer, I tried to hide the fact that I had cracked ribs while trying to prove my worth in the hayfield. I felt like I was dying, but later found out that every summer in the hayfield was just like that.

During the first fall, we hosted Grandma Betty for a week or two or three. After driving her from Maine, she informed us in the driveway that she would not be cooking for us. Little did she know that that was her best option because "the Smith's" always work until well after dark.

I will miss Pete for a long, long time. Being a quiet, thoughtful person, I was still trying to figure this whole bunch out. When I tried to make fun of the Smith's by describing them as *frequently wrong, but never in doubt*, they laughed and loved it.

As I think about the lessons learned from Pete Smith, I offer this one. So many people, myself included, say that they learned so many things from being with their horse. I now say that people owe far more credit to being with horse people, like Pete Smith.

One of Pete's tools that I marvel at is his ability to roar at adversity. Whether it was a run-away animal or an awful disease or an accident about to happen, Pete would do whatever it took to stop adversity in its tracks. With a little time to think and act, he would often save the day. Afterward, the outburst was long forgotten and no apologies offered. Pete would laugh and say that a lesser man might have cussed more than he had to.

Farewell to a Friend
Victoria Goss, Last Chance Corral

It is with the heaviest of hearts that I bring these next words to print…Our beloved friend, outstanding veterinarian and extraordinary man Dr. Abbott P. Smith, known as Pete, has passed away. A composite of so many fine qualities that he could have been Albert Einstein, Sean Connery and Jeremiah Johnson wrapped up in one. There are no words that could possibly capture his booming laugh or his quiet reflection. Nothing in our language could express his "*joie de vivre*". He was so much to so many that his loss will ripple across this land forever. Pete commanded every room he ever entered. I am proud to say that he was my friend. I'm honored to have had him as my favorite dinner guest. He was my mentor. He lived his life on his own terms. Goodbye, my friend…Happy Trails.

He borrowed a piece from every horse…
As paused to say goodbye.
And so in heaven their spirits soar…

301

As he rides them and they fly
If you see a tear in your horse's eye
It's not from fear or sorrow... but a tear of joy for
The honor of sharing in what he paused to borrow

Acknowledgements

Abbott 'Pete' Pliny Smith III, D.V.M., was an icon in Southeastern Ohio. His legacy will be in our hearts and minds for many generations. He was witty, wise, and whimsical – all at the same time. He was a highly skilled veterinary surgeon, combining knowledge, finesse, and strength; probing the entrails of a giant horse, grasping a steady rein on a runaway steed, cradling a newborn calf, or holding a child who just lost a family pet.

Traveling with Pete's widow, Jody, and their daughter, Jessica, throughout Ohio and West Virginia has been a great experience. Family, friends, and clients opened their hearts and homes to us as we collected stories about Pete. We talked with just about everyone - from horse trainers and equestrians, to neighbors down the road. I often told Jody that we needed to write a book about writing the book.

Everyone we encountered loved Pete. Most people believed him to be like a brother, near relative, or saint. People spoke eagerly of his miraculous and innovative veterinary procedures; how he saved their beloved pet from near death.

It was Pete's lifetime desire to have his own vet clinic. God sometimes brings us the desires of our hearts. Sometimes he throws in an anecdote that can be reflected on for many years to come, proving His grace, provision, and promise. We celebrate the life and times of Dr. Smith, and sincerely appreciate everyone who contributed to the contents of this book. Special thanks to Pat Smith, Jody Smith, Jessica Smith Fox, Tony D'Andrea, Kelly Lincoln, Richard Gilbert, and Grant Smith.

Gina McKnight

About the Author

From Ohio, USA, Gina McKnight is an author of children's literature (*The Blackberry Patch*, 2009; *Trail Ride to Snake Hollow*, 2017 Monday Creek Publishing; *Nawaab: The Great Quake*, 2017, Banyan Publishing, India), with endorsements from the Ohio Quarter Horse Association, WHOA (Water, Hay, Oats Alliance), Outdoor Writers of Ohio, and the Foundation for Appalachian Ohio. Gina is the author of Dr. Smith's books (2017), including *Milliron: Abbott "Pete" Smith D.V.M. The Biography, Tails of a Country Vet* and the production of *The South High Horseman: Stories and Poems by a Teen Cowboy* by Peter Smith. Gina has written two poetry anthologies (*To the Heart*, 2015; *Poetry from the Field*, 2016), as well as appeared in international poetry volumes and literary journals. Currently, she is a contributing columnist for *trueCOWBOYmagazine, Florida Equine Athlete*, and *Arabian Finish Line*. Besides being a freelance writer, she is an avid blogger about her life in rural Ohio. Gina lives on her family farm with her husband, son, and American Quarter Horses Zubedia and Mac.

Illustrator's Note

Many heartwarming stories of the colorful and talented Pete Smith, D.V.M. told by family, friends, pet owners, and professional associates inspired me to depict his life in three drawings: young Pete standing proud and strong in front of his family's home in Maine; Dr. Pete, the dedicated veterinarian, inoculating the author's family cattle at night in a thunderstorm; the family's touching story of how a red-tailed hawk responded to Dr. Pete's healing skills and kindness.

Special thanks to Bryan Shane, photographer, for permission to use his Red Tail Hawk photo.

Terry Fortkamp

About the Illustrator

Terry Fortkamp was born in 1951 in the rural flat lands of Mercer County, Ohio. She grew up in a loving, supportive family and community. Her illustrations, paintings and etchings reflect her introspective and sincere spirit. Sun drenched memories from early childhood are the subjects for much of Fortkamp's work; clothes drying on a clothesline, aprons, flowering bushes, and room interiors, all reflect her love for an earlier, slower way of life. A third grade blue-ribbon for her illustration of an alligator was the first of her many successes in the visual arts. Fortkamp received a BFA from the School of the Dayton Art Institute and an MFA from Ohio University. During and after graduate school, Terry produced hundreds of portraits of clients who completed teen and women's drug and alcohol programs. Her thesis show led to solo shows in England and Ohio. She presented in group shows in several states and was awarded honorary and monetary prizes for paintings and etchings. She treasures her People's Choice Award for *Symphony in Yellow*, a portrait of a forsythia bush, in the 2014 Ohio+Five Show at the Dairy Barn Art Center, Athens, Ohio, as well as Best of Show and Juror's Choice Awards from earlier invitational shows with the Lancaster Art Guild, Lancaster, Ohio. Fortkamp has been involved in many art endeavors: large community and private mural commissions; Ohio River Boarder Initiatives of Ohio and West Virginia Arts Councils mural consultant; resident artist for both the Ohio Arts Council and Greater Columbus Arts Council, Columbus, Ohio; resident artist and workshop instructor with Days of Creation - Arts for Kids, Columbus, Ohio, Paper Circle and Starbrick Galleries in Nelsonville, Ohio; illustrator of children's books and biographies. Her current focus is painting portraits of nostalgic objects from the 50's era, painting portraits of area flowering trees and bushes, and creating paintings using handmade paper with inclusions and mixed media. Terry currently lives a quiet life with her twin daughters in the picturesque rolling hills of Athens County, Ohio. Connect with Terry - terryfortkamp@gmail.com or www.TerryFortkamp.com